Jeremy Marre is an independent film-maker whose films for TV and cinema range from *Beats of the Heart* to the Japanese Martial Arts, and from *Forbidden Image* with Ravi Shankar to profiles of conductors Claudio Abbado and Herbert von Karajan. He is currently producing/directing two TV series: on British Music and on Animal Communication.

Hannah Charlton is an editor on the *Sunday Times* magazine. She has worked as a journalist, broadcaster, editor and translator. Her articles on music have appeared in publications including the *Sunday Times*, *Melody Maker* and *Collusion*.

Jeremy Marre and Hannah Charlton

# BEATS OF THE HEART

## Popular Music of the World

Pantheon Books, New York

Library of Congress Cataloging-in-Publication Data
Marre, Jeremy.
   Beats of the heart.
   Includes index.
   1. Music, Popular (Songs, etc.) – History and
criticism. I. Title.
ML3470.M35 1986 780'.42'09 85-43181
ISBN 0-394-74258-3

Designed by Ian Denning
Maps by John Grimwade

Manufactured in Great Britain

# Contents

800-733-3000

# Acknowledgements

With thanks for their work on the production of
the films or the book:
Mike Appelt, Roland Armstrong, Pete Ayrton,
Greg Bailey, Geoff Baines, Richard Bedford,
Bob Bentley, Egberto Bermudez, Georgina
Bishop, Melvyn Bragg, Bunyang, Yung Chang,
Sue Chambers, Zhang Che, Joe Conzo, Djalma
Correa, Stella Duggan, Diane Ellis, Bobby
Fulcher, Bruce Gaston, Tanya Giles, Chowky Goma,
Charlotte Greig, Rodrigo Guttierez, Shama
Habibullah, Anthony Isaacs, Noriko Izumi,
Gattu Kaul, Vanessa Kelly, Ben Tavera-King,
Bob King, Nik Knowland, Tunde Kuboye,
Martha and François Lesterlin, Felipe
Luciano, Diana Marre, Pepe Heredia Maya,
Chris Morphet, Chris O'Dell, Paul O'Dell, Ot,
Ian Owles, Andy Park, Dick Pope, Nik Powell,
Grattan Puxon, Alan Rayner, Tony Russell,
Jon Sanders, David Scott, Martin Shepherd,
Yukiko Shimahara, Mike Shoring, Sue
Steward, Prince Tony, Ernest Vincze, David
Williams, Zhang Zhimei.

# Introduction

My purpose in writing this book was to provide an account of my experiences in filming the television series *Beats of the Heart* around the world over a period of 7 years. A book allows more time and space to reflect on and elaborate the themes of the films, as well as to describe how and why they were made. There were many challenges, problems – even dangers – in exploring such diverse musical subjects, but all gave a further insight into those communities and their music.

I had wished, all along, to describe in writing as well as on film, the dynamic role played by popular music in the societies I visited. Then Hannah Charlton, a friend and journalist, introduced me to the publishers of this book and assisted my researches and recollections by editing the chapters into a manageable size.

The communities and countries featured in *Beats of the Heart* were selected for the different ways in which their popular music reflects the lives of the musicians and their audiences. The broadcaster Felipe Luciano has described salsa music as 'the conscience of the people'. Jimmy Cliff has called reggae 'the cry of the people'. Both were referring to the role music plays in portraying, shaping, even changing society. This is particularly true of the developing world, where music carries local news to a populace which often has good reason for distrusting the 'official' media. Many people in those countries have remained semi-literate, so modern

**The Queen of Latin music, Celia Cruz, filmed in a New York studio for Beats of the Heart**

recording techniques, amplification and mobile sound systems have updated the musical newsvendors of the past – the European troubadour and the African griot.

I did not restrict myself to the so-called Third World because music in many 'developed' societies also plays an important role. It may be a culturally binding force for immigrant or migrant communities, like the New York Hispanics or the Texas Mexicans. It may reflect the changes, pressures, ambiguities of the Japanese in their electronics revolution or of the Chinese following their Cultural Revolution.

I have not attempted a comprehensive overview or analysis of any particular culture; there was neither time nor space in the films or the book. Each chapter describes what we encountered when researching and filming *Beats of the Heart*, aided by musicians and friends in each community.

Of course, the choice of subjects was limiting. There were so many other places I would have liked to include, but the practical constraints, both financial and physical, meant making choices. Moreover, many of the authorities were politically hostile to our aims of showing the real relationship of popular music to society. Some made access difficult, some interfered with the filming and others had us followed and arrested. So each film became a struggle to present a 'sound portrait' as seen by the citizens of a community, whether gypsies, black South Africans or Appalachian preachers.

I wanted to escape from the awful television categories which treat music as high art, folklore or consumer pop. I wished, instead, to show the street musics – the beats of the heart – that truly mirror the mixes and changes inherent in every society. There is no such thing as a nationally 'pure' music. As we attempted to show, the music of one culture has always been subject to influences from many others, as well as to developments within its own. Like the rest of life, music is in a perpetual process of change.

Neither the book, nor the films, however, regard music solely as a vehicle for politics and propaganda. Music is also joyful; it is for having a good time – for dancing, courting, praising. It can be a release from daily pressures as well as a mirror of them. This multifaceted quality of popular music was what I wanted to film, examining each of the subjects through a contemporary perspective, yet at the same time incorporating the history, myth and tradition that underpins them.

I tried to achieve this aim by viewing each society through the eyes of local people. I was responsible for selecting images and sounds, and for editing them, but I did so – as far as possible – with the close help and guidance of local musicians. I did not want to filter their vision, but to present it directly, even uncomfortably, to the viewing public, who would be free to draw their own conclusions. For that reason, each film remains distinctive in style, rhythm and emphasis. The unity of the series, and in the chapters of this book, lies in what the music has to say. To paraphrase Felipe Luciano:

'Music is a double-edged sword. It is escapist, it is trendy, it is faddish. But it is also revolutionary, dynamic and progressive. It describes the experiences we have lived through, past and present. To that extent, music is the politics of the people.'

# 1 No. 17 Cotton Mill Shanghai Blues
## Music in China

On a misty October evening in 1983, on my second trip to China, I stumbled across the Shanghai 'Youth Palace'. A massive queue of adolescents led from its entrance around the block and past the snack bars and tea-houses packed with workers on their way home. I joined it and eventually pushed my way into the main auditorium where literally thousands of teenagers craned their necks to listen to boys with guitars, some wearing blue jeans, who were singing country and western songs like 'Take me back to West Virginia'. They must have learned the words off cassettes or from Shanghai radio which had recently begun to play selected western pop. What I was witnessing was the first pop music competition to happen in China after the Cultural Revolution of 1966.

On my next visit about six months later, I had yet another surprise. At the same Youth Palace, the same teenage crowd was watching the Dalong Machine Factory Orchestra playing tangos. The musicians were dressed in grey crimplene suits and their conductor was heavily made up with lipstick, rouge and eyeshadow. The applause was rapturous.

Music in China is seen as a barometer of the political climate and I was there at a time of thaw. Since Mao's wife, Jiang Qing, took control of music and the arts in 1966, they had been shaped to serve the state – 'a cog in the wheel of Marxism' – with an heroic realism depicting revolution at the hands of pioneering youth. It was this emphasis on propaganda through music and art that produced the name 'Cultural Revolution'.

As we were to discover, ten years of the Cultural Revolution had imposed a rigorously

dull and uniform, officially approved music through the vast expanse of the People's Republic of China. Over 1,000 million people live in 23 provinces, which stretch from the tropical forests of the southeast to the Gobi Desert in the northwest. Each province had previously boasted a distinctive music, language and culture. But the Cultural Revolution attempted to iron out many of these regional differences and even to suppress the great Chinese classics which were labelled 'anti-revolutionary'.

Since the end of the Cultural Revolution, the system had relaxed considerably. My visit coincided with an upsurge of excitement, not just for those in artistic circles, but for ordinary people everywhere in China. They suddenly found themselves able to sing and dance once again without fear of political criticism and punishment. But there were still difficulties. The authorities continued to regard music as a form of propaganda to be performed enthusiastically for a politely appreciative audience. Nothing should be questioning, disturbing or challenging. Time and time again, during my research trips, I was taken into empty

**Old acquaintance brought to mind: 'Auld Lang Syne' sung in halting English as a solo turn**

**Tangos and British folk songs from the Dalong Machine Factory's Orchestra playing at the Youth Palace in Shanghai**

theatres where local troupes performed optimistic folklore numbers on stage, just for me.

When I first arrived in Shanghai in spring 1983, a full year before filming began, I was immediately taken to the Children's Palace which was, in almost every respect, the opposite of the Youth Palace. Here, immaculately dressed children played Mozart sonatas on piano accordions, or were regimented into highly disciplined classical Chinese orchestras.

This was a showcase for foreign visitors and dignitaries, prettified and artificial. Ronald and Nancy Reagan were later taken there as part of their whistle-stop tour of China. In fact, the Reagan entourage had pushed us out of our hotel which had been taken over by 400 secret service men who strutted around Shanghai with crackling walkie-talkies and a spoon and fork displayed prominently in the front pockets of their jackets. 'I know how to pull the trigger of a 44,' spluttered one of them, 'but I sure as hell

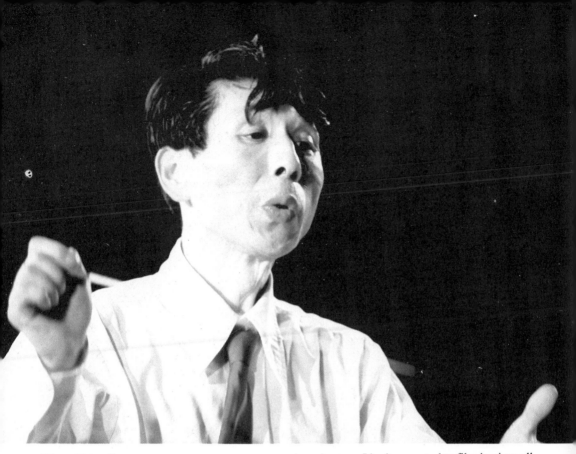

**Wang Jinhu, the leader of the Dalong Orchestra, in grey crimplene and camp make-up**

can't handle them chopsticks.' They had their own food flown in – hamburgers and more hamburgers – while they organized the President's itinerary. It was even arranged to have small Chinese children running 'spontaneously' across the road, playing games and music as the President's convoy made its way towards the Great Wall – a slice of everyday Chinese life.

The Youth Palace, with its Dalong Machine Factory Orchestra, was far removed from all this selective showcasing of Chinese life. Foreign visitors were not even informed of its existence. I had requested to film it, since all such proposals have to be made many months in advance and analysed by various local and party committees, but between the research trip and the start of filming there were a couple of government reshuffles and an old Maoist reappeared as the new Propaganda Minister. The pop competitions were banned temporarily and the authorities became clearly embarrassed by the excessively individualistic and 'camp' element displayed in the Dalong conductor's 1930s tangos. I had been informed by telex that several of the items I wished to film might no longer be possible, but by the time I returned to China there had been another swing of the political pendulum and the Maoist Propaganda Minister had been toppled. Not only had all my original requests been reinstated, but we were permitted to film and travel with an unusual degree of freedom, even holding unsupervised and spontaneous interviews with musicians and artists.

Many Chinese are still cautious when they speak to foreigners, and fearful of how far the pendulum might swing back to the 'Maoist clique'. The Dalong conductor, Wang Jinhu, played safe: 'In our factory, we hold song contests which advocate the guidelines and policies of factory management. Tonight we will perform the song that our own workshop wrote.' A chorus of girls in brown uniforms then marched on stage and formed a straight line facing the audience. They linked arms singing:

*We young workers of Dalong,*
*are strong-willed, work hard and contribute*
*   our wisdom,*
*superior-quality work and high output for the*
*   people.*
*We link our labour with the four*
*   modernizations.*
*Comrades, unite as one and strive for the*
*   happy life*
*of tomorrow and the glorious year of 2,000.*

The previous time I had seen them, the girl singers had swayed from side to side while singing. But they had been admonished by their factory leaders for not behaving correctly in front of foreigners. So when they performed for our camera, they stood bolt upright, as though glued to the floor, staring glassily into the darkness of the packed auditorium. After they finished, a young girl bounced on stage wearing a white polo-neck sweater, green slit skirt and gym shoes to sing one of the orchestra's standard numbers – 'Auld Lang Syne'. The programme for that evening listed Neopolitan ballads, British folk songs and Argentinian tangos. The clothes in which they performed were equally varied. My interpretation was that suddenly – at this moment of history – people had been allowed to push the door of self-expression just a tiny bit open and through it poured the images and sounds that generations had locked away in their memories, or in their attics. This was

perhaps the only place in China where such a thing could happen.

Having been told repeatedly how important factories and other work places were in encouraging music-making amongst workers in China, we wanted to film inside one.

We had decided against the Dalong factory since the authorities were becoming edgy at the degree of interest we were showing in that troupe. Instead, we went to No. 17 Cotton Mill, Shanghai. By delaying our decision, we had hoped to catch them on just another Saturday night – but it became clear as we arrived that the entire factory had been forewarned. It was a warm spring evening when we went to film, and as we pushed open the windows of the factory recreation room our hands stuck to the handles. The entire factory, we realized, had been repainted for our visit.

The No. 17 Cotton Mill works 24 hours a day, every day. As workers come off their shifts, they wash, change and then perform. They tend to spend their evenings in the cotton mill because the facilities and space could not be found elsewhere. On this Saturday night there was a vast communal dance with an enthusiastic instructress showing the workforce how to do Russian-style formations to some tinny 1950s dance records. Elsewhere around the factory were smaller-scale musical events, but as we went to film them we noticed that the same audience reappeared at every venue, disguised in different clothes and spectacles. These turned out to be 'approved workers' who were rewarded for their loyalty by a chance to appear on foreign television. So, to the confusion of our hosts, we swung open the doors and invited everybody from the factory to take part in the shows. The result was that the first few rows of the audience consisted of highly disciplined, clean and conscientious mill workers while behind them the room filled up with real Shanghai adolescents, sporting dark glasses and with cigarettes drooping from their lips in the style of Jean-Paul Belmondo. While the authorities were desperately pushing back the crowds and losing all control, a girl strolled up to

join the orchestra at the front of the room, clasped an antique microphone to her breast and began to sing the 'Factory give up smoking' song:

*Hey, comrades, listen to what I say,*
*Smokers pollute the environment.*
*It takes up too much of your budget,*
*And that causes conflict between husband and*
*    wife.*
*You're not liked at home, you're not liked at*
*    work,*

*So it makes life depressing and frustrating.*
*(Refrain) Yea, Yea, why do you do this,*
*    comrades?*
*Give up smoking quickly, yea, yea.*

As she left the stage, all the Belmondo characters deliberately relit their cigarettes while the authorities looked on, disconsolate at their failure to retain tidy control. The next song cheered them up: it was about cotton workers. But even sung in Chinese, it was clearly identifiable as a black American cotton-picking

**Cotton mill workers sit in organized rows to listen to their colleagues perform an evening of song**

noticed two boys strumming a bluesy number on guitar, so I asked to film them. The factory elders debated and agreed but then insisted on bringing their rent-a-crowd into the room. We spent the next half hour pushing everyone out again, since there was no way these two youths could play with any degree of spontaneity when watched by a crowd of several hundred people. For the first time, friction developed between us and the factory bosses who had begun to disapprove of our filming. Finally we got our way; the boys relaxed in an empty room and prepared their number. We quietly filmed them as they rehearsed. When we confessed to what we had done, there was much embarrassed laughter since the authorities wanted a positive, serious image of their country shown abroad and disapproved of this rough, sad, bluesy number. They could not understand how the realism of teenage kids jamming in a Shanghai factory storeroom, playing wrong notes while swigging out of orange juice bottles, could match the artifice of a carefully set-up piece about the people's unity. The problem was that their reality was different from ours. For over a decade they had lived in a society where all activities were regulated and controlled and where self-expression or spontaneity was

song called 'Poor Old Joe', originally a spiritual sung by Paul Robeson:

> Gone are the days when my heart was young
>     and gay.
> Gone are my friends from the cotton fields
>     away.
> Gone from the earth to a better land I know.
> I hear those gentle voices calling Poor Old
>     Joe.

Some time earlier that evening I had

regarded as part of the dangerous 'cult of personality'. Realism for them meant a social realism that showed only what was best in their society. Of that they were proud.

It turned out to be a day of problems for us. We did an interview in a rather run-down backstreet of Shanghai with a musical family. But in the time between our meeting them and returning to film, the local cadres had insisted that the mother change from her regular Chinese clothes into a brown, western, ill-fitting suit. She was told to have her hair permed and to move all the furniture around to create a more modern impression of her house. When it came to the interview, I politely asked her to change back into her normal working clothes and sat the family against some beautiful antique tea chests which were stacked in their living room. The interview itself went well enough, but afterwards the cadres complained bitterly that we were attempting to present a negative image of the interviewees and their environment by our 'selection' of clothing and tea chests: both of which had been there in the first place. They formally requested the termination of our entire film trip. Our determined and diplomatic Chinese production team fought tooth and nail to keep us working and they succeeded, but we soon ran into even worse problems in a commune near Shanghai.

The communes, which played an important role in the ideology of the Cultural Revolution, are homes of a vast amount of music and drama. They could not be omitted from any film about the relationship of popular music to Chinese daily life. But each commune I had been taken to on previous trips presented ever more carefully arranged 'spontaneity'. I did not want to film anything specially fixed for the cameras, and kept saying so.

Finally, we found a commune about two hours' drive from Shanghai where the resident arts troupe performed modern morality tales. One was about how happy the parents of a new-born daughter should be. This might seem innocuous, but it reflects a genuine problem in

**Closed down in the years of the Cultural Revolution, the Opera School in Shanghai is now full of eager pupils. Hours are spent in learning the art of traditional face paint in all its intricate detail**

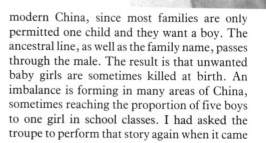

modern China, since most families are only permitted one child and they want a boy. The ancestral line, as well as the family name, passes through the male. The result is that unwanted baby girls are sometimes killed at birth. An imbalance is forming in many areas of China, sometimes reaching the proportion of five boys to one girl in school classes. I had asked the troupe to perform that story again when it came

to filming. But on our return everything had changed: the costumes, the music and the drama itself. When I declined to film anything other than what we had agreed – on paper – the commune elders bristled with indignation. Inside the rehearsal rooms our two sides seemed physically to draw apart.

In the end a compromise was reached and we agreed to film two different plays, both of which turned out to be interesting. The first was a pre-Cultural Revolution drama that had been adapted by Jiang Qing (Mao's wife) to become a political theatre piece. I was told that she had imprisoned the original playwright and then altered both the music and the drama to suit her political ends. It was called 'The red lantern':

'In old China, the jackal barred the way, fierce and wild. In darkness we anticipated the daybreak at the south lake. Spring thunder shakes the earth, and sparks of fire are seen on the red boat.'

Half a dozen girls, clad in revolutionary red, gestured heroically with lanterns.

The second piece was accompanied by the commune orchestra playing on traditional Chinese instruments with much hammering of drum and gongs. It was called 'Mr Stern apologizes' and concerned a social dropout who was rude to his parents and offended the commune chief. But he learned the error of his ways and, after much chastisement, became a model citizen. It was gently suggested that we too might learn from this play.

This performing troupe earned enough to buy costumes and props for their plays by making several thousand brown paper bags every day. They had a small workshop opposite the rehearsal room where 40 of them glued pieces of paper together.

Afterwards, we visited the commune fields where they were planting rice and rape seed. In the spring sunshine the countryside was a dazzling quilt of yellow and green, sown together by the waters of the many tiny canals that irrigated the fields. We heard music all around us and noticed the workers were planting rice – trampling it into the ground to the rhythms that echoed from loud speakers fixed to the trees. The planters explained that every commune had its own radio station which gave the local news and politics. It also played a variety of music, often of the westernized Chinese variety. After a lengthy debate, we were permitted to visit the radio station where, inside a rather dusty glass box, the commune disc jockey was doing his approved patter between numbers:

'The first session of the 10th People's Congress in the district of Yuang Tang opens today. The Executive Chairman delivered the following speech: "Heads of districts, comrades, I am making a report on behalf of the district government authority and emphasizing how our achievements in 1983 prepare us for the tasks of 1984. The leadership of the high-level party organization and the governing body must be carried out conscientiously and in the full spirit of the number one document sent down . . ." Dear listeners, now please enjoy our next number. We are going to play "An Evening in a Military Harbour".'

The DJ tripped the switch and through loudspeakers all across the commune rice fields floated the syrupy violin sounds and sweet girlie voice of one of China's new breed of pop stars. Another district report followed, and then came Neil Sedaka's 'Oh Carol', in Chinese English. The radio stations were originally set up to instruct people on what to do in times of invasion or revolution: now they are a propaganda outlet that takes Neil Sedaka directly to the people.

Before leaving Shanghai, we visited the Opera School where boys and girls from the age of five are prepared for a gruelling career in classical Chinese opera. It is a somewhat austere boarding school and on our first visit we were firmly discouraged from seeing the conditions under which the children lived and worked. But when we returned, we were permitted to film in the dormitories and dining rooms; though again they had been hastily redecorated and the food that day was so unusual that the children broke ranks to fight for fish and chicken. The Opera School had been shut down during the Cultural Revolution. All the ghosts, emperors and mythological figures that were the standard cast of ancient Chinese opera had been exorcized and revolutionary heroics took over. But a few years after the downfall of the Gang of Four, the school reopened. Teachers were brought back from the countryside where they had been banished and slowly, cautiously, parents started to send their children for a classical training again. Infants who had been born midway

**Bian Ren-Qing, a brilliant performer of the Chinese lute or pi-pa, works in the electronics factory writing propaganda**

**Dramatic sounds from the gu-qin, played in China for 3,000 years. Now there are less than 100 people able to play it**

through the rigours of the Cultural Revolution, entirely cut off from the traditions and ideas of ancient China, were being re-educated in the classics. Many of them came from families that had once had close connections with the performing arts and wanted their children to carry on those traditions, whatever the risks.

The training at the school is tough: children struggle for weeks to learn the stylized elocution of Chinese opera accompanied by all the minutest intonations, squeaks, laughs and gestures. Hours each day are spent in body building, painful acrobatics and even sword handling. Standard school lessons are interspersed with opera rehearsals, as well as with memorizing great chunks from the ancient

classics. We felt ourselves as near to the old China as we ever could be in this institution wholly devoted to the study of Shanghai opera, where even in their time off the children learned to play traditional instruments, talked in opera language and practised the ancient arts of face painting and makeup. Nowadays, the competition is fierce and less than one child in 10,000 gains entry. Success depends as much on his or her physique (for example, having longer legs than the average Chinese) as on the wishes of the family.

From Shanghai, we flew north to the capital Bei-jing, which – as the administrative centre and capital of China – is a far more grey and formal city. It is also much more cautious in its presentation of music and the arts. Above all, western classical music has taken on enormous prestige and has a diplomatic status all of its own. This attitude is rapidly spreading across China. Any visitor showing interest in Chinese music is immediately taken to a western music academy where students perform Mozart and

Beethoven on violins and pianos. The Chinese assume that westerners use their own cultural standards to judge musicianship, so the ability to play classical western music has acquired overriding importance. Under the Gang of Four, the western classics were condemned as unsound musical material. The Peking Philharmonic Orchestra and its conductor, Li Delun, were sent to the country for manual field work. Reinstated in Peking, Li Delun now likes to cycle to work, even though he is principal conductor of the city's major orchestra. He is a huge amiable man who did not escape persecution in the Cultural Revolution. Before being sent, as he put it, to a 'cow shed', he had been compelled by Jiang Qing to stop playing western classical music and to conduct instead the eight revolutionary pieces acceptable to her. These he conducted night after night and month after month with a placard on his back admitting the error of his former ways. Then, after 1976, came the performance of a western classic, for Henry Kissinger's visit. Li Delun pulled the scattered orchestra members together and

attempted a hopelessly under-rehearsed Beethoven symphony. It was a fiasco. So they were instructed to learn how to play the western classics properly. But even now, Li Delun informed me, there are strict constraints on what he can conduct. The standard western classics are acceptable, but most twentieth-century or modern music is still politically unsound. Li Delun and his colleagues fight these restrictions subtly: they invite foreign conductors and orchestras to perform modern works (a term that would cover, say, Britten and Shostakovich but nothing much later) which they can then build into their repertoires. The Shanghai film studios offer another way forward by incorporating into their feature film scores as much contemporary music as possible. If they get past the censors, they gain acceptance. All in all, western classical music is becoming China's latest cultural fashion.

It was in Peking that I first encountered the true brilliance of classical *Chinese* music. During my first research trip I was sitting through a dull show of popular songs in the main Peking music school when, as a final item, a little man with framed spectacles strode in carrying an instrument called the gu-qin. It was a block of wood with seven strings that had been played in China for 3,000 years. Wang Wen Guang turned out to be one of the greatest musicians of China: his own gu-qin was 500 years old. He played it with an intensity and lyricism building to controlled violence as he plucked the strings and hammered the sides of his instruments with his hand. His hair flopped across his face, his spectacles fell to the ground as he 'bent' and 'slid' the notes in a way I had never heard outside of North-American blues. The piece he played was 2,000 years old. It was

**Mo Zhong was once a Taoist priest and temple drummer. During the Cultural Revolution he drummed at home with chopsticks**

called 'Quanglingsan' – perhaps the world's oldest existing musical composition. It told the story of a blacksmith who, seeking to avenge the death of his son, learnt to play the gu-qin so perfectly that the Emperor invited him to court. The blacksmith concealed a sword beneath the instrument and, at a crucial moment, he drew it out and sliced off the Emperor's head. The passion of the story is matched by the music and makes a mockery of the emasculated, placid image of Chinese classical music that we have received in the west. It was one of the most exhausting and emotional musical performances I had ever witnessed.

Wang Wen Guang is an exceptionally brilliant musician, emanating a sense of joy as great musicians do, but he does not play too often today in China. Gu-qin music is still regarded with caution as the most elite of all the classics. The notation is itself extraordinary – it is all in Chinese written characters, each with detailed information: for example, 'Stop the fourth and fifth strings with the left thumb, while the fourth finger of the right hand plucks the rapid trill reminiscent of water running down a stream'. There are literally thousands of characters to learn. Wang Wen Guang explained that less than 100 people are now able to play the gu-qin in China. During the Cultural Revolution he was sent, as a punishment for

being devoted to his instrument, to labour on a farm for ten years. That was at the peak of his career in his early twenties. After 1976 he returned and took up the gu-qin again. Not only was it extremely difficult to play, he explained, but it was a sort of philosophy in itself. Volumes had been written about it. An ancient list of rules was drawn up as to where and when it could be played: when not out of breath or tired, not after drinking nor following sexual intercourse. Traditionally the gu-qin was a Taoist instrument and played as a form of meditation. Incense should be burned to create the right aura before the performance. It was said that the greatest gu-qin of all was the one that makes 'no sound'.

Following the Chinese classics to one of their sources, we travelled by train to the ancient city of Soochow about 50 miles west of Shanghai, which was once a centre of Taoist worship. Here on my first trip, I had met a Taoist who sat at dusk in an ancient rock garden and told me that the finest of all music was the sound of raindrops falling on lotus leaves. 'The only thing that spoils my meditation,' he added, 'is the appalling visitors I have to put up with.' By this he meant not foreigners but the Chinese themselves. Not surprisingly, he had been replaced, and on the filming trip we had to work with a stern party member who insisted on

**The ancient city of Soochow, once an important silk centre, is famed for its gardens and canals, many sadly polluted**

Xinjiang province in the far northwest has always been one of the crossroads of Asia: Turfan with its mosque has a large Moslem community

looking through the camera before every shot. He was anxious about the 'tourist image' of Soochow and the fact that most of the ancient canals – for Soochow is known locally as the Venice of China – are heavily polluted and blocked by a mass of hooting, belching barges.

I was anxious to find a young man, Bian Ren-Qing, who had been described as a brilliant virtuoso of the pi-pa – a Chinese lute and one of the most important instruments in the classical repertoire. I had heard about a piece called 'Ambush on all Sides' which depicted a terrible battle between the warring families of Han and Chan, and I wondered whether it could be performed for the film. It was several hundred years old and I was unsure if it was permitted. When I found the pi-pa player, he was indeed a brilliant musician, but was working as an assistant clerk in the propaganda department of a local electronics factory. This meant he was unable to practise or play. It was secretly mentioned to me by a local that the cadre families had wanted all the music academy places for their own children. But somehow, with almost no rehearsal, he played the famous battle piece magnificently. Its wild and untamed music was perhaps more extreme in its tonality than any western music I had heard. Once again, it was a piece of music to challenge our preconceptions of a quietly reflective and delicate classical Chinese music.

Bian Ren-Qing's father explained the problems his family faced back in the Cultural Revolution:

'Life was tough for us. They cut our wages and we became factory workers. There are seven in my family and together we earned only £8 a week. But my son loved the pi-pa . . . he often burned the midnight oil playing. There was no comfort at home, no cushions or stool. Sometimes he would get bed sores on his bottom or he would play till the strings cut into his fingers. But he would say: "I have to play".'

The son continued:

'After the overthrow of the Gang of Four, my parents were rehabilitated. We feel alright about performing now because importance is being attached to music by the central body of the Party. By Deng Xiao-Ping and Hu Yao-Bang. They show concern for "intellectuals".'

In the evening, our Soochow guides took us on to a folkloric show, where in the middle of a rather average folk orchestra sat a tiny old man, bald and with a hearing aid protruding from one ear. He seemed an anomaly, sitting bolt upright and playing his drums with an aura of power and certainty. Somehow he separated himself from everyone else on the stage. At the end of the performance I asked who he was and they told me Mo Zhong, a former Taoist priest who had learnt his drumming in the temples. Taoism relates classical Chinese music to its earliest folk roots – it is a popular and mystical religion that developed over thousands of years, incorporating music on a more spiritual level than the orderly and structured Confucianism. Drumming is highly significant in Taoism. It is both a call to the temple and a way to summon up the spirits of dead ancestors.

After much discussion, we managed to extract Mo Zhong from the indifferent performing troupe surrounding him and he told us about his family traditions:

'I am 72 years old and learned to play the drum from my father, who was a Taoist. In the old days, when lords and capitalists celebrated their birthdays Taoist bands were usually invited to give performances at certain houses. If they gave you gifts of money, you piped and drummed. But this is not practised any more. My father did story telling and ballad singing to the accompaniment of stringed instruments. But they needed a drummer and that is how I started. In the old days we were very poor. I continued drumming in Taoist temples, but when the Cultural Revolution came, I had to stay at home and do "neighbourhood work". Instead of playing the drum I beat on the table with chopsticks. I didn't give up. I continued practising because otherwise I knew I would never be able to play the drum again.'

I was told that Mo Zhong had buried his instruments at the bottom of his garden when the Red Guards came and, in frustration, they broke his hands. But by drumming on wooden blocks or on his dining-room table he strengthened the bones and was able to recommence his art after the Cultural Revolution. Now the Chinese government is opening and repairing the Taoist temples that were smashed by the Red Guards and is turning them into tourist sites for visitors to photograph. There is an increasing freedom to worship and one evening we heard the distant drums and gongs being beaten again in a Taoist temple in the Soochow market place.

Discussing religious freedom with my Chinese production team one day, it was suggested that a visit to Xinjiang province would introduce a totally different culture and music to the film: that of the Islamic community of a small desert town called Turfan. I had wanted to get away from the Han culture of the east, which is often presented abroad as being *the* music and art form of China. I wanted to go to the furthest provinces and see Chinese music on a different level, where it related closely to the way of life and was an accompaniment to social rituals and ceremonies. I travelled with my advisors extensively in the north and south and Xinjiang did indeed provide the contrast we had been looking for.

Xinjiang lies between Mongolia and the south Russian border. Its capital is Urumji. We flew there in a Russian plane accompanied by our excited Chinese interpreter for whom this trip was as much an adventure as for ourselves. Her name was Zhang Zhimei and it was she who

**The street market in Turfan attracts people from far away — reputedly one of the biggest private markets in China**

had been so helpful at times of misunderstanding, and who was to prove her worth again among the Ueger people of Xinjiang. After six hours flight we arrived at the provincial capital – a disappointingly ugly, smoky, industrial city, quite close to the Russian border. It revealed a high cultural mix: old Buddhist and Taoist temples converted into mosques and street markets packed with rogues peddling narcotic substances and fake antiques. There was a heavy military presence in Urumji since it was so near the border. We saw armed coaches going by in convoy with bars on their windows and mattresses piled high on their roofs. Inside were

prisoners with shaved heads, their faces pressed against the glass as they were driven to a giant prison camp deep in the Gobi desert.

It was a hard, hostile desert of stone, surrounded by white-capped mountains and green valleys. That evening we were taken to a local wedding in Urumji and the music was totally unexpected. The Uegers are a Turkic-speaking minority and their music is based upon the Twelve Maqam – an ancient Turkish court music. Their instruments are of Turkish origin too, like the hand drums and the tambura. The wedding music started slowly, a mystical and meditative piece with an opening like an Indian

**At an Islamic wedding
in Turfan, the women
gather together in
one room to lay out all
the bride's gifts**

raga. Abruptly it changed its rhythms into a whirling Turkish dance tune. The guests leaped from their trestle tables onto the dance space where they swirled and spun with piles of cups balanced on their heads, their necks undulating from side to side, Indian-style. Here we could see the history of the silk route which had run from Turkey down through India and into China. Indeed, there is a substantial Indian influence in the area, and the nearby caves of a Thousand Buddhas had been horribly mutilated during the Cultural Revolution. But what a contrast in atmosphere from the rigidity and formality of the east! Here were fiery, emotional people who dragged us onto the dance floor, laughing and gesticulating with pleasure.

Our Han guides were amazed, even a little frightened; for a moment they couldn't believe that this too was China.

The next day we drove for about three hours into the Gobi desert, down to an ancient market town called Turfan, which was once a stopping place on the silk route. It is a hot and dusty place built of mud and clay bricks near an oasis. Again, before starting to film, we had to pass through a baptism of fire. The local foreign affairs committee decided to accompany us and were so suspicious of foreign film makers with their Han guides (there is ill-disguised hostility between Uegers and Hans) that they refused to allow us to film or record any images or music that we wanted. Instead they took us to a street filled with 1950s Russian-style buildings and instructed us to film them. We refused. My interpreter suggested there was one way out: I had to make a speech that would convince the foreign affairs committee of our good intentions. I spoke for five minutes, during

**The family and guests meet the night before the wedding to dance to their fiery Turkish music**

which time our cameraman, Chris O'Dell, filmed unnoticed. Zhang Zimei translated my speech from English into Han, embroidering and elaborating. It was then translated from Han into Ueger and grew from five to nearly 15 minutes. At its conclusion, the foreign affairs officer announced a lunch break. We sat on separate tables in a hostile atmosphere. We started to make contingency plans, trying to think of something that would fill the gap left by

this failure. The foreign affairs officer then approached our table and told us to follow his car. Once again, he drove down the street of 1950s Russian buildings and we were sure we had failed. But his car drove on through old Turfan and up to an ancient mosque on the outskirts of the town. 'There,' he announced, 'we've changed our minds. You can film whatever you want. You are our guests.' So we had the freedom to film anything and everything

**The night before the
wedding, the elders
in Turfan gather
to discuss the terms
of the dowry**

in Turfan, even inside the mosques to which the
faithful are called to prayer by an imam who
simply stands outside the doors, sticks his
fingers in his ears and belts out a prayer call –
until his voice is gone.

What we had come to film was a wedding.
Not a cadre one with extravagant amounts of
food and organized entertainment, but a
genuine local wedding. Yet the only one in town
was planned for July and not May, as we had
been told. When we visited that family they
happily agreed to bring the wedding forward,
although the new couple had nowhere to live.
They were trying to build an extension to the
groom's father's house and at that point only the

foundations and a foot or two of wall had been
constructed. The foreign affairs committee
worried that it looked ugly, but we assured them
that we would point the camera the other way
and film the courtyard hung with vines. After
further discussions it was agreed that we would
return in two days' time. When we did, and
entered the courtyard, we thought we must have
walked into the wrong house. In 48 hours they
had built a totally new home. The roof was on,
the walls were finished, even the doors and
windows were painted and the glass panes
fitted. Electricity lit the rooms and they were
ready for the wedding.

On Sunday morning at dawn the families
climbed into their donkey carts and drove down
the tree-lined lanes to Turfan market to buy
their presents. They shopped among the sheep
and camels, at privately owned stalls selling
silks, tobaccos, false teeth, tortoiseshell
spectacles and cures for tape worms or boils.

IAN OWLES

**Filming in Turfan required careful negotiation with the members of the foreign affairs committee**

Cassettes were playing in all the food stalls where clouds of steam rose from tin buckets filled with noodles and sheep heads. This, we were told, was the largest private market in China.

At the bride's home preparations were made for the imam who was to officiate the wedding in traditional Islamic style. The dusty roads were packed with carts bearing colourful gifts and barriers had been built at every corner to force visiting guests to give a bribe or gift towards the wedding, and where violent but playful arguments ensued. At the bride's house all the women had assembled to display the gifts which were lifted one by one out of a giant tea chest for the inspection of the assembled guests. Silk scarves, shoes, photograph frames, dresses, even a watch were shown; and the elders murmured their approval as the names of donors were called out. The imam came and said his prayers and blessed the couple who, by local custom, were not themselves present but symbolically represented by some elders. Then the bride, covered in a white shawl, was carried by her uncle to a waiting car, all the while wailing and crying in the manner prescribed for a Ueger bride about to leave her family. Suddenly everything stopped. It was lunchtime and the foreign affairs committee insisted that we eat for an hour. We protested. How could we miss filming such an event? They waved their hands and whisked us away into a neighbouring house where we unwillingly ate our way through a magnificent feast. An hour later we returned to the wedding, only to find that everyone had waited exactly as we had left them, as though frozen in time. The drums and flutes began again, the bride recommenced her hysterical wailing and the whole procession sprang back into life and continued on its way to the groom's house.

There we had our final skirmish with the local powers. To start the celebrations a troupe of incredibly smooth and costumed men filed in and performed some theatrically acrobatic dancing. They could not possible have been genuine guests and we refused to film. In all the heat and flurry, I overreacted: 'You're insulting the people here; what you're saying is they can't dance well enough to be filmed at their own wedding'. Sure enough, the foreign affairs committee had decreed that a visiting folkloric troupe should put on a show for the film. We finally got rid of them and the celebrations proper commenced. As the wild and unself-conscious dancing began, the musicians played the ancient melodies that had accompanied such celebrations for centuries along the silk route. An ensemble with Turkic instruments appeared, seating themselves in the courtyard, and a comic mime dance was performed for the assembled guests. At dawn, we left them. The skies had turned grey and a heavy dust storm

**The bride is carried by her uncle from her family's house: happy to be married, she still weeps and wails as befits her**

**The Imam arrives and blesses the young couple whose wedding was brought forward for the film**

swirled around the town obliterating the snow-capped mountains that surrounded it. I asked the leading dancer, Mr Hasimu, whether he would say a few words about what the music meant to him and the Ueger people. He consented, pulling up a chair in the empty courtyard. But before we could get started, the foreign affairs committee arrived and hovered menacingly. I asked, 'Has the music changed much since the Cultural Revolution?' Mr Hasimu glanced nervously around him and at the heavy-set cadres in blue and failed to answer. I tried again, 'Mr Hasimu, has life changed much here since the problems of the Cultural Revolution?' He replied, 'I am a happy man, married with a wife and two children. They go to school, I do my work and we have enough.' Then he rose from his chair with a hint of a smile and walked away.

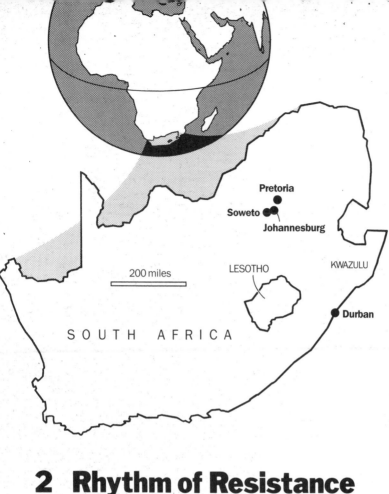

# 2  Rhythm of Resistance
## *The Black Music of South Africa*

Late on a Saturday evening at a black workers' hostel outside Durban the inmates were preparing for an all-night song contest. We smuggled ourselves past the police guards who kept a 24-hour watch on the hostel gates and perimeter walls. Inside the main hall, the organizers hastily drew thick blinds across the windows and put the finishing touches to a wooden stage. The all-night contest is an almost weekly event in black South Africa when different groups of workers sing in competition against one another and when the traditional prize is not money but a goat.

Groups of competitors filed in from segregated black townships further afield, all of them serving the white industries and businesses of the resort city of Durban. Soon it was dark outside and to our surprise we were led back out of the hostel, surreptitiously, by the contest organizers. We wandered with them through the poorly lit backstreets of Durban and at every bar or restaurant they pressed their faces to the windows, peering inside as though searching for someone. Finally reaching agreement, they abruptly swung open the door of a run-down cafe and grabbed a white man who was

attempting to eat a doughnut at the counter. This, they explained, was their way of selecting a judge for the contest. He should not be black, for a local man might have tribal or family preferences for some of the groups. So the judge had to be a white man who would know nothing of their customs and traditions and would be so ignorant as to be unbiased.

Their choice was particularly apt. This 'judge' had just been released from prison after serving ten years for armed robbery. He had been wandering the streets aimlessly, delaying the moment of going home, when suddenly he

**After 12 hours of a song contest, the winners step up to claim the prize goat — real wealth, not white man's money**

found himself bundled out of a diner by half a dozen black strangers in pinstripe suits. In bewilderment, he agreed to become judge for the evening. His pallid face, blue, glassy eyes and ill-fitting suit all bore witness to his recent incarceration. He was led down the street

**A white outsider has been abducted from a bar to judge one of the weekly song contests — in his ignorance he is fair**

through the gates and half-lit courtyards to where several hundred hostel dwellers were gathering for their all-night session.

Inside, in the dark impersonal hostel dormitories, groups of contestants were changing into fancy costumes and rehearsing harmonies with a total disregard for the others trying to rehearse around them. Fifteen hundred men lived, sixteen to a room in this all-male hostel. It was policed and controlled by the city authorities so there could be no spontaneous protests by the inhabitants against their living conditions. That night women were allowed to come and watch their men take part in the contest.

Each group of competitors filed in singing, past the judge – the only white man in the hostel other than ourselves. He sat at a rickety, wooden table directly below the stage. The groups wore a variety of costumes: blue coats and white gloves, black suits or smoking jackets. Each performed a selection of songs: some hymns, some gospel, some local Zulu lullabies. The pasty-faced judge stared back at them impassively. Puffing clouds of blue smoke from a narcotic cigarette, he attempted to make some sense of this event. Singers stood on their heads with pipes stuffed in their mouths; they balanced on their hands; they executed perfect choreographed routines. When they finished, each group descended from the makeshift stage and passed back through the audience – wildly clapping and cheering – to their own partisan section.

The contest began at 9.00 in the evening and by 9.00 the following morning the last weary participants finished with a lullaby. 'Sit down, sit down,' shouted the black organizer to the confused white judge as he tried to leave his chair and stagger to the lavatory. 'Your job isn't finished yet, stay there.' A blackboard and a piece of chalk were placed in his hands. Then came the awesome responsibility of marking up the number of the winning group – a dangerous matter, as losers were unlikely to take failure kindly. The judge thought long and hard. He finally decided to make two groups equal first. Amid a welter of boos and whistles, the prize was hauled on stage, kicking and butting at all the contestants, to be shared out later amongst them. The window blinds were drawn to let the morning light fill the room and we were ushered out, again secretly, into a bus and away to the 'white side' of the city.

All over Durban, we passed black road gangs who toiled all day under the supervision of white men. They sang Zulu songs that their white chiefs could not understand, like 'The whites be damned they call us Jim'. For six days a week, men like these do the dirty jobs of the city: they are the road builders, cable layers, hospital cleaners and unskilled workers who at night are forced to live in segregated hostel compounds like the one we had just visited. One white road gang supervisor did not want us to film the men singing – he had guessed the song's content. He demanded to know what we were doing and then threatened trouble – 'Big trouble, man.' He noted our car number and phoned the police. Back in our hotel room, the door suddenly burst open and four burly white policemen thundered into the room, attempting to grab our film stock. We countered their threats with reason and a little bit of subterfuge, showing our permits and explaining that we had permission to make a film about the black music of South Africa.

Any music that truthfully reflects the life and problems of the blacks would not be found in the white city but in the black townships. Though we were forbidden by law to go to those places, we made our own arrangements with black musicians and went.

That was the start of our many problems with the South-African police during the making of the film. In Johannesburg they often followed us at a close distance, in shiny cars, with their pump shotguns and mirror shades clearly visible, presenting a constant warning that we should not stray out of line. Remaining for a while on the right side of the tracks, we visited a wealthy white suburb where we found Sipho Mchunu working as a gardener in the house of a prominent business man.

Sipho was one half of a well-known duo, 'Johnny and Sipho'. He had to take this manual job as no black person was allowed to be in a white area for more than 72 hours at a time without a white employer to sign his papers. Sipho had consistently refused to bow to the pressures of the white music business and would not make the kind of music that the white-

**Blacks and whites are not allowed to play together on stage for a mixed audience: the duo of Johnny and Sipho has defied this rule for many years**

controlled record industry wanted of him. His most recent song, 'Don't run from the gun', had never been published because of the 'inflammatory' nature of the lyrics.

Sipho explained:

'I was brought up in Kwazulu where my father sent my seven brothers to school. But he kept me home because he loved me. He made me herd his goats and cattle out in the fields. I learned to play a tin guitar made from a petrol can. When my father died I was forced to become a migrant worker to support my family. I couldn't read or write, but became well known as a street musician. I refused, however, to learn English. I wouldn't learn the white man's language.'

But realizing it was necessary to understand the white man's tactics and to communicate with him, Sipho decided to attend Harry Oppenheimer's school. Oppenheimer is the head of the Anglo-American Corporation and one of the wealthiest men in the world. His wife had started a school for their 80 gardeners when she felt pangs of conscience after the 1976 Soweto uprising. Its purpose was to teach the Zulu gardeners the kind of language they would need in a white man's world. In class the teacher asked, 'The madame she was go town. Is that good English, Sipho?'

In 1979, Sipho and his musical partner Johnny were unique in South Africa because, unlike Sipho, Johnny is white. Johnny explained how the duo evolved:

'I had always been interested in playing guitar and one day when I was 14 and was at a store I saw a Zulu guitarist sitting on the wall.

**Sipho standing in the hills surrounding the village where he grew up in Kwazulu, one of the bantustans or African homelands**

English with their cannons and rifles and those stories had a childish, romantic appeal. I began to learn things which are not in our school history books. To be with the Zulus I had to become humble and to learn how to behave. I was lucky because I was still a child and had not yet achieved a white man's status which would have made this friendship impossible.'

That evening Johnny and Sipho were performing together in a mixed club hidden away inside the Johannesburg Market. They played haunting Zulu melodies, using a mouth bow (similar to a jew's harp) and guitar. Johnny introduced the last number for those whites in the audience who were ignorant of Zulu mythology:

'This next song describes two fighting bulls. One is large and strong with huge horns and one is small with tiny horns. But as they fight it becomes clear that the little bull is going to beat the big one. From this story comes a Zulu proverb which says: the bull does not stab with his horns but with his fighting knowledge. It is the spirit that counts, not superior weaponry. This is a tale that symbolizes the victory of the underdog over his oppressor.'

Johnny and Sipho had seen some hard years together. Another recent record of theirs had been banned: it was considered by the authorities to be 'an incitement against work' and unacceptable because it used slang:

He was a cleaner who lived close to our house and I asked him to teach me. But then he returned to his village in Zululand. One day I saw Sipho playing in the street: we got to know one another and decided to play together. This was very difficult because legally blacks and whites were not allowed to play on stage to a mixed audience. But we organized a few little hidden venues where everyone, blacks and whites, could come together and enjoy each other's music. For us, music is a feeling. I'd rather struggle all day to discover a chord than learn how it is part of a logical progression.

'The more I got involved with Sipho and the music, the more I began to understand about the Zulu people – which in South Africa is difficult for a young white. I had read about the battles where the Zulus with spears beat the

*Father! the world is heavy,*
*Father! work is bucking me,*
*Father! the money I get is nothing*
*And I wish that the week would end.*
*Come, come Friday, my darling,*
*Come, come Friday,*
*Work is haunting me.*
*Come, come Friday, my sweetie,*
*You are the girl to whom*
*I'm really betrothed.*

The duo's lyrics – mainly Sipho's – always related to the experiences of the black people around them, yet one of their numbers was banned by the white authorities as 'an insult to the Zulu nation and an indictment of social relations in the city'! But Sipho's music *is* the music of the Zulu nation. We travelled back with him to his homeland village in the rolling valleys of Kwazulu. Only the old and sick, the wasted and the very young lived there: all the able-bodied men had been forced to leave and try to make a living in the cities or the mines. Sipho's wife and family were not allowed by law to live with him in Johannesburg, so he could visit them – just once a year.

Getting to the village was not easy for us. Being white and, even worse, a foreign film crew, there was no question of receiving formal permission to record the genuine life of a depleted Zulu village. So we drove at night without lights to shake off the police cars tailing us. We gave false addresses, checked in at one hotel and then immediately departed by the back door. But the police were hard to shake off that night. Finally I pulled onto a mountain path where we sat still, in silence, hearing cars go by for about half an hour, until we knew we had lost our tail. As we reversed onto the road, I discovered that a front wheel of the car had been hanging over a precipice several hundred feet deep which, in the darkness of the night, we had failed to notice.

We then located Sipho's village by means of a prearranged sequence of headlight flashes in a sort of schoolbook morse code, and were received with warm hospitality. We were given a small kraal, or hut, to ourselves and a welcome hot dinner of chicken with mealie. We settled down for the night, hoping to rise at dawn to start filming life in a Zulu village – the lullabies and work songs for herding and drawing water, the traditional rhythms by which they lived their lives. But that night was not a peaceful one. Around two o'clock in the morning the village was violently awoken by what sounded like loud gunshots coming from all directions. Sipho and the village elders rushed into our kraal. They told us to lie low and on no account to run back to the car because we would be shot down. Their fear was understandable; our fate would probably be no worse than to be thrown out of the country, but they faced possible prosecution, beating or imprisonment if we were caught. The awful responsibility of what we were doing came home to us. We concocted all sorts of stories to make our presence seem

**Sipho's yearly visit to the village — empty except for women, the sick and children — is a cause for dance and celebration**

accidental. The 'shots' continued and Sipho, armed with a huge stick, disappeared into the darkness to confront the enemy.

Twenty minutes later he returned with blood on his hands. By now we had been hidden in a women's kraal under piles of blankets and when we saw Sipho we anticipated the worst. 'It's all right,' he said, laughing, 'it's just my drunk brother. He was told by other villagers we had white men hidden here so he lit a load of fire crackers he'd bought for a local wedding to scare the wits out of us.' Sipho looked at his hands and the stick: 'But he won't do that again in a hurry.' The next morning we saw Sipho's brother limping uncomfortably around the village filled with self-pity and genuine remorse. We had experienced a fraction of the oppressive paranoia these people live under every day.

While in the village, we filmed not just the sounds that had inspired so much of Sipho's music-making, but also the warm celebrations

**As an urban worker, Sipho had to leave his village and can only visit his family once a year**

that greeted his homecoming. His wife and family and other villagers gathered in a circle as he drank mealie from a huge earthenware pot which was passed around. Old women with sad, drawn faces clapped their hands and swayed their heads wrapped in polka-dot scarves, and a small child in a red smock and paper hat danced with happiness.

Back in the black townships of Johannesburg, many hundred miles away, we spoke with workers who lined the streets in search of a job. Some had been there for months. Street musicians played amongst them beside the peeling wall posters and the shells of battered cars. This kind of urban street music is

called 'Mbaqanga'. It is highly creative, largely improvised and its lyrics are tough, as a local writer pointed out:

'These guys are in the forefront, being kicked and called kafir. These are the invisible people who work in the streets. Professional musicians have at least got some kind of "Ithunzi" or shadow because they're looked up to. But these amateurs are really confronting reality every day in an immediate way; through their music they are saying strong and critical things that other people do not dare to say.'

On the same streets, at five o'clock the next morning, domestics and cleaners hurried to the buses that would take them to the white man's town where they would work 12 hours a day before returning, compulsorily, to their own black townships. Some of these domestics were the Sisters of Zion who, every Thursday, the

**The toughest kind of music is Mbaqanga — street music which is often played by wandering musicians openly defiant in their song lyrics**

**Ladysmith Black Mambazo is one of the best known groups in South Africa: a blend of African and western harmonies**

servants' day off, gathered in a small, pink house near the township of Soweto. Robed in white and blue, they immersed themselves in a fundamentalist religious ceremony which involved calling on Jesus to help them, together with a speaking 'in tongues' and laying on of hands. It was an ecstatic gathering in a stiflingly hot front room beneath a calendar depicting the Resurrection. As the Sisters pledged their faith in God to lead them out of bondage, they clasped small wooden sticks tied in the shape of crosses.

Protest and defiance take many different forms in South Africa, and the church has often been a focal point for the black communities. This Sunday morning a yellow van climbed the township streets with loudspeakers blaring the vocal music of Ladysmith Black Mambazo. These are the famous group of 'Mbube' singers, with their unaccompanied male vocals that verge on gospel. They have sold over half a million records, and though they are a household name to blacks, few whites have ever heard of them. They are musically unique, having developed their song style – a lyrical blend of African and western harmonies – amongst the migrant workers in the men's hostels. That Sunday they were performing in a small suburban church. Dressed in red or shocking pink, with white shoes and velvet collars, they danced each song with a choreographed routine of flying feet, waving hands and swaying body movements. One song quite shocked the elders of the church – it was in praise of the beauty of a young girl's body, full of pagan imagery, sex and superstition. Black Mambazo insist that their music is a celebration of all sides of life and they take it into church because there it will reach large numbers of people. In general, they avoid overtly political lyrics. Their pleasurable and colourfully presented music is a statement of defiance in itself. It was described for us by a black South African poet, now living in exile:

**Record shops in the black townships are packed with customers eager to hear or to buy a copy of the latest record**

'It seems strange perhaps that black South Africans can sing, can dance, can still create music that is an expression of life in the face of violence and oppression. Even the man who is walking to his execution, for example, sings. But the songs that are created and played by black musicians throughout South Africa are songs of opposition, of rejection of the apartheid system that makes a black person a fourth-class person in his own country. Music created by black South Africa is a direct response to the apartheid system under which we are forced to live. In that way it is uniquely South-African music. It is defiant. It expresses the determination that every one of us will win freedom one day. It cannot be explicitly political, so it is subtle. It expresses in its tone, in the sound of the voice and sound of the instruments, the soul of the black South African.'

To counter these 'rhythms of resistance', the South-African authorities have evolved a system of broadcasting controls that keep the black radio service on a tight leash. Of course,

the white radio service would not play any black South-African music at all. But there were at the time seven black stations (including Zulu and Xhosa) totally controlled by a committee of white Afrikaaners. Lyric sheets still have to be submitted with every record, which the committee has absolute power to accept or ban. The music permitted is broadcast between a heavy load of government propaganda and commercials. Everything has to pass through the central committee of censors and only the records cleared by them can be played on the air by a programme producer or DJ.

We interviewed one black producer who preferred to remain anonymous and who, on his way to our interview, had been beaten by several thugs on a street corner. His head bandaged, he described the censorship system for black music:

'They use a thick pen on the cover of the records they send us to obliterate the title itself so we can never see what the original title was. On the actual record, they scoop out the title so it is just not there. On the track, they use a sharp

instrument like a knife or razor and cut across it so that when you play it the needle jumps from track to track and you will never understand what it was all about.'

The censorship committee had recently banned a Bob Marley number, recorded in Jamaica, called 'Catcha Fire'. They had, without humour, ruled the word 'fire' to be 'inflammatory'. So the title track was prohibited on Radio Bantu.

The most commercially dominant music on radio and in the shops was Mbaqanga and records of this kind could sell half a million without the artist being credited. In the same way, without hit-parade listings, major record companies in South Africa, like Gallo and EMI, could employ musicians to jam in the studio doing cover versions of western hits. These artists were often exploited by their own black producers like West Nkosi, who in their turn, were exploited by the white company chiefs. We filmed Mpharanyana (who died a short time later from TB) and the Cannibals recording

'Rivers of Babylon'. It was a sorry affair. The record was being hurriedly produced and distributed before rival versions could be marketed. But the title of the song had a special irony for the performers: for them 'Babylon' symbolized a system of iniquity and slavery that would one day be destroyed. Of this the censor was unaware.

The fear of censorship leads many artists to play safe. We talked to blind Babsy Mlangeni, a popular 'middle of the road' singer, who had just flown into a Johannesburg studio with his manager to record a song about mother love. Babsy's lyrics were all about love or God. But even he and his manager admitted: 'Our music always has some kind of message for people. We sing a song encouraging a person to be not disheartened by obstacles. We give some examples whereby a person can overcome anything provided he tries hard enough. Things will come right.'

Other musicians hid political or social messages in lines of symbolic poetry, for example, Johnny and Sipho's 'Africa kukhala ambangcwele' ('Africa the Innocent, weep'). Still others, like the great jazz-rock musician, Philip Tabane, and his group Molombo, saw the act of playing jazz as being in itself an act of defiance for a black South African. It was a victory over the system since it meant ignoring pass laws and restrictions on movement; it meant forced separation from the family, problems with the police and danger of imprisonment. It meant official unemployment. Tabane played an electric guitar ('Chuck Berry style') against highly complex cross rhythms. Two percussionists wore wrist and ankle rattles and beat with hands and mallets on 16 cowhide-covered drums carved from the baobab tree. The name 'Malombo' had a special meaning in the Venda language of Tabane's homeland:

'It means spirit. That's why I perform with these guys. If I don't really hear the sound of drums, I can't get the feeling of the spirit. Malombo drums are like the call of a witch doctor. My father would play, for example, if

my mother was not there and he wanted to call her back. He would beat some drums and she would come. If something was happening at home like a celebration or a wedding we would beat the drums because we were happy, and if we were sad we would beat the drums, though the rhythms are different each time.'

Tabane went on to explain how different the black South-African music experience is from American blues:

'There is nothing down in the mouth, nothing sorrowful or self-pitying about this music. It's a statement about the love of life. You see, when I played in San Francisco once, the owner of a club said to me, "Philip, I like your music but there's one thing lacking in your performance."

"What?" I asked.

"Before you go on to play," he said, "why don't you tell the people about your country?

**For 20 years the great guitarist Philip Tabane and group Malombo have been drawing widely on traditional sounds for their jazz rock**

low bad your country is, how bad the situation how bad apartheid is? That way you can't "

I told this guy I hadn't come there for sympathy. If I tell people before I play that I'm from South Africa and that it is very bad, well, when I play they wouldn't listen to my *music*. They would say it was a shame, it's sympathy he's after. But that is not what I'm after. I want people to listen to my music. My music says it all.'

In every black township we visited, the record shops were crammed with customers

**Wrist and ankle rattles combine with hands and mallets on drums for the cross rhythms of Malombo's music**

**The Mohotella Queens are an all-women group with an outrageous stage presence**

anxiously searching for some new album, listening intensely on their headphones and then carrying home their treasured possession. Every record was a big investment: at 4 rand it was one-third of a worker's weekly wage. But it was not to be played just at home. The whole street shared it at weekend dances where the beer flowed all night in packed shebeens.

One of the most popular acts in black South Africa was Abafana Baseqhudeni, an all-male group who toured from township to township, playing in dance halls to ecstatic crowds. They arrived on a local bus with a startling all-woman group called the Mohotella Queens, who shared the same Mbaqanga backing group. 'Mbaqanga' is a heavy, doughy cake, symbol of the thudding bass that underpins the heavily amplified Zulu guitars. The Queens had been

around for 15 years, brightening the bleak changing rooms and makeshift stages of such halls with outrageous and provocative clothes (or lack of them) and squeezing into tight, brown wigs. They burst on stage to the thudding beat of Abafana's backing group with absurd dance routines and wild gyrations. This was a rare, free concert. The wooden chairs were filled with children and workers who had hurried back from a long day's manual work on the other side of town. Outside the reverberating tin hall rows of smoky food stalls offered local mealie meal and light refreshment.

Daringly, the show was interrupted by an orator dressed all in black with a heavy brimmed hat pulled down over his eyes. He jumped on stage, grabbed the microphone from the MC and began to shout: 'You know I can feel right now that I'm black. You can feel too in your blood that you're black. Can you get it right, we're black. Happy everybody, happy that we're black.' As he launched into further monologue, he was hastily replaced by the all-male Abafana group who rollicked and rolled

**Abafana Baseqhudeni
are an all-male
group who present
their music with
a rollicking show**

onto the stage, somersaulting and cartwheeling, jumping in and out of each other's arms while the audience erupted with hysterical enthusiasm. For a moment the show was out of control. But Abafana were clever with their lyrics. They had suffered from radio and record censorship too often in the past and they wanted to maintain their popularity. So here, in a township hall where there were no whites to come between them and their audience, they quietened the pace with a jokey number about a black man who has to pull himself out of bed each morning to go and do a lousy job in the white man's world. It was full of good-humoured fun and cynicism and the audience's frenzy was quietened into laughter at themselves and the humiliations they go through every day of their lives.

After the show we tried to go with one musician to a restaurant on the white side of town but we were refused service, time and again, because we were accompanied by a black man. Finally, to our relief, we found a small Chinese restaurant and sat down at a table. The Chinese waiter apologized that he could not serve us; he would be willing to bring our food if the black man either ate in the kitchen or out back with the dog. We left in awkward silence. The cruelty of the system is impossible to avoid. Yet through our travels all round the black townships where as illegal visitors we endangered many people, we met nothing but kindness and generosity. They wanted us to take their music and show it to the world outside for what it really is.

Throughout this century white colonizers have imposed their own cultural forms on blacks as a means of domination. And the black people of South Africa have taken up those forms and transposed them into their own rhythms of resistance. These range from work-gang chants to church songs, from pop hits to street music;

**Away from the tourist
circuit, a private
dance of defiance
from Zulu workers**

they can be heard when the crowds sing freedom
songs at political gatherings, or at strikes in the
barren townships to which they have been
forcibly moved. Whites have appropriated
black music, transforming tribal instruments
into polished museum pieces, into emasculated
anthropology or ethnomusicology, into bland
commercial 'Ippi Tombi' musicals that tour the
world as a phony representation of black South-
African music.

Most publicized of all the tourist traps are
the so-called miners' gumboot dances which we
were asked to film one day. Nattily dressed
miners in polished gumboots performed in a
sort of circus for the avid, chattering tourists
who photographed the show to take back as a
'real slice of black South-African life'. It was, in
fact, funded and staged by the mining
authorities. This travesty is a political
manipulation of Ngoma, a Zulu group dance

with song. Far away from this contrived event
we found the real Ngoma in a workers' hostel
inside Johannesburg.

After their historic victories over the
British army, the Zulu pride of spirit and
aggression towards an enemy were embodied in
this form of dancing. It was brought to the cities
by displaced migrant workers. Its home is now
their hostels.

Amongst the milling, tired workers,
marched a procession of Zulu workers beneath
the harsh glow of a setting sun. They were naked
except for loin cloths, wrist and ankle
decorations and the spears they brandished.
They followed the big bass drum, derived from
the invading British army, accompanied by
whistles and shouts. The drummers and
dancers took up their positions and with
stamping feet and ferocious cries they slowly
acted out their symbolic resistance. Every week
they danced and sang their message of defiance –
towards the enemy within.

# 3 Chase the Devil
## Religious Music of the Appalachian Mountains

Spring snows were melting in the Appalachian Mountains which run for 1,000 miles down the east coast of the United States. Rivers swelled and their waters rose and tumbled past small mountain towns like Hillsville, Virginia. Beside the New River, surrounded by steep slopes, stood a congregation in their Sunday best with coloured umbrellas and a smattering of guitars, singing 'Yes, we'll gather at the river'. The Reverend Bobby Akers, a preacher of the Holiness Church, was preparing to baptize the faithful in the dangerous river waters. The musicians strummed and Akers chanted while the congregation swayed and sang on the river bank in a deafening unison punctuated by cries of 'Praise the Lord', and 'Thank you, Jesus'.

Afterwards Akers led the faithful – clasping at the rope he had tied around his waist – into the swirling waters. At the last moment some of the congregation remembered the cash and wallets in their pockets which they hastily removed before the waters soaked them

through. Then, one by one, he immersed them fully in their Sunday clothes. Suddenly, the newly baptized started to call 'in tongues', a sort of wild and formless babble language, vibrating their tongues against the roofs of their mouths while jumping and twisting in ecstasy, their arms outstretched to heaven. With river water pouring from their hair, they were hauled back onto the shore. Akers quoted from St Mark: 'And these signs shall follow them that believe in my name. They shall cast out devils and they shall speak in new tongues.'

This literal belief in the word of the Bible and in the power of the Holy Ghost is one of the hallmarks of the Holiness Church. Another is its fundamental faith in the power of music. Akers explained: 'We believe in using music to praise and glorify God in our worship. I feel that music is a great blessing. It is a talent that comes from God, and people who are really talented ought to play. Other white American religious sects do not permit instruments other than piano or

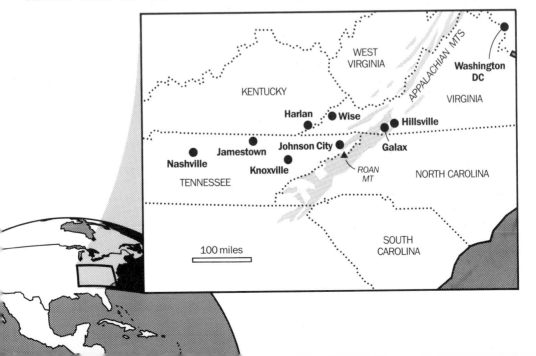

organ in church. But for us, guitars and drums and rock-'n'-roll are the instruments of God.'

When I first met Bobby Akers in the spring of 1982 I was researching the subject of religious music in the Appalachian Mountains with Tony Russell, an English devotee of country music and blues. We hired a car and, starting in Nashville, drove a circuitous and lengthy route around the mountains with an ever-expanding list of contacts to try to get to the heart and spirit of Appalachian music.

Life in these mountains is hard and has changed little since the British and European settlers arrived 300 years ago. Fundamentalist faith in God has been untouched by the pressures of urban America, though splintering into a dozen different and defensive sects. At one extreme, the Baptists regard any music as 'The Devil's work', at the other, the Holiness church goers, whom Baptists still call 'the geese', centre the fervour and intensity of their services on music.

Many of the mountain folk were at first hostile or suspicious of our motives through a natural reserve and fear of the outside world. Many have never stepped beyond their townships, fearful of what they might find outside this essentially poor and unchanging region of America. They have clung fanatically to traditional values in the face of economic hardship and geographic isolation. Stripmines and smallholdings have given little to the generations who have worked them.

Bobby Aker's house was a typical wooden structure with a painted stoop and a plaster angel on the front lawn. Inside, he was sunk in a cushioned armchair, eyeing us suspiciously and weighing up carefully every word we spoke. His wife and children treated him with awesome deference. Around him, as in many Appalachian homes, was a variety of colourful bric-a-brac. Hundreds of porcelain bells filled one glass-fronted cupboard, miniature glass animals filled another; flying ducks and plastic fruits covered the striped wallpapers and everything was polished clean and shiny.

Over the next few days, Akers warmed to

**Plunging into icy waters, faithful members of the Holiness Church are baptized while gospel music is played**

us and our project. He began to talk about himself:

'I was raised in the country and I was more or less backward. I had a great impression that the spirit of the Lord was with me and that if I failed to warn people of their sins, their blood would be recorded on my hands. I was real backward. I didn't want to preach, or to carry the gospel; I just wanted to work quietly and make a living for my family. But through it all, I kept having the impression that the Lord sat upon my shoulders. So I would go out into the woods and pray. Sometimes I would even

preach to the trees because the call was so great. The first time I preached before a group of people I saw a vision of the great multitude with their hands raised as if needing help. That was why I accepted the call and started preaching the gospel to try and win lost souls for Christ. It felt like I had won a great victory.'

Akers worked by day in a steelmill, about 30 miles' drive from his home. But his evenings and weekends were devoted to spreading the gospel. With his own hands he had built a tin church shaped like a garage. It housed a small but fanatically devout congregation. Life is tough for small-time preachers in the States: there are too many bigger, fatter ones around who have turned religion into big business to reap their heavenly rewards here on earth. For Bobby, though, it was a matter of scraping the cents together from a hat passed round at the tent revivals he held every summer, where he found relief from the heat of his tin church in the cool canvas pegged to a village green.

On our first trip that spring, we attended a Sunday service at his church. It was a truly devastating, almost miraculous event. Akers himself was transformed from a quiet, severe,

and sinners leapt up to howl confessions in this communal, cathartic gathering of mountain souls.

Later, driving away from Hillsville, we heard Bobby Akers preaching his Sunday-lunchtime hour on the radio. All over the Appalachians, tiny radio stations broadcast their sectarian messages endlessly. Akers could only afford one hour a week to send his words to the citizens of Hillsville and it was preceded by a riproaring number called 'I know my Lord is going to lead me out from this fearful land'. Akers had crammed half a dozen local musicians into a recording studio about large enough to stable a mule. They pressed between a portrait of the crucified Christ and a pepsi-cola machine. Gearing himself up to a well-rehearsed pitch of frenzy, Akers delivered his message across the airwaves in a rhythmic, staccato pattern:

'America is supposed to be one of the greatest religious nations under the sun. Amen. But we have vastly fallen from God. Amen. Our young people are bound on dope and alcohol. Amen. Sin is rampaging in the streets. Amen. Father rising against father and brother against brother; murders being committed throughout the land. Amen. Since I found Jesus I've got joy. Thank God it's joy, it's unspeakable and it's full of glory . . . until next Sunday, this is Brother Bob saying so long and may the Lord Bless you.'

The commercial spin-offs from the fundamentalist faiths are hard to escape from in the mountains. Every seedy, clapped-out hotel and every fast-food restaurant sells books with titles like *If God Loves Me, Why Can't I Get My Locker Open?* Many are aimed at converting the

shy steelworker into a wild and intense preacher using a hot gospel and rock-'n'-roll backing to get his message across. The pianist was a truck driver and the drummer was ten years old. The guitarist was Akers' own son. Together they pounded out rhythms that rocked the congregation and shook the tin walls of the church till they rattled in response. The congregations cried: 'I can feel it in my hands, I can feel it in my feet, I can feel it all over me,' and soon lost control. They jived in the aisles or raised their hands to heaven and talked in tongues with all kinds of unknown languages spilling from their lips. Others fell into ecstatic trances; tiny children twitched and fell semi-conscious to the floor; old ladies wobbled and shook and hopped around flapping their arms; tough old steelworkers broke down and cried

**In the atmosphere of wild rhythms and song, small children fall into a complete trance**

Larry Richardson used to play banjo with the country greats, then turned to Jesus. Behind him on the diner wall, the vibrant colours of The Coming Rapture, (right)

adolescent before he or she takes 'the wrong path' out of this economically depressed region with its deserted gas stations, tumble-down houses with a dozen kids playing hopscotch on the front steps, and shiny white fundamentalist churches 'holding body and soul together'.

We stopped for a coffee at Herb and Mary's Christian Diner on the road south of Galax. We were looking for Larry Richardson, a brilliant banjo player and guitarist who once played with the legendary Bill Monroe and his Blue Grass Boys (now made a 'National Treasure' by

Ronald Reagan). We knew Larry lived in a trailer halfway down the hillside behind the Christian Diner. The diner was his contact point. Like others, he was initially suspicious, but then warmed to the prospect of getting his message across to millions through the medium of TV. So he strapped on his banjo, and launched into an old mountain song:

*I'm using my Bible for a roadmap,*
*The Ten Commandments will tell me*
*what to do.*

On the walls above him was a painting of the Last Supper in lurid vibrant colours. There was another, more curious painting called 'The Coming Rapture'. This depicted a modern America filled with skyscrapers below which was every kind of motorway abomination. Trucks, limousines and pickups collided, smashed to pieces, and sent bodies spilling across the road into 'The Peaceful View' cemetery. From there the corpses, clad in white sheets, floated upwards towards a glowing image of Jesus high in the clouds. Beneath him, another symbol of decadence – a Boeing aircraft – smashed into a skyscraper and disgorged its sinful passengers. Meanwhile Larry continued singing:

*The twelve disciples are my roadsigns*
*And Jesus will see me safely through.*

I looked down at check-clothed tables and noticed that each one had a ticket, a free ticket.

Mine was printed with the number 777 and admitted me to spend 'eternity in heaven with Jesus Christ'. But when I turned it over, the reverse side read number 666, an invitation to spend 'eternity in the Lake of Fire with the Devil'. A trucker at the next table flashed his credit card: a 'Bank on Christ' card dated 'good thru eternity'.

Then Larry Richardson described why he threw up fame and fortune as a country music star in Nashville and turned to Jesus.

'Well, it seemed with everything I tried to do as a boy, I thought I'd be happy. But there was always something missing. I tried everything I could, but I did not know what to do. My mother, up there in the Blue Ridge Mountains said: Boy, son, you need some help, and she told me where to go. So I asked the Lord Jesus Christ to help me and on 15 March 1970 I gave my heart to the Lord and I knew that things would change. I walked outside and I had never seen the sky so beautiful in all my life. I saw a big tree standing there and the tree seemed like it was just clapping its hands together and praising God because I was born again. I said then: "I'll tell you one thing. Everybody ought to know what I've got. I'm going to tell everybody in the world all I possibly can about the Lord Jesus Christ with my music".'

Nashville, Tennessee, where Larry had once been a star, is the headquarters of the country music business. Its symbol of success is the Grand Old Opry, through which every name from Hank Willliams to Bill Monroe to Dolly Parton has passed. But the Opry casts a shadow: a skids row filled with out-of-luck musicians who have failed to replace the 'big time' with anything more than alcohol or drugs and who end up playing country music to pimps and whores in the bars. Skid row is filled with pawnshops and porn shops and triple X-rated movie theatres. We found Vernon Oxford gazing in the window of one of these, though he made haste to point out he was 'just checking the Devil's work, boys'. Vernon is one of country music's most distinctive singers but he has failed to make the big time. He told us how he had refused to toe the line at drunken parties or make drug deals which, he said, are essential for success in the country music business. Instead, his life had become a search for Jesus and an escape from the clutches of the Devil:

'I first started drinking when I was about 14. Just stayed at home and played the old Hank Williams stuff and cried, just being miserable. I wasn't like the other teenagers. At the time, the rock-'n'-roll age was on and I was considered a square because I still parted my hair and didn't have a duck's tail at the back and didn't go round in gangs and wear motorcycle jackets . . . the Devil blinds everybody . . .'

To illustrate the point, he launched into a song:

*I wandered so aimless, life filled with sin,*
*I wouldn't let my dear Saviour in.*
*Then Jesus came like a stranger in the night.*
*Praise the Lord I saw the light.*

Before showing us the new church he had helped build for his congregation, Vernon had more bitter memories about the country music business:

'Things might have been different if I hadn't spent so much time in the taverns, trying to be the image of what people think is a country entertainer. It's time to let people know that country musicians are not all dope addicts or drunks – just those that haven't met Jesus. The problem was, when I moved down from the mountains to the city, I moved from God. It took me a long time afterwards to rediscover what I had felt in His presence as a child.'

In his Nashville church the inaugurating service began with a 'laying on of hands' – a healing ceremony during which an enthusiastic reverend tried to persuade blind members of the congregation that they could see a whole lot better than they thought they could. Then Vernon sang an old Ray Charles number called 'Lord, I've tried everything but you'. The congregation clapped and wept while Vernon stared into space. Behind him the American flag hung limply from a newly painted flag pole.

*I guess I've tried everything*
*From drinking to hiding my wedding ring . . .*
*I've lived like a fool till I'm just plain tired*
*And I feel all dirty inside,*
*Lord, I've tried everything but you.*

The idea that something precious,

**Vernon Oxford uses
his voice to crusade
against the Devil**

mysterious or spiritual belongs to the mountains
is often part of country music songs. The
romantic attraction of people's roots has been
given a spiritual twist. In fact, in the poor
communities of the Appalachians, from which
most of these musicians come, life is anything
but romantic or picturesque. It is a long struggle
against the elements, and against a depressed
economy.

In Jamestown, Tennessee, life continues
much as it has for centuries. Basically a one-

horse town with a motel and a couple of general
stores, it is a community which has little contact
with the world outside. Jamestown was the
home of an American movie hero, Sergeant
York, who was played by Gary Cooper, and
rounded up half the German army single-
handed after shooting the rest down like
turkeys. He returned a hero. Oddly enough,
Sergeant York was a true hero and his wife is still
alive. She used to hold musical evenings and
invited an old-time fiddler called Sharp to play.
His son, Junior Sharp, now runs the local
honky-tonk, which is safely placed on the
outskirts of town. The honky-tonk is something
of a mountain tradition – a place where citizens

could go to let their hair down with impunity. We had been told it was a thing of the past, but here at the Mountain Top Inn, Junior Sharp's band swung into a number called 'It wasn't God who made honky-tonk Angels', about women 'of loose virtue'. One such lady described her life of squalor and hopelessness. She asked how old I thought she was and I said 30, playing safe. But she was 19, and the reason she looked so old was that her makeup was caked and thickly smeared all over her face. Her family was too poor to install gas or electricity so she put her makeup on each night by candlelight in her wooden cabin. Her father was doing 16 years in jail for murder. Her brother had shot himself between the eyes out on the bluff just a couple of years back, his brains scrambled by the local moonshine (bottles of which were to be bought under the counter at the local police station). Her mother turned out to be the fat lady sitting next to her who opened up her bag to show a snub-nose pistol she always carried. 'In case of what?' I asked. She stared at me uncomprehendingly, tossed back another bourbon and

**Roy Gunter, one of the mountain's great recluses who can 'talk to the Lord at any minute of the day'**

explained that she was there to guard her daughter's virtue. In fact, her daughter had never left town in all her 19 years, never gone beyond the used car lot where the skeletons of pick-ups, green Chevys and burnt out Oldsmobiles were piled five high, and where some families still made their homes in the shell of an old bus together with their ducks, cats and geese.

We had been brought to Jamestown by an enthusiastic character called Bobby Fulcher, who was so modest that we only later discovered that in his own right he was a banjo player, record producer and forestry worker. He took us places nobody had heard of. First to meet Roy Gunter, whom Bobby described as 'one of the last old mountain men'. Roy Gunter lived in a tumbledown shack at the back of a cabbage patch. He was 50 years old, wore ragged old overalls and carried a broken-off car aerial which he used as a 'direct link with God'. Roy believed that churches did no good; that the spirit of the Lord and of the mountains were all around him. 'I doubt,' he said, 'if there's a man a-living in Jamestown, or in the State of

**At the local square-dance hall, they play traditional mountain tunes, regarded as sinful by many locals**

Tennessee, who can talk to the Lord at any minute of the day like I can.' As for music, Roy could not listen to it, not even on the radio. All music, the Lord had privately informed him, was the Devil's work. He pointed a finger in the direction of a wooden cabin explaining Jesus would not even want him to go in there. 'It's not a place,' he said, 'for a Christian man to go. Pride and fast women are the biggest threat to our belief.' The wooden cabin to which he referred was the local square-dance hall. To Roy, dancing was every bit as sinful as music. We shook hands and said goodbye, and I noticed his hands were covered in broken callouses: 'Just piles, boy, just piles,' he muttered and limped off for another meal of Campbell's mushroom soup with locusts – the only food 'the Lord approves of'. The stern life led by Roy Gunter and others like him is a sort of self-imposed exile; they deem themselves sinners and retreat up the mountain to grapple with the conflicts of God and the Devil. These mountain recluses, together with bandits, witches and demons, are still part of mountain mythology, as are the serpent handlers.

Handling snakes is no isolated phenomenon; it happens in Holiness churches throughout the Appalachians, accompanied by electric gospel or rock music. In a Holiness church near Carson Springs rattlesnakes were kept in a padlocked box with the sixteenth chapter of St Mark painted on the outside. 'Jesus said: in my name they shall cast out devils, they shall speak with new tongues and they shall take up serpents, and if they drink any deadly thing it shall not hurt them.' As hysteria mounted in the course of the service, the box was opened and the serpents lifted out. But first came a trial of faith: the preacher invited some of the congregation to gather and drink poison, either carbon tetrachloride or strychnine. They believed that the strength of their faith in God would immunize them. After the poison drinking came the ritual of serpent handling – which carried with it all the excitement of touching the Devil. As the slimy, coiling bodies of the snakes were held up, the congregation

grasped them. The serpents were stroked. One man was bitten. The congregation screamed. No doctor could be called because no-one was allowed to interfere with the workings of God. If the man recovered, then the strength of his faith had seen him through; if he died, then he did so in the service of the Lord. In fact this victim recovered but another, Jimmy Williams – later died from drinking strychnine:

'We believe that the serpent may represent evil, the spirit of the Devil or even the spirit of a man who is bad. And, for that reason, Jesus sent rattlesnakes down amongst us to test our faith in handling them.'

Before leaving Jamestown, Bobby Fulcher took us on our most ambitious trip. We drove our battered vehicles high up the mountainsides, through streams and forests until we arrived at the swaying rope bridge that divided the forest from the home of Virgil Andersen. Virgil was a sparkling, rotund, 80-year-old banjo player with a distinctive style called 'claw hammer'. Despite his years, he still played a subtle and exciting music. Virgil was born in 1902 in Wild-Cat Rock City from which 'no visitor shall leave unfed or unhappy'. Wandering the countryside and taking any job that came his way, as a lumberjack or a miner, he developed his own style of two-finger banjo picking. He learnt how to bend a melody line with impressive bluesy phrasing from the black men he had worked alongside. One of the numbers he loved most was 'I'm leaving you, woman', a mountain blues made slyly amusing and satirical by this hospitable recluse who explained that he and his wife slept with a gun under each pillow.

'I've always been as poor as Job's turkey and Job's turkey was so poor he shivered as he walked. Of course times is better nowadays when God has increased his wisdom to us. It

**Old Virgil Andersen plays white mountain blues which he picked up when working in the lumbercamps**

suits me here at Greenford. Population: one man and one wife. Speed limit: 15 miles a week, the roads so crooked the black snakes jerk their heads off trying to run them. Drinking moonshine whisky and dancing has been my occupation for the biggest part of my life. But now I live out here, alone except for Mabel.'

Virgil had built himself a private church in his front garden where he gave thanks daily for all the blessings bestowed on him since the days his family had arrived from Sweden – bandits who earned the name 'Black Andersens'.

Leaving Virgil, we went in search of another set of old-time recluses, whose music embodied the rich traditions of the Appalachian

**The Roan Mountain Hill-Toppers played their square-dance tunes and were escalated to pop fame via 'Buffalo Gals'**

**Fiddler Joe Birchfield of the Hilltoppers, shunned for years by God-fearing neighbours**

mountains: the Roan Mountain Hilltoppers in East Tennessee, the Birchfield family. An old lady wrapped in a coloured quilt who could never find her teeth, played washboard; Joe Birchfield, cross-eyed, skinny as a rake in denim overalls, played fiddle; Cousin Creede picked banjo, and together with other younger members of the family, they filled the mountain air around their aged mountain shack with the bouncing melodies of old-time square-dance tunes like 'Sugar Hill' and 'Sally Anne'. We talked about their lives and music and the stern religious traditions around them that caused people to regard their carefree dance music as 'the Devil's work', shutting them off from the rest of society. An ironic end to our visit was the subsequent appearance of pop impressario, Malcolm McLaren. After seeing our film, he drove a multitrack mobile recording studio up to the Birchfield family shack, put some

hundred-dollar bills their way and got them to play backing tracks for his record, 'Buffalo Gals'.

Not far from Roan Mountain at Knoxville, Tennessee, a World Trades Fair had just been opened by Ronald Reagan. It transformed a sleepy provincial city into a brash industrialist's Disneyland with gold-dome convention centres and a mass of colonial-style motels. On its outskirts, in a country lane, stood the bright-green wooden homestead of Nimrod Workman. Nimrod was in his seventies, a wizened, tough little man who sang, with a clarity and intensity that belied his years, the old ballads of the Anglo-American tradition. Many dealt with the obsessions of murder, death and family feuding. On the porch of his house Nimrod lay back in his rocking chair, pulled a wide-brimmed hat down over his eyes and sang 'Death of a wayfarer', a haunting, unaccompanied song about the fate that awaits us all. Nimrod had learnt music from his family and perfected his rough country singing style when he worked as a miner. But music-making had always been frowned upon in the community where he had grown up. He talked about the conflicts and ambiguities his family had felt towards music-making.

'Now my daddy, he played banjo and the family played fiddles. But not my mother. Neither she nor my grandmother, who was 118

father and brothers. She herself is intermittently ill. She has seen persecution and financial hardship but her spirit is irrepressible. Hazel sometimes sings together with Nimrod and they joined in a rendition of 'Amazing Grace' which silenced even the neighbourhood dogs and birds. Hazel then picked up the theme of parental guilt and opposition towards music.

'My Daddy grew up in a religious family and I guess it instilled a sense of religion in him, although in his younger life he was pretty rough and carried a gun and made moonshine liquour. But then he got religion and joined the church. He found it hard to reconcile with his gifts as a singer and player of the five-string banjo. After he became a minister, this was frowned upon and considered the music of the Devil – a worldly thing in which they were not supposed to participate. So in his older years he just sat around the house doing nothing. He was also pretty sick at that point. We tried to take a banjo into him so that he could pick at it and feel better, but in fact he felt so condemned by it that he made us take it out of the house. There was an even more extreme case: an old mission friend of ours who was a music collector had made a record of old-time mountain people playing. He had included my dad on the record. My dad was proud of it. So I went to great trouble to get a copy. While he was ill and dying in bed, I brought it home, but that night my father felt so condemned by it that he crawled out of bed at three or four in the morning, when no-one was around, and he scratched that record all to pieces and threw it in the garbage.'

The next day he felt another kind of remorse at having done that to his daughter's gift:

'So he asked me to get him another copy and then he destroyed it – he felt so guilt-ridden. The fact that the church frowned upon his music made him afraid of being excluded from it and from the community.'

Crossing the railways track that led down from the coal mines, we drove on through blinding rainstorms across the mining district of Kentucky, through into Virginia, past the strip mines that had destroyed not only the

years old by then. They said it was a sin to play music, especially in church. When I asked them why, they said they had read in the Bible that the apostles took up their harps and hung them on the walls and never did pick them up afterwards. They said that to listen to music was a sin, even to pick up the instrument was a sin and to play it surely was.'

We arranged for Nimrod to be joined by an old friend, Hazel Dickens. Hazel is not just a fine singer of Appalachian ballads; she is also a committed political activist for miners and for the women's movement. She has seen more than her share of troubles: many of her family dying from 'black lung' mining disease, including her

countryside but also the lives of the people who worked them. There we met up with the Reverend Joe Freeman. He was a smooth, ruddy-faced man of the world, dapperly dressed and with a swept-back 1950s hairstyle. As we drove towards his home in Wise, Virginia, Joe told us how he wrote the song he had recently recorded, 'There'll be no black lung up in heaven'. 'I wrote the song about my dad and the other men who work in the mines who go before their time to meet their Lord and Saviour Jesus Christ, through the black lung disease.' He sang:

*There'll be no black lung up in heaven.*
*No smothering when they walk on streets of*
  *gold.*
*The coal miners that make it in*
*Will be breathing good again –*
*There'll be no black lung over there.*

Like so many other ministers, Joe Freeman was building his own House of God, but finding it hard to meet the bills. It looks as though more money is spent building churches than on anything else in the Appalachian Mountains. Seated in the pulpit of his unfinished church, Joe told us how he came to make music. He had been a sinner, a drinker and a womanizer. His marriage had been on the rocks. Then one day he 'found the Lord' and became a minister. He had always loved music, especially country music and gospel. He explained:

'Elvis started out in gospel too. You could feel God in Elvis Presley's songs in the early days. In all that agony and alcohol, you could hear the spirit of the Lord fighting to get out. I loved that man and his music. Well, I listened to country music and I'd say: "I can sing that and make it into something." So I'd take a country song and make it into a gospel song. If the Devil can steal one of ours why can't we have one of his?

'A lot of the songs would have a kind of rock-'n'-roll beat and I'd be hollering away and some lady would come up to me and say, Joe, you're God's little Elvis. And that's how it all

began, that's how they came to call me "God's Little Elvis".

'I believe that God gave me that musical talent to help me get his word over. A lot of people would come into church to hear the song; singing brings them in and you can get a message to them that eats their hearts and souls and causes them to be saved.

'I'm just an old country boy who was brought up by a coalmining Daddy who preached for 44 years at this church right here and which I'm building up again. Right here, I used to cling to his breeches while he preached the fiery word of God, and some of it rubbed off on me. I believe that Jesus Christ wants us to be a joyful people and that he came to bring us out of the river and out of drudgery, by singing. Jesus offers us the streets of gold and one way we can get there is by busking it, by singing our way into heaven.'

It was a wild and frenzied service where Joe

An ex-miner, the Reverend Joe Freeman has adapted commercial Nashville songs into a religious idiom

rocked and rolled across the pulpit and cried, 'Let's all have a good Holy Ghost time.' His cousin, Emery Freeman, punctuated every line with a 'Thank you, Jesus'. Joe urged his people to the Lord with numbers like 'Wake me, shake me, Jesus' – adaptations of other people's country music. As the service reached a pitch of frenzy there was a 'laying on of hands' by Joe. The faithful who needed healing or help came up to him, clasped his hands, shook and jabbered in tongues and fell in ecstasy, unconscious, on the floor. The musicians joined them, writhing and twisting their bodies, as the congregation swayed and fell upon them. A cripple in a wheelchair rose to praise the Lord, a blind man screamed out his sinfulness, asking for communal absolution. The music was pounding, heavier and louder. Joe leapt from the pulpit dancing around the church to inspire the congregation into feeling the spirit of the Lord.

In the long silence after the service we made our way in convoy through the darkness of a moonless night to a mountain lake. The cars were driven in a semi-circle around it, their headlights shining onto the waters. Joe and Cousin Emery, oblivious to the cold, waded in, shoulder-deep, and called to the faithful. Young and old stepped in to be baptized, dipped in the freezing waters to be reborn, with cries of 'Thank you, Jesus, thank you, Jesus'. Wet, shivering and with ice forming around their socks and skirts, the congregation climbed back into their battered cars and slowly drove back to Wise, Virginia. The headlights caught their cold, pale faces, all of which held a special expression of ecstasy. All believed that a benign force, greater than themselves, was leading them home and that it would ultimately lead them to those streets of gold they knew they would never find in this world.

# 4 Salsa!
## *The Latin Music of New York and Puerto Rico*

A silver-grey Rolls Royce with the number plate 'Salsa 1' pushed its way through rush-hour New York traffic on a hot summer's evening in 1979. Inside, in combat army gear, sat Jerry Masuchi, millionaire boss of Fania Records.

A few miles away in the ghetto of New York's South Bronx, the homely bearded figure of pianist Charlie Palmieri was hunched over an upright piano in a schoolroom. He was enthusiastically attempting to reintroduce migrant Puerto-Rican children to the musical rhythms and culture of their homeland.

On the island of Puerto Rico, 1,000 miles away in the Caribbean, a spirit ceremony of the Santeria sect was taking place around secret effigies – black plaster dolls, red-Indian chiefs with feathered headdresses, a brown, turbanned Madonna with a cigarette between her lips and the smiling figurine of an Irish New York cop. All these were images of the African-based Santeria cult. The musicians who pounded the drums for this ceremony chanted words of the Yoruba language of West Africa which their forefathers had brought with them when shipped as slaves to Puerto Rico and Cuba.

In Cuba itself, a group of cane workers gathered round an antique record player where they stooped, hands on knees, listening to a rumba dance record that Xavier Cugat made in the 1930s.

All these are aspects of salsa music. The children who sat around the piano in Charlie Palmieri's South Bronx schoolroom ranged through every shade of white and brown. They were what New Yorkers call their 'Hispanic community'; others call them the 'New Ricans'. They were the children of migrant workers who had come from Puerto Rico or Cuba to find work in New York. Charlie was explaining salsa to them:

'Now "salsa" means literally a sauce, the kind your mother makes. It's hot and spicy and that's how we describe our music. There was a phrase that started down in South America whenever they heard a New York Latin band – they'd call it a "salsa" band. But basically the rhythms they were playing were those that have been with us since the 1940s.'

He played a mambo from Cuba, a plena from Puerto Rico and then the children in their baseball hats and Mickey Mouse T-shirts were given sticks, drums and cowbells by Charlie to beat out the rhythms of their Caribbean homelands – the Latin rhythms that are their last real link with their past.

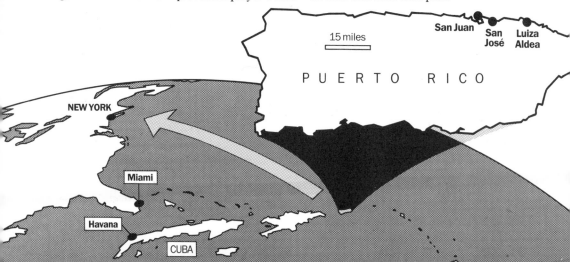

In a garishly painted, noisy bar on 116th Street in the middle of New York's 'Spanish Harlem' I met Felipe Luciano. He was former head of the New York 'Young Lords' – a fight-back vigilante group with the express purpose of asserting the rights of Puerto Ricans. Felipe described his own history:

'I'm part of the second generation of Puerto Ricans, born in New York. My grandmother came here around the turn of the century and I still remember the stories she told of slavery, of the Spaniards leaving Puerto Rico and the Americans coming in. The Americans took over our island in 1898 and it was hard for a black

**Felipe Luciano is an outspoken activist for the New York Hispanic community**

woman at that time to make a living. She washed shirts and married a man named Ulmo, who was a gangster, and had eight children by him. She brought them all to Brooklyn, which was the first Puerto-Rican community here. Then Puerto Ricans migrated to what they call the "Barrio", which is a piece of land they carved for themselves around 110–116 Street in New

A wedding in New York's Bronx district: a guest of honour is premier percussionist of Salsa, Tito Puente

York, roughly bounded between the black community and the Italians, with a sprinkling of Jews and Irish. That was where I was brought up in what I call "sub-poverty", living on the streets and listening to the street music that transcends generations.

'Cubans came here in the 1930s and 1940s. At that time there was a serious race and class problem in Cuba and many people left. They brought with them their music – the danzon (violin music of European style, mainly French-influenced) and the rumbas – from the black ghettos of Havana. They thought the danzon would survive here in New York, but it didn't. What survived was the rumba, the mambo, the cha-cha-cha. These were African rhythms, street rhythms and they survived because they

had intensity and energy and they preserved the cultural consciousness of the people. It's the street music – the music of the people – that will survive. It has had to adjust from a country rhythm which was slower and guitar-orientated to an urban-paced music, and it has survived that. Our music is now much faster than it was 40 years ago. If you compare the clave (the rhythmic pulse) of the 1940s with the clave of the 1980s, it's almost twice as fast now. It has adjusted to the speed of cars, airplanes, of modern life.'

I noticed the jukebox had stopped playing and that silence had fallen in the bar. Lights had come on in the darkened streets outside and we could hear salsa floating out from almost every doorway in 116th Street. We could hear the

complex drum rhythms punctuated by shrill brass and strident, repetitive lyrics – always in Spanish – to which passers-by shuffled their feet. An old grey-haired lady in a red T-shirt and football shorts began to dance with a storekeeper from across the road. Felipe went on:

'There's always a danger. Music is a double-edged sword. It is escapist, it is trendy, it is faddish . . . but it is also revolutionary, dynamic and progressive. It is the politics of the people that determines what will live and what won't. Their experiences will determine whether the music lives or dies. It's where a people's vision lies.'

The next weeks were spent travelling the streets of New York and the island of Puerto Rico to record that vision. I had wanted to film

in Cuba too, but the authorities insisted I could only record what they regarded as 'politically acceptable' music. Moreover, if I filmed in Cuba, they wished to deny me the right to include any sequences of New York 'salsa' in the same programme. I was not prepared to be dictated to in this way.

A friend of Felipe Luciano's, Joe Conzo, was getting married that week in New York's South Bronx district. It was a warm, emotional event surrounded by the worst images of desolation and poverty that any metropolis could have provided for its citizens; an area that politicians, in their pre-election speeches always promised to clean up, an area that is forgotten as soon as the election is won. Indeed a salsa band headed by drummer Tito Puente had visited the White House the week before to try and persuade Jimmy Carter to do something for the Hispanic community. Tito had played 'the peanut vendor' ('*El manicero*' – the most famous of all Cuban tunes in the States) to Carter, whose aides had then treated him and his band with arrogance and contempt. They returned from Washington embittered.

Tito Puente attended Joe Conzo's humble wedding. Tito is known in New York as the 'high priest of salsa music'. Joe had been a junkie some years earlier and his family had despaired of him. But Joe loved salsa, especially Tito Puente and his big band sound, so when he went cold turkey his family bought him every Tito Puente record they could find and played them to him day and night while Joe suffered, swore and sweated through his agonizing withdrawal. Joe pulled through – 'I paid my dues' – and finally the great man came himself to visit. Tito had now come to bless the newly wed couple and play, along with percussionist Ray Barretto, at the reception that followed.

The following day Tito and his 20-piece band were giving a free show in a school yard in the South Bronx. Charlie Palmieri came along to add his jazz-flavoured rhythms on a fuzzy, funky electric piano that had spent the night in the rain. (Charlie is brother to one of salsa's all-time greats: pianist Eddie Palmieri, who has

always invested salsa with fresh styles and sounds.) Soon the crowds were swaying to the Latin-jazz rhythms. The master drummer, the 'high priest', left his band behind with flights of percussive fantasy and complex cross rhythms. The crowds screamed and whistled their excitement. Tito burst into a violent solo on the high-pitched timbales. He chewed his tongue and hunched his shoulders and screwed his face into rhythmic contortions as he pounded the taut snare-drum heads and then executed a miraculous roll on the large cowbell. No-one was paying him that day, his performance was 'for his people'.

But even among the Puerto-Rican community it is not common knowledge that Tito Puente is also a priest of the Santeria faith. For a year, I was told by Joe Conzo, Tito dressed in white and had his head shaved as part of his initiation into its priesthood. Now at night, in the back streets of New York's Upper East Side, Santeria drum rhythms, which once formed the basis of all Afro-Cuban, Puerto-Rican and salsa music, can be heard again, accompanied by ritual prayer and dance.

I was shown some Santeria 'sacrificial rooms' at the back of a 'botanica' shop which sells religious effigies and herbal cures. Inside was a

**In a school yard in the South Bronx, Tito Puente and his band give a free show: he has been playing since the 40s and is master of the timbales drums**

gutter down which the sacrificial animal blood ran and incense was burning – in New York, far from the Cuban roots of the ancestral culture. The original animist faith, brought from Africa to the Caribbean and into slavery, survives. It is no longer hidden behind Christian images of saints and white Madonnas, but has adopted many shapes and forms, in each of which a spirit dwells.

About the same number of Puerto Ricans – around 3 million – live in New York as on their island. There, a busride east of the busy capital city of San Juan, is a small 'black' town called Loiza Aldea, tucked away amongst the coconut groves. The town is affectionately known as the home of the plena dance rhythms of Puerto Rico. On the beach, sitting across the trunks of fallen trees, we found young hopefuls strumming their cuatros (eight- or ten-string guitars) and singing about an American who thought a Puerto-Rican fish was his friend. Instead it attacked him and ate him up. Maybe, suggested the singers, it came from Cuba?

Today, as part of the 'American Commonwealth', the island has become entirely dominated by the US economy. Tax-free businesses and low wages for workers make it a haven for the multinationals. Puerto Rico is also part of the huge American tourist trade and its beaches are filled with condominiums and American-owned hotels. In the Condado Hilton local waiters, dressed up like cowboys with sheriff badges and polished six-guns, serenaded their customers with wild west songs while they piled their plates high with T-bone steaks. When I joined the waiters in the back room later, they were whistling salsa rhythms as they unbuckled their gun belts and spurs.

In the Holiday Inn a folkloric event developed disturbing overtones. A troupe of local performers presented a bomba dance, another traditional Puerto-Rican rhythm. The musical story was about the violent death of an African slave girl at the hands of her white plantation owner. The American audience was intrigued, amused and even a little bored. They could see no relevance in the story at all; for them it was just another charming item of organized entertainment, safely anaesthetized for visiting tourists. In fact what happened on stage was a remarkable example of the schizophrenia of modern Puerto Rica: while performing cameo stories for tourists, the dancers became gradually and hypnotically

**Puerto Rico depends heavily on tourists and the dollar. At the Hilton, waiters dress as US cowboys**

possessed by the power of their own movements, together with drum rhythms pounded furiously out from the wings of the stage by five local percussionists. The organized choreography broke up, movements became blurred in a flurry of frilly white costumes that flared beneath the stage lights as the dancers turned, twisted and fell upon the stage. This magnetic, violent performance ended with a piercing communal scream which echoed around the Holiday Inn's convention hall and brought the house lights up for a polite if hasty exit by a bemused audience.

Outside, I met up with a young salsa musician from a group called Moliendo Vidrio who are radically opposed to US 'occupation' and cultural domination of their island. We talked about the bomba rhythms which, like the plena, are attributed to the mystical seaside town of Loiza Aldea. 'The Puerto Rican

**On the beach at Loiza Aldea in Puerto Rico, young musicians play their cuatro guitars and sing anti US songs**

rhythms,' he explained, 'are clearly African; the Yoruba drumming evolved here much like the Afro-Cuban rhythms of Cuba. But when these are accompanied by a guitar you have the bomba which involves descending chords that go back to the Spanish influence.'

In the slum district of La Perla, which sprawls beneath the walls of the Spanish castle in Puerto Rico's San Juan, the wooden shacks are filled with the sound of bomba and plena rhythms, while street guitarists and bar jukeboxes offer the latest in commercial salsa music. Over the past 25 years, America has poured in millions of dollars to keep the island politically 'in line'. A new middle class has evolved, for whom American domination means security. To them any mention of revolution or political independence is anathema. This is nothing new. Many years ago even the songs of Rafael Hernandes (one of Puerto Rico's most famous composers) had their references to 'political independence' censored, and today those pieces are performed on stage at the local Holiday Inn with no lyrics at all.

By chance, our filming trip coincided with the release from American prisons of four Puerto-Rican 'independence fighters'. Victor Collazo had tried to assassinate President Truman in 1950; he was shot and jailed for 29 years. The three companions, with whom he was returning to Puerto Rico that day, had been jailed for firing pistols into the US House of Representatives. Their leader was a woman called Lolita Lebron. Thousands of Puerto Ricans, waving their national flags, encircled the airport in the burning midday sun, while from roof tops American secret service men recorded the event. Lolita Lebron grabbed a

**Puerto Ricans gather at the airport to welcome back four 'Independence fighters'**

**Puerto Rican band Moliendro Vidrio play for the return of the revolutionaries**

microphone on a makeshift stage and cried to the waiting crowd: 'People of Puerto Rico, my people! How wonderful it is to be back home after so many hardships, after so many years. It's up to you all to make sure that this flag I hold in my hand is never torn down, never trampled on again. This flag, which today they attempt to make inferior to any other in the world.'

With clenched fist salutes and tears streaming down their faces the ageing revolutionaries were led away through the crowd. Moliendo Vidrio, with whose cuatro player I had talked the previous night, serenaded the parting 'heroes' with a song:

*The Puerto Rican will not be downcast,*
*Even though she has no home to love,*
*since her island is not*
*really her own . . .*

It is not only the revolutionaries of Puerto Rico who put politics into their music. One of salsa's biggest stars, Ruben Blades, also records songs with uncompromising lyrics. Ruben is a Panamanian who trained as a lawyer and later became one of Latin America's top performers. Many of his songs identify with the victims of oppression – not of any particular country, for Ruben Blades looks at the Hispanic people as a whole, not according to separate nations. He has recently adapted one of García Márquez' stories, *Nobody Writes to the Colonel*, into a salsa number, replacing the old man who waits for his pension with the figure of a corrupt dictator. 'In Latin America we don't have too many heroes' he points out, 'so musicians carry a heavy responsibility. I'm very much concerned about the young people who listen to our music. But I don't ask myself if music is going to change things. I ask only whether my music will make somebody ask something – put a question into a kid's mind that might otherwise not have been there.

'I think that for too long this business has been run by people who don't understand the music. They always felt the less you say, the better off you will be. In other words, don't get too deep because people don't understand that, they don't want to be bothered by it. It's also the case that a lot of musicians – and I'm sorry to say this – are not too creative. They fall into a pattern that works and they stay there. That is one of the reasons I got involved with salsa music. It is the folklore of the city – not of one city, but of all cities in Latin America. There are so many subjects, so many problems to be sung about. So that's why I said: I've got to get involved in this. I've heard enough of that crap.'

Ruben Blades, accompanied by superstar Willie Colon and a band of 30 top salsa musicians, launched into a new number. It described how a man returned home, walking very slowly, so slowly that his shadow was always behind him. He was not in a hurry, he knew what awaited him in his neighbourhood – the same corner with the same trash cans overturned, the same noise from the bar. These are constant images for the people who buy the music.

Outside the studio, where Ruben and the others were recording, on the streets of the Lower West Side, Felipe Luciano picked up the theme:

'We've got to get away from lyrics like "We love you, the sky is blue, how do you do . . ." We've got to make our lyrics speak and make sense. We're saying to our composers, arrangers and lyricists: "Our sons and daughters are listening to this music. Can we say something in the music about the kind of life they are leading, about their options or lack of them?" Ruben Blades and other are doing that but it's an uphill battle. It is up to the community to buy those records and allow them to succeed. The irony is that the big record companies will still make money.'

Hopeful young Latin musicians filled the corridor that led to top promoter Ralph Mercardo's office in a multistorey Manhattan block, round the corner from where Fania Record's boss, Jerry Masuchi, ran his salsa empire. I had last seen Ralph with Jerry and the boys living it up and throwing parties in Puerto Rico. Now they were back in New York, running Fania Records which in 1979 had a tight monopoly on the music. Since then, Fania has become a shadow of its former self; Willie Colon and Ruben Blades have left to record elsewhere with smaller labels. Younger musicians found Fania's monopoly and its conservatism hard to deal with. Outside Mercardo's office a disillusioned trumpet player told us: 'The major problem is that most of the people running these companies are not musicians or artists. They are businessmen and they look at business in a typically American way – if you find a formula that sells, then flood the market. But Latin music is a lot richer and deeper than that. It has a heavy heritage.'

Inside Ralph's office the walls were predictably crammed with portraits of the salsa greats. Mercardo towered above his polished desk and forcefully gave his point of view: 'I tell some of the guys they are just little stars trying to get bigger, because we have only got one superstar – one star who sells all over the world. She is from Cuba and has been singing for many, many years. Her name is Celia Cruz and she is

FRAN VOGEL

**Ruben Blades, one of the new wave of Salsa musicians, writes lyrics with a message for the Hispanic community**

legendary band had been put together, in the mid 1960s, by Johnny Pacheco. He is a Latin-jazz arranger who started Fania Records with Jerry Masuchi and is still a power to be reckoned with in the Latin music business. He was there that day in the studio, an admirer of Celia's immaculate style.

Celia is a large dynamic lady with a powerful presence, now in her late fifties, who shows no signs of letting up or losing her grip as Latin music's number-one and only woman performer. She is idolized by the Hispanic community – both male and female – and so I put the inevitable question to her: 'Why only you, Celia?'

She replied: 'Many Latin women are fine singers, but we're very badly paid in comparison to American stars. We can't expect to be like Donna Summer in Las Vegas with a full house each night. Latin people have to get up early and go to work and go to bed early, so we can only afford to go to clubs at the weekend. Therefore, we singers earn less. But Latin women can be fine singers.'

Celia launched into another Cuban-based song as if to illustrate what she had been saying to us: 'If a man is good to a woman, she'll be good back but if he's bad, she'll give him nothing. If he treats her like a slave, she'll clear out.'

Celia Cruz was graceful, even regal in manner and waved away our offer of payment for recording her music. In fact, we found this throughout the work we did with salsa musicians. They were pleased to get some 'positive exposure' away from the Latino stereotypes that commercial American TV imposes on them.

On their nights out to listen and dance to their Salsa music in clubs like the Corso, Latin kids dress with obsessive care. Others go to

the Latin Ella Fitzgerald. She is just great. I've never heard her voice crack or get sore – she just knocks it out every time. She's so dynamic; she's like a goddess to me.'

'How would you describe her voice?' I asked.

'It's hard to describe,' he replied. 'It just gives you a good feeling.'

'Why are there so few women singers in the Latin music business?' I asked.

'I don't know,' sighed Ralph. 'I guess there just hasn't been that many around.'

The salsa music business, like so much else in the Latin-American way of life, is heavily 'macho'. It is a man's business in a man's world and Celia is the great exception to the rule. We found her recording some Cuban-based salsa numbers in a New York studio – backed by the Fania All Stars. This

clubs on the Lower East Side or the South Bronx where charanga bands (traditional flute and fiddle) play through the night alongside household names like Hector Lavoe and Ray Barretto. On our way to the Corso Club we had an ugly run-in with some black bootleggers on the street, whom Felipe dismissed with a quiet threat. His reputation as former head of the Young Lords gang was still good.

We walked up the tinsel and mirrored staircase of the Corso to watch tiny Puerto-Rican children hammering away at Tito Puente's drumkit while a vibrant and good-natured crowd packed the floor with complex and intricately choreographed dance movements. Felipe explained:

'What has happened is that, due to the influence of record companies who want to dominate the market with a bland salsa sound, our music, almost insidiously, takes on a status quo role, a pacifist and defusing role. It takes people away from having to look at the reality of their own lives and at the shit-encrusted walls they have to work in.

'Here in New York city we are among the most oppressed people. You've seen the dancers and what I call the cultural priests – the musicians. You've seen the joy, the very life, the pulsating rhythms which are in our community. But all that belies our political reality. You can see the musicians playing three gigs a night, high on coke, for something like 30 or 40 dollars a night, their lips down to their knees, exhausted, trying to support families.'

During a break in the show we went to talk to one of the musicians. 'I go blank,' he admitted. 'I let my frustrations rip about what you have to go through being a musician – travelling, not getting enough recognition, busting up the family. It's the only way to let my frustrations out – closing my eyes and beating the hell out of the bell.'

Another musician butted in: 'That's where the feeling comes from. Because during the 1940s people said, "That's monkey music, African music, we're never going to use it." Today, everywhere you go they have a conga

Celia Cruz began her singing career in Cuba in the 1940s: now the undisputed queen of Salsa, she is still a rare woman in Latin music

drum, a timbales drum, maraccas.'

Out on the streets that night people were celebrating. As on almost every weekend through the summer months, there was a street party: another of the salsa bands had settled down on the corner. Many of the houses on the block were burned out, their windows and doorways blackened and their rooms filled with migrant families or squatters. The store windows were boarded up. Yet despite the squalor and deprivation, there was a sense of community and humour that held families together. Old and young danced beneath the orange street lights with an intensity that blotted

out everything but that moment.

I asked Felipe if the majority of New York's Hispanics felt they were oppressed. 'Without a doubt,' he replied, 'except that we are not a minority. We're actually about 3 million Hispanics in this city. With a city of 8 million people that means that we are more than a quarter of the population. If you include the illegal aliens we could add another million. We are the largest ethnic group in this city and it's imperative that we hold on to our identity.'

As we talked, one of the oldest names in the salsa business, Latin jazzman Machito, was starting up a street concert with his immaculately decked-out band. Felipe continued: 'Every one of these musicians playing on the streets of New York is in his own way a keeper of tradition. There's not one musician playing conga or trumpet, whether Puerto Rican, Cuban or "Hispanic", who does not understand what the roots of his culture are.

'Ours will be the music of the Americas in the 1980s and 1990s. It's the street music that will survive, because there are more street people, poor people. It is the music of the people because it is their conscience. That's what salsa is.'

# 5 Konkombé
*Nigerian Music*

A blind beggar shuffled his way up a Lagos high street. He sang 'praise songs' to the passers-by, in the hope of earning a few pence. He was pushed and jostled off the broken paving stones into the road where the traffic was blocked in a huge, steaming, ill-tempered jam that ran the length and breadth of Lagos, capital of Nigeria.

The beggar's name was Benjamin Kokoro. He accompanied the praise songs on a tambourine, his thick fingers pounding the hide. At the end of each song, he held up the inverted tambourine for passers-by to drop some coins in. A few did so, but others took coins out and put them in their pockets. The blind man knew

what was going on but was powerless to stop it. He carried on up the street without a stick, tapping his tambourine and singing more traditional songs. He knew his way by heart: he recognized every broken paving stone, the stench of every sewer and the distinctive sounds and smells of every street corner.

On a February day in 1979, Benjamin Kokoro went his usual route, but this time with a radio microphone hidden under his beggar's smock. We were filming him from behind a bush and through the railings of a Lagos graveyard. We were not alone. There were several putrifying corpses piled up beside the

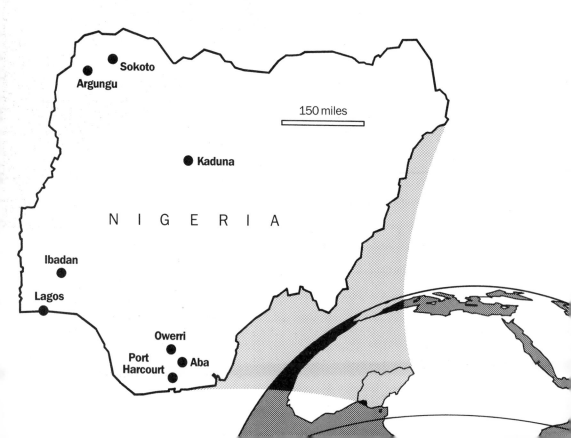

**Blind Benjamin Kokoro inspired many of the newer African musicians**

railings, and another lying out in the road – an everyday occurrence in Lagos. We were hiding from the Nigerian authorities because we had not yet received permission to make the film, so we attached a telephoto lens to the camera and a radio microphone around Kokoro's neck and filmed him from a distance of several hundred yards.

Benjamin Kokoro is acknowledged throughout Nigeria as one of that country's most influential musicians. A whole new form of West-African music evolved when Lagos guitarists tried to imitate the layers of rhythm Kokoro had developed with his simple hand drum. In so far as he is a wandering minstrel who sings local news and individual praise songs to paying customers, Kokoro is part of the oldest traditions of West-African music. But he has also developed a modern, very personal style of presentation and self-accompaniment, mixing drumming rhythms with new urban slang and vocal inflections. The fact that Kokoro is reduced, in his blindness, to this penniless state is of little concern to those Nigerian musicians who have flourished since borrowing from him. In his one-room slum dwelling Kokoro spoke proudly of his art: 'I don't care about what others do. I don't care if they have borrowed my music. I feel that the right place for my music is here with poor people on the streets of Lagos.' His words were interpreted for us by our guide and adviser, Tunde Kuboye, another leading musician. Tunde was as shocked as we were by the conditions Kokoro was living under: open street sewers ran past his door, the only toilet facility was one huge, rusty oil drum with a wooden stepladder.

Yet the curious neighbours who gathered around his house that day showed deference and respect. The very effort of his daily round of begging reminded people of his rightful place in the development of urban Nigerian music. 'I'm not a recording artist,' he explained, 'although I did once make a record. I didn't see any money and don't know what happened to it, but I believe many musicians listen to it. My aim, however, is to sing directly to people in the streets and to give them the message of my songs face to face. I sing about my society and update old-time stories. I sing people's praises and if I make them happy they give me a few pence. My life is simple: I'm a minstrel, a beggar.'

Making this film about Nigerian music was the most difficult and dangerous of the series. When the Nigerian authorities learned that my intention was not to make a comfortable, folkloric propaganda film but to reflect the trends and contradictions of current Nigerian society through its music, we ran into angry and sometimes violent censorship.

When we arrived at Lagos airport without the appropriate filming documents (despite several 'brown envelopes' that had passed surreptitiously through the hands of immigration personnel at their request) we were immediately stopped and our equipment piled up to be confiscated. Suddenly, alongside the sweltering customs shed, a fleet of open-topped Mini-Mokes pulled up, each plastered with clenched-fist emblems and the name and picture of Sunny Okosun. Sunny is one of Nigeria's leading pop stars, who had (as a member of the disadvantaged Ibo tribe which lost the civil war some years earlier) fought his way to the top by a mixture of cunning, determination and some talent. Sunny had

promised in London that he would get us into Nigeria, and now he was as good as his word. He burst in through a side entrance accompanied by a massive entourage carrying piles of his latest album. Leaping up onto a desk, he proceeded to distribute these among customs officials who pushed and shoved with outstretched arms to receive the free gifts, flamboyantly signed by Sunny. In the meantime, several of Sunny's brothers had ushered us into a waiting bus and our equipment followed, actually carried by the grateful customs officials with their new albums under their arms.

We relaxed with Sunny's family and entourage in his Lagos home and he talked about the influence of western music on him and on current popular music in Nigeria. The irony of this is not lost on Sunny. Nigerian musicians are only too aware of how the drum rhythms of the West-African slaves became the basis of popular western music: they arrived in the Americas in the form of Candomblé, macumba and Santeria ceremonial drumming. These developed into distinctive dance rhythms as they mixed with the music of other nationalities – European and American-Indian. From South America came such rhythms as the samba and

**As a teenager, Sunny Okosun tried to imitate Cliff Richard and Tommy Steele. Now one of the top Nigerian pop stars, he blends traditional sounds with reggae rhythms. Flamboyant in style, he hurls albums to his crowds of fans**

the cumbia; from the Caribbean came the Afro-Cuban dance rhythms, reggae and many others; and from North America came jazz and blues.

Indeed, when the talking drums were taken by Africans across the Atlantic, they proved so powerful that they were banned because the plantation owners feared their communicative power would rouse the slaves to fight for their freedom. The playing of talking drums became for a while punishable by death in North America. The blues that moved up from the southern plantations to the northern cities, and later, rhythm and blues, which became the essence of so much American and British pop music have their roots in this 'slave coast'.

With some humour, Sunny describes his early musical influences:

'It all began for me when I watched films: I saw *Loving You* with Elvis Presley, *The Tommy Steele Story* and Cliff Richard in *Expresso Bongo*. These were my biggest influences. Then we all started playing the guitar. We grew our hair to look like Cliff Richard and Elvis, although we were black. But after living in Lagos and opening my eyes to what was going on, I came to believe that if I was going to write music, it had to be something my people would want to listen to, digest and maybe act on. I strongly believe my music can change people's lives. It's good to write a love song, but if you want to pass a message to the world it has to be a real strong message. You can make money that way too. So I wrote songs like "Fire in Soweto" or "Papa's land" or "Let my people go". I use Nigerian rhythms as well as heavy reggae rhythms to back my message.'

Later that afternoon, Sunny's musicians gathered round and worked out a new number: 'Give power to the people . . . that's right . . . power to the people' started Sunny. 'I think that's how the chorus should go.' He told one of his assistants 'Write it down, man,' and started singing and talking again:

'Give power to the people, power to the people . . . Now we are going to talk about democracy. By the people, for the people, with the people, to the people, if possible, in the people. There must be a message in the music. Listen, we're talking to the rulers now. There is so much inflation in this country, so much corruption, confusion, commotion and oppression. We have to fix all that for once.'

Sunny's rebel stance is a carefully calculated affair. He has built his image on it and he knows it sells records. It has made him immensely popular in his own country, across West Africa and abroad. He took us in Mini-Moke convoy, with the drivers all hooting and punching the cloudless sky with clenched fist salutes, from his house to the rather downbeat EMI studios and pressing plant where he was treated with colonial condescension by the white managing director.

That afternoon Sunny was not recording his album but some television jingles and we left him smiling expansively at a group of pretty girls. We were called into the pressing plant which had its own typically Nigerian story. A corpse lay at the bottom of the acid tank, slowly decomposing. No-one dared touch it, any more than they dared touch the corpses by the roadside or the graveyard on the Lagos high street. Touching a corpse suggests involvement in the crime or death, and gives the police an easy victim. But the problem in the pressing plant was that the corpse was 'affecting the quality of the product'. They showed me some forty-fives where the stylus bounced wildly from groove to groove, making them impossible to play. It seemed that decomposing pieces of flesh had been pressed into the vinyl – hence their joke of the day: 'We have here the original stiff records'.

We waited for Sunny around the corner at the base of an unfinished flyover which stopped abruptly, with no warning, some 50 feet above the streets. It was said that at night many a car

JAK KILBY

**Fela Anikulapo Kuti, rebel musician and outspoken critic of the government, now in prison in Lagos**

The same combination
of showmanship
and fervour is present
in Fela Kuti's life,
in his shows and in his
revolutionary news
sheet, *Yap News*

had driven over the edge, so a small encampment had growth beneath it ready to pick apart the car and its unfortunate occupants as soon as it smashed on the ground. At the time there was a curfew in Lagos and it was quite dangerous to travel at night, not simply because no-one used lights, but because certain soldiers liked taking pot shots at passing cars. On one occasion, our car was stopped and we were ushered onto the roadside at rifle point and told we were breaking the law by 'having too many people in one vehicle'. They demanded an on-the-spot fine, unspecified in amount. The danger in this event was that having received it,

they could then rearrest us for bribery and fine us even more. So we had to wait for a passing Nigerian driver and bribe *him* to bribe *them*. Then we could move on.

After negotiations, we managed to persuade Sunny's record company to let us film the live show they had planned for the launch of his new album, 'Power to the People'. The event itself was chaotic. Loudspeakers and radio stations made incessant announcements like, 'The superstar prophet out with another excruciating revelation. Sunny Okosun now declares what we are fighting for.' On a high stage Sunny and his band, decked out in multicoloured feathered headdresses and pink tunics with cat skins or rugs, belted out his latest numbers with the powerful backing of heavy brass (saxophones, trumpets, trombones) and pounding drums, while swaying girls in tribal dress danced around him. The amplification shook the paving stones. The highlight of the event was reminiscent of our entry into Lagos: Sunny was teasing the audience with free copies of his album. Pausing between verses, he would hurl an album at the crowd who fought to get their hands on it, in the process tearing the record to bits. At the end of the event, I asked an exhausted Sunny if the show had not been somewhat demeaning to his audience and fans. He was genuinely surprised: 'They love it. That's how we do things in Nigeria.'

Because the whole of Lagos suffered from a sort of arterial sclerosis by day, with every road toally jammed, we travelled mostly at night in Tunde's battered Ford, while he negotiated the backstreets of Lagos to avoid the police and army. The political system was tottering. Democracy was about to give way to the military and high on the hit list was the rebellious musician Fela Anikulapo Kuti. Fela had been trying to start his own Revolutionary Party, and was openly critical of the government and bureaucracy that controlled Nigeria. They had tried to silence him by beatings, imprisonment and even attempted murder, but without success. There had been several recent attempts on Fela's life, all of them bungled. He had just been released from prison, and had immediately put his experiences onto record:

> *Look at fence them break,*
> *Look at gate them fall,*
> *Look at girls them run,*
> *Look at head them break,*
> *Look at blood him they flow . . .*

Fela was hiding out now somewhere in a suburb of Lagos. But, as good fortune would have it, Tunde was married to one of his nieces. He was able to take me late at night to visit the political rebel.

Fela's house was in total darkness when we arrived and Tunde pushed me in first. I tripped and fell in the dark amid hot, heaving bodies and naked legs. A high-pitched babble broke out and a light was turned on above a sofa on which the figure of Fela Kuti reclined, wearing only pink underpants and smoking a gigantic joint. I looked up from the floor. 'Hey, white man,' Fela asked, 'What are you doing with my wives?' A short time earlier, Fela had married 27 wives simultaneously because it was his 'right as an African man'. Now in political exile, they were forced to live all in one room, the wives on the floor and Fela on the sofa. A small TV set flickered in the corner, showing a Nigerian game show. As the lights went on, the girls got up. Beautifully dressed and exquisitely made up, they perched around their chief on his sofa.

Fela is renowned as the first exponent of 'Afrobeat'. I asked how he had developed it.

'Before I went to England to study in the mid-1960s, people had been making us think that jazz was European and white. They brought Glenn Miller films or Bing Crosby or Frank Sinatra. You never saw a black artist. I went to Trinity Music College in London and we were made to study classical music which I didn't rate at all. But I got exposed to what they called modern jazz and I started playing something called high-life jazz and also listened to the records of traditional African musicians. Then I thought deeper into what the African musical experience really should be. That was where I found Afrobeat.

'You see, in England your society has reached a stage where music can be an instrument of enjoyment; you can sing about love, you can sing about who you are going to go to bed with next. But in my society there's no music for enjoyment, there's only a struggle for people to exist. Art has to be about what is happening at a particular time of people's development, or underdevelopment. So as far as Africa is concerned, music cannot be for enjoyment, it has to be for revolution.'

Fela showed me a copy of his revolutionary newspaper *Yap News*, full of slogans and cartoon drawings, which he had helped to print and distribute illegally in Lagos.

'I am trying to use music as a weapon. I say: play music and act. Do something about the system. If you feel bad about it, do something. I'm singing in pidgin English – because it's the only language common to all Africans, so the only way to communicate is in pidgin. We just released a record called "Suffering and smiling", you know how every African smiles – but you don't have to smile in a bad condition. That is making matters worse. So I wrote a tune called "Suffering and smiling" which attacks religion and other ills of our society like police brutality.'

Fela carefully placed his joint in the ashtray, grasped his tenor saxophone and unsteadily played the melody from this latest hit. At that time, he could not appear publicly on stage. He claimed he had also suffered badly at the hands of Decca, his British-based record company, and that they had refused to pay him royalties. In protest, Fela and his wives had invaded Decca's head office and barricaded themselves inside for several weeks. Two of his wives gave birth to children in the managing director's office and, I was told, the placentas were found in the wastepaper basket after they had left.

Our own impression of Decca's Nigerian operation was not particularly favourable: the managing director refused us entry to his home or office, preferring to spend time talking to his parrots. Decca's set-up seemed remote from the

**Kehinde and Taiwo, the Lijadu Sisters, are exceptions in the very male world of African music**

street life of Nigeria, and they were suspicious of our contact with the musicians. An exception was a Nigerian Decca producer called Odeon Iruji; he was constantly fighting to get a square deal for his artists and trying to get funds for promoting new and exciting Nigerian talent.

With Odeon's help, I came to meet two of

Nigeria's top female performers – the Lijadu Sisters. We travelled up to their house in Ibadan where I spent the first night discussing the legacy of white colonialism. Under attack, I explained how I felt. In some ways TV is the last outpost of colonial rule: Europeans come, film and record a so-called 'primitive' culture and take it away with them in cans to be shown as instant entertainment. Finally the sisters, Kehinde and Taiwo, decided to take us through a filming experience that would give some idea of the problems Nigerian artists suffer. They talked first about their life as women musicians

– a rarity – in West Africa:

'We are twin sisters and we think that has helped us survive in the business. It would be terribly lonely without people around you – we can lean on each other. In the past women were relegated to the background in Nigerian society, but now they realize they have as much right to work and to social responsibility as men. In the past our men believed the wife should stick to the kitchen, but now we are telling our men we no longer want to be at home. Women have been playing important roles in nearly every aspect of life here. It is only this industry that has a shortage of female artists.'

About a dozen local musicians gathered round the house next day and the sisters, each holding a baby, jammed with them. It was a sexually explicit number called 'You can touch me if you want to'. They were well aware of the glamorous image they projected on record covers and publicity material, but they talked with bitterness about the role of the record company: 'Nigerian musicians cannot afford equipment, so we are forced to buy from the record company and they take the cost out of your royalty. When you sign with them you sign away your life. As far as they're concerned you keep owing them and paying back until you die.'

The air conditioning had broken down that evening in Decca's sweltering studio. Kehinde and Taiwo were trying to record in too short a time that same number with a backing of electric instruments and talking drums. It was a hectic and ultimately ill-tempered affair. As time ran out and the guards at the studio gates rattled their keys impatiently, the atmosphere in the control room, where they listened back to their last efforts, was filled with recriminations and a deep sense of artistic frustration. 'They don't give one fig about the artists,' muttered

**I.K. Dairo, MBE, is a musician and preacher in the Aladura Church. He also pioneered the early styles of ju-ju**

Kehinde, 'they just sap and sap . . .'

Our filming also suffered frustrations: stones were thrown at us; a secret service man ploughed into our van with his VW to prevent us filming street musicians through its windows; I was arrested and interrogated to the extent of having to pass an elementary test in European music. 'Where did the Beatles get their music from?' Any answer other than Nigeria would have been judged incorrect. I finally passed with flying colours, although my passport was rejected as being no proof of identity. They claimed it could have been a CIA forgery.

It was particularly important for us to be

officially acknowledged as we needed permits to travel outside of Lagos. Kicking my heels one day while waiting, I had the good fortune to stumble upon the Aladura Church of Mr I.K. Dairo. He lived in a backstreet slum where the holes in the road were so deep that the vehicle in front frequently dipped almost from sight and where the pavements were lined with processions of women with bananas, laundry buckets and beer crates stacked on their heads. His house was not difficult to find, because he lives in a street named after him – Kehinde Dairo Street – which is a rare honour for a musician in Nigeria. I. K. Dairo was made an MBE in 1960 when Nigeria became independent and the British colonial system was supposedly dismantled. I.K. Dairo is a charming and gentle man and deeply religious: 'All the music of Mr I.K. Dairo is a lecture and prayer. When I play music it is to inspire people

to do good in life and so I also play my music in church.'

I.K. takes electric instruments backed by several drums into his church services where the blue-and-white clad congregation sways and claps and prays and little children sleep on the benches. The Aladura Church was founded by Moses Tunolase Orimolade (otherwise known as Baba Aladura, founder of the Cherubim and Seraphim, who was born in 1879 in Western Nigeria, his birth being preceded by wonderful signs). I.K. Dairo gives this missionary offshoot a distinctive West-African twist: he was – and still is – honoured for his pioneering of a style of music called ju-ju.

Most of his numbers are in two or three parts – songs within songs. For example, 'Aiye fotito pamo' is a satire which tells of a time when the whole country was eclipsed by a cloud of dust. Those responsible claimed ignorance: 'They preferred to call black red or red white.' In another song, 'Emi iba n'egberun ahon', I.K. thanks God for being able to form a new and better breakaway band called Blue Spot. It was with Blue Spot that he became famous throughout West Africa and beyond as the initiator of ju-ju. This introduced western instruments – guitars, saxophones, trumpets and even an accordion – to traditional Yoruban drumming. On the balcony of his apartment, overlooking Kehinde Dairo Street, I.K. played accordion accompanied by a relative on talking drum, and then took time to explain how the intonations of the Yoruba language were mimicked by the drum so that it actually 'talked' to people. Music and language in West Africa are closely interwoven – the rhythms of one spilling into the other and becoming inseparable in a way that is hard for a westerner to understand. Later ju-ju musicians like Chief Ebenezer Obey and King Sunny Ade owe much in their music to Mr Dairo.

There was a strong contrast between the latter two. Sunny Ade, in a most serene and gentlemanly fashion, had tea brought to me on a silver service by a white-gloved servant as we discussed details for filming him that night. He

**King Sunny Ade —
his ju-ju band with
its massed guitar
and drum sound**

rumoured that night) a Mercedes Benz. Furthermore, while the musicians play (and a normal ju-ju gig can last for five or six hours), they are subjected to the traditional Yoruba custom of 'dashing' in which paper money is stuck to their faces or clothes by enthusiastic fans.

On this occasion Sunny Ade's performance was restricted to a mere five hours by the fact that one of Lagos' intermittent blackouts happened as he was about to start and so none of his amplifiers would work. When he got going, his band produced the most stunningly choreographed and tightly organized performance with layer upon layer of brilliant virtuosity, heavy talking-drum rhythms pounding as money and liquor flowed liberally.

This is the sort of ju-ju which Sunny Ade has now made internationally famous; it is brilliant and spectacular but perhaps lacks something of the music's original lyric content. I.K. Dairo made ju-ju lyrics a matter of opinion, newsworthiness and social relevance. It was I.K.'s song 'Kasora' that so outspokenly and chillingly warned – years before it happened – of the terrible consequences of a Nigerian civil war.

> *Houses will begin to fall and the earth will
> shake,
> The mother will no more know the child nor the
> husband know the wife.*

The effects of the civil war which pitted the Yoruba and Hausa majority against the Ibos in Biafra is still in the forefront of Nigerian consciousness. Its horrors are not easily erased. The victors were aided by the United States, Britain, France and the Soviet Union. The Ibos were helped by virtually no-one and yet they held out for years with great suffering, their land and families devastated. It was a war inflamed

was aware of our 'illegal' status and had arranged a location where no-one would dare touch us: the Oba's (King of Lagos) palace party. Sunny Ade was His Majesty's favourite musician and the Oba's palace would be packed that night. Kings in Nigeria no longer have much political power but they wield social influence behind the scenes. And such is their wealth that they can afford to pay the top ju-ju musicians with a refrigerator or (as was

**The Oriental Brothers from the east, are Nigeria's foremost High Life band**

far beyond tribal conflicts by the importance of oil, and hence the involvement of the 'world community', greedy to wrestle it from the Ibos.

After arriving in Biafra, as it was previously known, the differences between East and West Nigeria were immediately apparent. Broken bridges remained unmended, shelled houses scarred the townships and wreckage still floated in the river waters. We went to visit the East's foremost high-life band, the 'Oriental Brothers'. High life has been one of West Africa's most popular music forms since the 1940s. It is basically a dance music which evolved as a cross between African rhythms and the brass bands that came with the missionaries and regimental armies. The fusion of military brass sections and pounding drums became known as high life and the 'Oriental Brothers' were the leading exponents of the Nigerian style. In the battered township of Owerri young boys and girls who had grown up in the extreme hardship of the postwar years danced their nights away to Ibo high life. Girls swigged beer from bottles and the boys swayed on the dance floor beneath the dark, torrential clouds. Several of the youths were limbless – victims of a civil war which left its scars on every Ibo family.

Getting out of the townships with their rain-drenched roads and endless motorbike display rooms, we headed off into the forests to the hut of an infamous 'witch doctor', or shaman, called Area Scatter. His home was filled with bones and skulls and paintings of the power of good and evil. A muscular, humorous man, he explained how, after living through the civil war, he had gone into the wilderness for seven months and seven days and had

**Crowds gather for a
boxing contest which
is accompanied
by talking drums**

**In eastern Nigeria,
Area Scatter
plays for the local
king and queen**

reappeared transformed into a woman. The day we visited him he headed off, dressed in white smock, polka-dot skirt and a shamanist bone necklace, to the residence of his Royal Highness Eonunnoke to play for the local king and queen.

Area Scatter was a highly accomplished performer on his thumb piano which was decorated with a distinctive skull and crossbones. When the king and his wife ceremonially entered and seated themselves on their thrones, Area Scatter bowed deeply and started to sing in a soft, rich voice. The palace entourage sat around the blue and pink painted walls hung with ancient hunting photographs, leopard skins and spears and an elaborately framed print of Constable's 'Salisbury Cathedral from the River'. As is so often the case with Ibo songs, there was a poignancy and biting relevance to his humorous lyrics. His song was about a man who suffers because he is smaller than anyone else. But one day at the market he meets a man even smaller than himself. Then he is happy, happy to know there is someone even worse off than himself.

From Iboland, we travelled north, to the city of Kaduna. Northern Nigeria, bordering on the Sahara desert, is the territory of the Hausa people, said to be the most wealthy and powerful in the country. There had recently been riots and street killings, so we stayed only long enough to catch a bus up to the far northwestern township of Sokoto. The landscapes were stunning: Saharan sands dotted with mosques, oases, camel trains and tiny market towns. Music here was still a daily accompaniment to work – with wandering bands playing flutes and drums, wearing mirror shades carved into the shapes of hearts and diamonds. Because of curfews and 'national security', life became even more difficult for us. Every morning in Sokoto I had to leave our hut at 5 a.m. to request permission to film the event

for which we had travelled north: the Argungu Fishing Festival. And every day they refused.

We became anxious but turned the delays to our advantage by touring the countryside. Hidden away within four ruined walls of an ancient desert house, we found a boxing contest where the fighters bound their hands with raw hemp (a centuries old tradition) to cut and bloody their opponents' faces. Two dozen talking drums accompanied the fights which happened several at a time. The audience was brilliantly dressed: decorated women covered their faces in fake shock at some of the terrible brutality meted out by their favourite contestants and a frantic witch doctor sang and danced between the bouts, waving a magic gourd and uttering obscenities.

Outside the walls, seated in a circle beneath a tree on the main tobacco and camel route to town, sat Alhaji Dan Anace. He was surrounded by a group of deep-voiced accompanists with talking drums, singing a haunting boxing song in praise of the fighters' spirits.

On the desert sands beyond we came across three wandering minstrels – the original West-African 'griots'. These were magnificently dressed, proud musicians who carried local news from town to town since neither radio nor newspapers could be relied on for accuracy. Their instruments were carved bamboo and hollowed-out gourds. They wore decorative headpieces covered in beads which hung in strings down across their shoulders as they strolled across the burning sands singing of the latest politics or gossip from the neighbouring village.

On the fifth day of waiting I was finally told that we could film the Argungu Festival. Early that morning thousands of fishermen armed with nets, rods and giant fishing pots poured over the banks of the river, wading into the waters summoned by the giant drums that blue-robed musicians beat in their canoes. They were calling up the spirits of the fish. It was a kaleidoscope of robes and pots and nets, floundering and splashing, until the entire river seemed aflow with human bodies. Fish glistened in their hands as they dragged them

**Further north in Nigeria the Arab influence is felt: Alhaji Dan Anace praises the boxers**

West African griots hold a special place in music and culture: traditionally it was they who were the professional musicians, but they were also the bearers of information, news and local gossip Overleaf: The annual Argungu fishing festival in northern Nigeria

from the waters and plunged them into pots. The drumming became more incessant and louder and mingled with the cries of the fishermen, some of whom answered in a kind of call and response pattern. The same talking drums that filled the Lagos recording studios, the Ibo dance halls and slum suburbs were being used to communicate with the spirit world – a communion of man and nature. The climax was reached as the largest fish of all was carried proudly, head high, to the judges and the first prize was awarded to a tumultuous reception.

It was only afterwards, wandering round the back of the judges' stand that we found rows of army lorries parked in the burning sun. The trucks stank. They were filled with gasping fish in melting ice cubes which had been driven up from Lagos to fill the river for this spectacular event.

It took several more days to get back to Lagos to return home. But leaving Nigeria was much the same as arriving there: our British Caledonian flight was delayed by the further impounding of our equipment, followed by threats and its hasty release. Finally we sank back in our seats with relief, as the plane began to taxi to the accompaniment of the pre-flight musak. I recognized it as Abba's 'The winner takes it all', whose beat goes back in time to the black drumming rhythms of West-African music.

# 6 Tex-Mex
## *The Music of the Texas-Mexican Borderlands*

Just outside San Antonio, Texas, the number-one name in Tex-Mex music, Little Joe Hernandez jumped around a makeshift stage with a 20-piece band playing what he called 'the unofficial anthem of the Tex-Mex people'. The name of the music in Spanish was Las Nubes – The Clouds. The lyrics were about the loss of identity and pride of the Spanish-speaking people of the Texas-Mexican border, many of whom have over a generation abandoned their homes in Mexico.

Little Joe is one of the most political of the musicians who play along the border to committedly enthusiastic Tex-Mex audiences. His music is dance music, but it sometimes carries serious lyrics. Little Joe sees himself as a political spokesman. Many Tex-Mex people still like to think of Texas as a part of Mexico, even though it was lost to them in the Mexican-American wars in the mid-nineteenth century

when the USA invaded and claimed Texas for itself. Little Joe has given up his more extreme ideas like founding a Texas-Cuban federation. He has in recent years become blander and more commercial. His music is now for Saturday night dances, and the lyrics have been watered down. But in his pop star trailer, a plushly carpeted chocolate-brown caravan, he talked about the violence that his people still suffer at the hands of the Texas police and the big farming combines. 'Some people call it political,' he said, 'but to me, through my music, I'm making people aware of everyday issues and giving them my opinions.' He described how in Dallas, Texas, a twelve-year-old chicano boy called Rodriguez (chicano is the local term for a person of Mexican descent) was thrown into the back of a police car and forced to play Russian roulette with the officer's revolver. On the third or fourth pull of the trigger the little

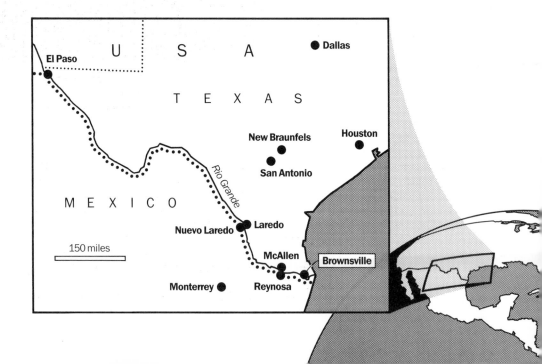

boy blew his brains all over the inside of the car. No-one was held responsible. 'There are many, many more cases like that,' added Joe. 'We've got to put a stop to it. We can only do that by organizing.'

The United Farmworkers Union, which has offices all along the border and is still traditionally linked to the Catholic Church, provided us with secret videotapes which the Mexican-American community had acquired. These had been made by the local Texas police who, for some unknown reason, chose to record themselves beating up Mexican-Americans at a police station near McAllen, Texas. Similar incidents allegedly happen in all the police stations along the border. These were particularly brutal. The Texas cops hammered their victims' faces against the sergeant's desk, then picked them up, threw them onto the floor and stamped on them. The videotapes were acquired by lawyers acting for the Mexican-American people and have been broadcast nationally in the United States. However, as in the case of Rodriguez, no indictments were brought against any police officers and no-one was disciplined.

The history of the Texan-Mexican border is fraught with politics, warfare, revolution. Once Texas became part of the United States in 1836, the Rio Grande became the 1,000-mile border and achieved a kind of mythical status. Many songs called corridos were spontaneously composed and sung all along the river. They tell of border crossings, violence, loves, intrigues and murders. Folk heroes were often created by the repetition of these ballads which also played an important part in the Mexican Revolution. Pancho Villa had corridos written about him which described his battles, his courage and even his death. So the corrido performed a dual function: entertainment and poetry at the same time as news and propaganda.

There are still many corrido writers, one of the most prolific being Salome Gutierez. Salome is unique in that although he owns a little record store in San Antonio, he writes his corridos 'in the one place where I can find peace and quiet – in my car'. Accompanied by his wife and

**Little Joe Hernandez is a fervent spokesman for the Mexicans who live in Texas**

clutching notepaper, a pile of records and a cassette, he climbed into his battered beige wood-framed Chevrolet and drove through the Mexican part of San Antonio, past graffiti-covered shacks, scores of children playing football in the road, through the huge puddles left by rainstorms and bad sanitation, past garages whose walls are decorated with other people's hubcaps, past the cantinas serving spicy Tex-Mex food and the record stores from

which different sorts of Tex-Mex music blasted across the streets.

Then Salome dictated with increasing enthusiasm, first by word and then by phrase, his latest 'creation', his latest corrido. It was called 'El gatto negro', 'The black cat':

> *They call me the black cat.*
> *All the lawmen are chasing me . . .*
> 'Yes, that will sell well – it's a song about smuggling.'

In fact, 'The black cat' is quite a popular corrido character: he is another of the local heroes who kills a few cops, crosses the border, and gets arrested and imprisoned in San Antonio city jail. From the fifth floor he makes a dramatic escape.

Besides his own corridos, Salome's record shop was crammed with different styles of Tex-Mex music. One best-selling record was 'Mama solita', the story of a mother left alone because her husband had gone to be a 'wetback', crossing over the river into the States; and she was fearful of what would happen to him. Another record is 'Miquerida Reynosa', a

A chili stand in San Antonio in the 1930s when Mexicans crossed the border in search of work — cheap labour for the US

but proud image of Reynosa that earns the description '*querida*' – dear or beautiful – in the songs. On the American side of the border in its twin town, McAllen, the stores are crammed with cheap mass-produced electronic products. Reynosans cross the border, buy these in vast quantities and either smuggle them back (with a

Santiago Jimenez Jr., son of famous border accordionist and the brother of Flaco, carries on with the corrido tradition

nostalgic song about the 'Mexican border town' of Reynosa, which is a divided town. It offers restaurants and antique shops for American tourists, while on the other side of the railway tracks traditional forms of Tex-Mex music are still played in the cantinas at night. It is this poor

bribe to the Mexican border guards) or arrange to get them flown across illegally from private airfields all round the border towns. Pilots still fly by night with their Cessna aircraft packed full of electronic gadgets, often returning with a load of marijuana.

Salome and his record store were important to the Texas-Mexican community in San Antonio: he was not just a writer/producer, he also pressed and distributed all his own albums – an entire record company in himself. When something newsworthy happened on the border, Salome not only wrote his ballad and recorded it, he could also distribute it within

days, like a hot newssheet. The day we were with him, Salome was going to record 'El gatto negro'. Having composed it in his car, with his wife intently scribbling the lyrics he dictated, a new creative excitement possessed Salome, leading him through red lights and onto the wrong side of the road.

We arrived at his one-storey town house and went into his front room which had been converted into a recording studio, dominated by a large space filled with a dozen microphones and music stands. The other half of his room, separated by glass and wood panels, contained the 'control studio', inside which Salome not only produced his records but also recorded himself doing harmonies and chorus. He sat there adjusting the volume, pressing the buttons on his cheap twin-track recorders and singing along with the star soloist he had brought in – the famous borderland accordionist, Santiago Jimenez Junior. Santiago was given ten minutes in which to learn the entire corrido, both music and lyrics. When he attempted to record it, he was pulled up every 20 seconds by Salome who complained that 'it does not sound the way it did when I sang it in my car'. Salome, for all his amateur equipment and living-room studio, was, in his own words, 'a real perfectionist'.

He wanted his corrido to feel right and sound right – it needed spontaneity and Santiago even dared to improvise, encouraged by Salome. Half an hour later the recording was finished. The next day, Salome would transfer the tapes to vinyl, press the records, design the covers and print them. The records would be on the streets and in the shops within a few days. With piles of copies in his rusting Cadillac, Salome would drive the length and breadth of the Texas border, selling his latest creation direct to customers or placing it in record stores.

**Flaco Jimenez, the king of accordion, plays rootsy norteño music but has also played with Ry Cooder**

Tex-Mex is minority music: 'It's made cheap and sold cheap.' If you barter, the price is cut. To survive, one man has to do it all. Yet Salome sees himself not just as a contemporary record producer, but as a music and myth maker within the history of the border.

After leaving the studio, Santiago Jimenez went to visit his parent's house: it was Mothers' Day. All Tex-Mex musicians visited their parents on that day. So Santiago played his favourite songs in the street outside his mother's house, with unashamed emotion: an expression of filial love.

Santiago is the son of one of the most famous accordionists of the border: Santiago Jimenez Senior. Santiago Senior's other son is currently the favourite accordionist of the Texas-Mexican people. His name is Flaco Jimenez and he has attempted to cross over into jazz and into the pop scene, playing with rock musician Ry Cooder on such albums as 'Chicken

**Originally settlers for the breweries, the Germans played their accordions in Texas**

Shack'. He was to play in two days time, downtown in San Antonio, for the Fifth of May Mexican Independence celebrations. Flaco had prepared a new song called 'Blue jeans' with double-edged lyrics. It was in praise of the so-called 'American dream' – wearing blue jeans and looking 'Anglo' – but, at the same time, making a gentle, satirical dig at Mexican Americans who choose to turn their backs on their Mexican heritage. 'People who wear blue jeans become like all the others around them – indistinguishable – losing their culture, forgetting their language, turning their back on their history and merging with the mass of Anglo-Americans who control our society.'

Flaco brings to his music certain jazz breaks and cross-rhythms that are new to Tex-Mex music. What he plays are not corridos but a different style called norteño music. This is North-Mexican border music – rootsy, gutsy Mexican border music. The rhythms of norteño are those of the polka and its instrument is the button accordion, all stemming from the German immigrants who, at the end of the last century, came into Mexico and Texas to farm and build breweries. Every Saturday night they held dances where German families would polka to accordion bands, dressed in Tyrolean hats and lederhosen. The most famous of the German settlements was New Braunfels, near San Antonio, and as a child Santiago Senior used to creep up to the high walls around those houses and listen to the German accordionists playing polkas. He knew that was the kind of music he wanted to play. When he was old enough to purchase a button accordion, it was polka music that he, and others like him, adapted into the norteño idiom.

During my travels, I met a German American called Chris Stark who makes and repairs accordions in his terraced house in a secluded Anglo suburb of San Antonio. He is middle-aged and he has an 'oompah' band with accordion, tuba, trombones, trumpets and

**Guitarist and singer Lydia Mendoza, known as La Gloria de Texas, has been playing Mexican-American music for over 50 years**

**Lydia Mendoza played the mandolin on her parents' first record in 1928, aged ten**

drum, which still plays at German dances at weekends. Chris Stark explained how the Mexicans had borrowed 'German music', and how more recently the Germans had borrowed back some of the unique spirit of life that the Mexicans had brought to the polkas. Every Hohner accordion arriving from Germany is adapted by him to 'sound right' for Tex-Mex music, before being offered for sale in the local shops. Another distinctive instrument is the 'bajo sexto' which developed from the orchestral double bass.

Norteño music now has other names like 'musica chicana', but is most commonly known as Tex-Mex music. A current hero is Steve Jordan, a Mexican American despite his name, who plays a peculiar blend of Tex-Mex with Latin rhythms, has a black patch on one eye,

knuckle dusters and a reputation for violence. Violence has been a major theme of border life and music for as long as anyone can remember. So has the drug scene. Even Pancho Villa's song called 'La cucaracha', perhaps the most famous corrido of them all, extols the pleasures of marijuana smoking. It was sung during and after the Mexican Revolution.

I had seen photographs of Pancho Villa's wife talking to a young girl singer on the border in the early part of this century. Her name was Lydia Mendoza and she is still singing today, with a large 12-string guitar. Lydia is one of the last of the great border corrido singers; she sang 'El tango negro' ('The black tango') for us, with which she used to entertain Texas-Mexican workers in the hard years of the Great Depression.

'I called myself "a singer of the people", so I played anywhere I was asked to along the border. I would work in bars, in nightclubs, dances, theatres: wherever a "singer of the people" could reach her audience.'

Today, Lydia is regarded by many as a 'national treasure' and she subsists on a

foundation from the University of California. She had arrived back in San Antonio to take part in the Fifth of May celebrations. But what Lydia found there was a caricature of her people. The image the Mexican Americans presented on the streets of San Antonio, as they passed in their multicoloured floats, was a tame symbol of independence; people hiding their own culture beneath glossy smiles and folkloric costumes. Following the floats came a contrasting vision of Mexican American culture – the Low Riders.

The Low Riders are a culture of their own; Tex-Mex music or rock-'n'-roll beat out of their custom-built flashily painted and ornate cars, filled with border symbols. Crowds cheered and clapped as they paraded past the Alamo – a tourist site and symbol of the struggle for Texas between North Americans and Mexicans.

One of the heroes of the Low Riders is Frank Rodarte. He had just made a record called 'I wanna be a Low Rider' – and the record cover was a striking mixture of symbols: the Alamo was there but dominated by the prayer tower of a mosque, beneath which an armadillo was scratching away at the foundations of the historic monument. Below the Alamo were two Mexican-American faces with hats pulled down, shoulder-length hair, mirror shades, an angry snarl and hands clenched in fraternal union. On either side of them a girl slumbered in some long grass beside Low Rider cars – the whole an ornate, rebellious image of Tex-Mex culture. The name of the band is The New Aces. Frank Rodarte's bizarre and violent visual references to border life also reflect his music and where he plays it.

On 6 May there was a prison concert in San Antonio City Jail. Frank Rodarte sang a number there about a convicted prisoner's last meal: the lyrics were as strange as the actual prison setting. Tough female warders, armed with truncheons, led in a group of young gay men – their faces painted like women – with pouting lips, mascaraed eyes and shoulder-length hair. They were greeted by jeers and whistles and took their place at the front, coquettishly posing

to the other black and Mexican-American prisoners. The 'girls' had come to mob Frank Rodarte and his band in an all-male prison.

After the City Jail, the authorities granted us permission to drive up to Bay View Detention Center in the wild marshlands beyond Brownsville. Seagulls called and circled around the wire-fenced perimeters of watch towers, submachine guns and heavily armed guards. We talked to one internee who could not speak a word of English but who had come north to America in the hope of starting a new life. Like many of the refugees who cross the border, he was not in fact Mexican but Nicaraguan. Hundreds of Latin Americans are daily trying to cross into the States, as one of them explained:

'The real problem why we end up here is that our fathers are so poor. We never had a chance of any sort of education or even a job – not a good one or a regular one. So we keep on crossing into the States illegally to find work for

**A particular cult of San Antonio is the Low Riders, based on their low-slung cars. Frank Rodarte is a Low Rider musician who plays San Antonio rock'n'roll with his New Aces band**

ourselves and our hungry families, but we end up in prison.'

The US Border Patrol has the task of attempting to prevent illegal entry along 1,000 miles of the Rio Grande Valley. We met up with them on the night of 12 May and travelled in a jeep to their favourite hiding place behind the local MacDonalds hamburger joint on the outskirts of Brownsville. Their idea was to set up a sort of triangular trap around the river bed beneath the Brownsville bridge, one of the busiest illegal crossing points on the Texas border.

There are various ways of crossing the border: some people creep across bridges, others swim, some float on inflatable rafts (one had stuffed his coat full of parrots – selling the illegally imported birds over the border could earn him more than drugs) and still others arrive in the false panels or flooring of trucks. At Brownsville, most people either swim or walk across the bridges. Leaving McDonalds, we climbed down the river bank and hid in some long grass. Our two border guards were playing cops and robbers with their walkie-talkies, guns, truncheons, handcuffs and keys, all of which jangled and rattled as they crept 'soundlessly' around the long, damp grass by the water's edge. Suddenly the walkie-talkies crackled into life and pandemonium broke out. There were hollers and shouts, torches flashed and we raced across the pitch-black banks of the Rio Grande, stumbling into holes and tripping over bushes until we arrived at a clearing where two illegals had been cornered. With torches shining in their faces, they were frisked. Then, found to be carrying nothing (any illegal substances would have been got rid of during the chase), they were locked into one of the jeeps. A third man escaped back across the bridge into the darkness and safety of the Mexican side. 'Vermin!' exclaimed our patrolman. 'Little vermin. But they'll try again, as often as three times in one night and when we catch them we'll just take their details and kick their skinny butts back over the border. There's nothing else you can do. It's an impossible job.'

'Certainly,' continued his partner, 'a person has to look at the morality of the whole thing and it does worry me. On occasions I get terribly depressed. It just gets you into a terrible frame of mind. They are mostly economic refugees and, in the end, is that any less valid than being a political refugee?'

Most of these border patrolmen are very different from the hardened Texas police. They are often ex-Vietnam veterans, quiet family men who have been given an impossible job – to keep out thousands of desperate immigrants determined to get over the border one way or another.

The next day we spoke to the chief of the local border patrol, Larry Richardson. He had a gold name-plate on his desk, at either end of which stood a Smurf. He said:

'I'll have to do a little guessing, but we must apprehend, around this part of town, about 40,000 immigrants a year. Well, in truth, I guess we catch one out of three, so you could say there's over 100,000 of those guys running through here. Now if you're an enterprising individual over on that side and you want to make some money, then there's a demand for alien labour in this country.'

The point he was making was that while it is illegal for the Mexicans to work on American farms or businesses, it is not illegal for Americans to employ them. Consequently, if cheap labour can be brought over the border on a large scale, the big farming combines can make huge profits. They neither have to pay federal minimum wages nor ensure sufficient housing or hygiene for the immigrant workers. The border patrol chief continued:

'There is a way of making money if you are an enterprising person. You make arrangements to buy transport, guides and mules. You bribe for a crossing of the river to a pick-up point on this north side. Then transport is arranged to take the workers to a destination in the interior of the States. Then you do a deal with the farm bosses and provide the cheap labour they want.'

All along the border the migrant field workers are represented by the United Farm

**Bay View Detention Centre: for the many hopeful economic refugees who cross the border north**

Workers. The union tries to help the workers both with improved conditions and legal assistance. Their president is the legendary Cesar Chavez, who in the course of his working life has suffered beatings and intimidation. When we went to see the local union they were holding an evening of farm workers' entertainment. It consisted of short plays performed by the educated children of immigrant workers, each telling a simple story that might improve the comprehension and consciousness of older working people. One of the plays dealt with their low wages – far below the standard minimum wage. Another dealt with the appalling levels of disease and illiteracy which parents and children suffer when

working in the fields. Most employers do not provide toilets or drinking water for the labourers, so illnesses like hepatitis run rife. Child labour is common: children as young as five are seen working alongside their parents in the fields, endangering their health with pesticides, machinery, insects, heat and sun. In the evenings, farm-worker families gather in groups beneath trees and beside pick-up trucks. With their accordions, they sing their polkas or corridos. This is a sentimental link with the land they left, but with the full realization that each season many will have to cross over and do the same work again in order to survive. Others will stay, moving from farm to farm for seasonal work.

Some illegals do settle in the States and finally become legal citizens. We went to see one such family in a suburb of San Antonio. Their maid – a newly entered Mexican immigrant – was cleaning the floor of the porch while inside the fashionably dressed daughters of the family were sitting with their mother, sipping Mexican coffee. 'I'd never go back, never in the world. To visit maybe,' said the first, 'but over there women like us are just housewives. You don't get educated, you don't get a job, you're stuck. There's no middle class there; you're either poor or rich. But here in the States, after my parents became legalized, my husband and I are in the middle category – you know, we've sort of made it. We recently bought a home, a car and a pick-up truck. My kids go to private school, my kids have swimming lessons – we're not rich, we have to work, my husband has to work, but we're not poor any more and we're not going to stand in line for any food stamps.'

South of the border tens of thousands wait to cross into the States. They live in shanty towns with their chickens, doves and horse-drawn carts. The area is known as 'North America's rubbish dump', where whole families rummage by day for food or valuables. The little cantinas are full of music. We spent some days there with musicians whose guitars were kept between the bottles on the bar shelves and whose double basses were stacked against the wall, on sawdust, behind clapped-out jukeboxes. In the evening, the bars filled up and the musicians played their dramatic corridos about the great days of Pancho Villa and Emilio Zapata, of heroes like El gatto negro and about crossing the border. Many of the songs told of

**South of the border are the run-down shanty towns of the thousands who wait, hoping to cross over**

**Musicians keep their instruments in the cantinas or bars and at night time sing the ballads of heroes like Pancho Villa**

men who never came back, and of those who died violently at the hands of gringos on the other side.

Just outside many Mexican border towns is their '*zona rosa*'. We visited Reynosa's red-light district on an evening when the streets sank beneath six inches of torrential rain. Cars sprayed their ways down the muddy sideroads between brothels and dance halls, where the roughest forms of norteño music were played by three-piece bands with cheap and deafening amplification. Here all-night shows attracted not just Mexican workers but also hoards of Americans crossing the border in search of cheap sex and thrills. In a pause between the rain, three local musicians waded across the '*zona rosa*' thoroughfare, knee-deep in water. They were playing a love song, norteño style, about a man who mistreated all his women but who ended up king of the castle. We followed them into a bar and were talking about how their music survived, even flourished, in this area – though there was little work elsewhere – when a man entered who looked as if he had just arrived from outer space. Round his neck he wore pig-leather straps at the end of which was a square, metal box with half a dozen dials and two metal handles. A customer paid a few pesos and then grabbed the handles. The 'spaceman' wound up an electric current inside the box, higher and higher, so that it became increasingly painful. The man who clung on longest was the most macho and won the approval of all others. It was a typical display of border machismo, one of the powerful motives behind all the border stories, myths and music.

The following day I talked with Placido Salazar. Placido had accompanied us on our previous night to Reynosa's red-light district and had quickly hidden when we were chased out of one bar at gunpoint for daring to film out of a cardboard box. Placido described his childhood:

'Well, I wasn't much of a field worker myself, but being out here with the family – quite a few times you know, we would have to dodge the aircraft that would come in real low and spray their insecticides. All that spray would fall on us, and it would stay there. You couldn't just take off and have a shower . . . so

**Placido Salazar plays guitar and sings mariachi music for any event from a rodeo to a wedding party**

**A Mexican cowboy at a charro — a style of rodeo common to both sides of the border**

many of our people now suffer from health problems.'

During the Vietnam war, Placido used to sing for the soldiers at night. He swears that was the only time the Vietcong gave them any peace. They would, he said, creep silently up to the camp's wire fence to admire his Tex-Mex music!

Placido was a small, rotund figure in his late thirties, with a podgy face and twinkling brown eyes. His family had grown up working in the fields where he had learnt his music. His father was an old-time violin player who had crossed the border in the 1950s under one of America's programmes for 'controlled immigration' (cheap labour for American farmers).

The next day Placido was going to perform at a charro, a Mexican style rodeo, that takes place both on the south and north sides of the border. This particular rodeo was held at a sizeable ranch, owned by the wealthy Mexican-American Diaz family. The oldest son explained proudly that the Mexican cowboys who performed at these charros were the origin of the stereotyped American cowboy.

These rodeos also have their musical accompaniment. Not norteños or corridos but mariachi music, which the wealthy in Mexico

find much more to their taste. Mariachi stems from the word for 'marriage' and means music which accompanies all sorts of social events. All across Mexico and Latin America, groups of mariachi musicians play anywhere from funerals to serenading a new girlfriend outside her lover's window. Placido Salazar told us how he had decided that mariachi music suited his temperament better than norteño. At the opening of the rodeo Placido sat astride an unruly mare, singing as he rode, supported by a small band who were also on horseback. It was an expressive mariachi song about love and death on the border, continuing even while he dismounted, emitting a mild squeak as he caught a tender part of his anatomy on the saddle handle. At the end of the number there was a polite smattering of applause, the bulls came thundering in and the mariachis fled for their lives. Then Mexican cowboys entered to display

**Amidst the dust and thundering hooves, mariachi musicians play tubas, guitars and trumpets**

their extraordinary control and acrobatics both on horseback and bareback on angry, black bulls. Controlling the bull – a symbol of untamed sexuality – was the ultimate in machismo.

Meanwhile Placido was singing at the top of his voice, his lungs straining to compete with the musicians with trumpets, tubas, bajo sextos and guitars who accompanied the tumbling bulls and thundering horse hoofs.

To make a living, Placido has to do more than play at rodeos; all he earned that morning would pay for some gas for the pick-up and a couple of bottles of beer or tequila. So he went to do a live show at the local San Antonio radio station. It was hosted by Ricky Davila, who had been a friend of Placido's for years. Ricky Davila was a tough, bearded, fast-talking Mexican American who saw the entire history of his people laid out in music. It was his job to broadcast every morning from an upstairs commercial radio station in the backstreets of San Antonio – to all the Mexican Americans and Spanish-speaking immigrants who could tune in from the fields, shops, garages, cantinas, or wherever they worked.

'That's what I really feel,' explained Ricky. 'My radio station gets to the roots of the music. It helps teach the young chicanos and those people who want to learn about their roots, why we are the way we are. All you have to do is listen to find out our history. We play stuff from Pancho Villa, through the 1920s, through the 1930s, with musicians like Lydia Mendoza, through the 1940s and some of the first norteño music recorded in San Antonio. It gets people back to their roots.'

Ricky's DJ patter was a unique mixture of Spanish and American down-home phraseology, a continuous machine-gun verbal assault on the microphone, interspersed by records spanning 70 years of border history.

He also played the current hits of Little Joe Hernandez, Steve Jordan and Frank Rodarte – the full spectrum of a Texas-Mexican music that other commercial network stations would not touch. Ricky continued:

'Yeah, when I went to school here, it was real bad; they didn't want to hear the Spanish language – they thought it was dirty. Even then they'd tell you, if you're a chicano you should be ashamed of yourself and ashamed of your language. You should be ashamed of your music. Even in the history books we were taught that it was us guys, we were the ones who put the Alamo down, who killed Davy Crockett. It's that mentality we have to struggle against. Our music stands against all that; what it stands for is a continual reminder of what we are.'

Ricky Davila dropped the stylus on another record – the latest recording that

**DJ Ricky Davila plays the new records and keeps the Spanish language alive for a new generation**

Salome Guitierez had made in his front room. It was 'El gatto negro' – the story of a mythical character who came north to America and kept his pride and his identity and whom they couldn't kill. It was sung over the pounding bass rhythm of the bajo sexto and Santiago Junior's gentle accordion rhythms. The music went out across the Texas airwaves and along the Rio Grande, keeping alive the legends of the borderlands.

# 7 Shotguns and Accordions
## Music of the Marijuana Regions of Colombia

At the foot of the Sierra Nevada mountains sprawls the dusty town of Valledupar. The day we arrived, there had been another murder. A storekeeper lay dead by the roadside, enshrouded by yellow and white butterflies shimmering in the heat. From the central square we heard the sound of amplified accordions competing in the Valledupar festival, which is held every spring. But that June of 1983 it was two months late because the guest judge, Nobel Prize winner, Gabriel García Márquez, had been 'unavoidably delayed'.

From the temporary bandstands, where coloured canopies protected musicians from the midday sun, vallenato musicians performed before groups of judges who solemnly entered their verdicts in notebooks, assessing the players for the spontaneity of their rhymes and social satire, as well as the rhythmic quality of their Caribbean-flavoured music. The accordionist was accompanied by a drummer and a guacharaca (scraper) player who would occasionally break into an improvised solo to the delight of the crowd that packed around the bandstands. These had been erected in front of the crumbling colonial colonnades of a city unsung for the other 51 weeks of the year.

Vallenato music has a fanatical following. [I was constantly reminded of how García Márquez had taken a band with him to Norway to serenade his reception of the Nobel Prize for *A Hundred Years of Solitude* which was written about this region.] The festival attracted audiences from all over north Colombia. They were a racial mix of Indian, black and white. The blacks had originally been imported to work the banana and coffee plantations by the Spaniards who had enslaved or murdered the original Indians. These racial confluences are all reflected in vallenato music.

**Nafer Duran, one of
the top vallenato
accordionists, too
good for a prize
at the contest**

Colombia has many different styles of regional music. The Indian flutes and drums of the Andes mountains in the south; the black marimba music of the Pacific coast; the llanero harp music of the eastern cattle plains and the vallenato of the north. It was the last form that came to fascinate me, for it mirrored in its rhythms and lyrics the social decline and disintegration of Colombia's north coast through the drugs trade centred on the Sierra Nevada.

The mountains of the Sierra Nevada de Santa Marta remain a spiritual and economic force today. Their triangular peaks form the geographical boundaries of a magical cosmos for the Arhuaco Indians. Because of this, all the people of that area are deeply superstitious of the spiritual power they contain. Economically they remain important as a centre of the drugs industry that has replaced bananas with marijuana, and coffee with cocaine. The week we arrived in Valledupar, a dozen canvas-covered dance halls called cassettas had sprung up where musicians performed at all-night dances or at cockfights and roulette games. Dirty money could be lost or laundered there by the drug runners, who jammed the streets with their 1950s Chevrolets stripped of bumpers, boots and bonnets. In the background stood the backstreet cocaine-processing plants and stores for the marijuana brought down from the mountains on mules.

As darkness fell, the judges announced whom they had selected to play in the finals

One of the greatest vallenato accordionists is Nafer Duran who explained to us that because of his age and the traditional style of his playing – deeper and less flashy than his younger competitors – he did not stand a chance:

'In the end, all one can say is that the festival results are fixed. It's very easy for them. The organizers decide beforehand who is going to win. And the winners are those who have been sponsored and sent to the festival by the big record companies. However well you play, if you aren't sponsored, if you aren't backed by a record company, you must lose. I don't feel bitter, but I just don't think it's right.'

As he strode to the microphone, Nafer was determined to show he was the best. Whereas his rivals had performed flamboyantly with lyrics about loves and doves, moons and spoons, Nafer was intense, solemn and dignified. His song was a biting critique of the small-town mentality and corruption that predicted he would lose:

> *The governor is an ass because he's easily led.*
> *The police chief is a goat.*
> *And while the poor suffer in the burning sun,*
> *The 'poncho' just looks on and laughs.*

García Márquez turned up with a whole cavalcade of women, journalists and hangers-on and joined the inebriated judges by the side of the stage. They unanimously declared Nafer Duran out of competition because he was 'too good and therefore not eligible for a prize or recording contract'.

The following day, Nafer returned to his home town, El Paso, which was one of the first black settlements in Colombia. The radio had carried the news of Nafer's humiliation and, by way of protest and sympathy for the loser, the whole town laid on a party with the black tambura music and dance the slaves had brought with them 200 years earlier. In response, Nafer unpacked his accordion from its green box, polished the keys with the sleeve of his shirt and sang, in a minor key, a most unusual vallenato number:

**New, brash vallenato superstar, Alfredo Guttierez finds a reward in praising the local mafia**

before a crowd of thousands that was already pushing back the crash barriers in the central square. Police with sticks and guns took up guard as protection against the scenes of spontaneous violence that had broken out the previous year after an unpopular decision. As everyone knew, the competition was fixed. It was financed by Colombian record companies who would invest huge sums in promoting the winner into a new vallenato star.

*In a sad way, with this sad song,*
*I am trying to tell you what my heart is feeling.*
*I am running out of patience.*
*I live in sadness.*
*Because you are the guilty one*
*To have left me like this.*

A friend of Nafer's explained to us, 'It's more than a sad love song. It's about the guilty people who have turned the rest of us into victims.'

These people are the victims of a corrupt and crumbling economy. Until a few years ago, the local marijuana – called 'Colombian gold' – was sold in increasing quantities and at inflated prices to the United States. In the late 1950s and early 1960s, when marijuana became as much part of American culture as Mickey Mouse and Coca Cola, the Colombian mafia terrorized and murdered workers on the coffee plantations and took over their fields to cultivate dope. They became immensely powerful: they built airfields for planes to ferry the drugs to North America; they stole the entire flight control equipment from Valledupar airport and rebuilt it on one of their own landing strips, high in the Sierra Nevada. But then the dealers became greedy: they started to mix their 'Colombian gold' with leaves, plants and horseshit. As soon as the Americans discovered this, they paid in counterfeit dollars. As a result, the local Colombian banks collapsed and with them the whole region's economy. Meanwhile, Americans extracted the marijuana seeds and today the plants are grown in California and Arizona.

In a Valledupar backstreet we had hired a battered green and yellow bus with no suspension and with a front nearside wheel that one night parted company from us and left us stranded. Its drivers were Orlando and

Guillermo, whose mirror shades gleamed from below the brims of their homburg hats and who nostalgically recounted their past adventures as drug runners:

'We just knocked back a few bottles of rum and drove like crazy. We had a whole busload of marijuana – even had to take out the seats to fit it all in. Someone else bribed the police. It was

**The drugs boom gave reign to the dreams money can buy: a safari park and disco dedicated to Lennon**

well organized. We pressed it into thousands of little packs and I just drove for three or four hours with my foot flat down till we found the plane and the gringo who was going to take it to the States. Sometimes he was already dead or the plane was burning by the time we got there. A rival gang or a bad payoff.'

When we returned to Valledupar for the last day of the festival, the celebrations had almost been washed out by a torrential tropical downpour. But in a packed cassetta, whose canvas roof kept out the rains vallenato superstar, Alfredo Guttierez, was being paraded head high on stage by his sweaty musicians as he belted out a song that typified the corruption this music has suffered – from the same sources that had affected much of the rest of north Colombia:

> Aren't I great, aren't I great,
> I've got two women;
> You've only got one.
> Don't you envy me?
> Aren't I the greatest?

Such musicians become rich by finding favour with the big-time mafiosi. They do this by naming the gangsters in their songs. The mafiosi are so thrilled to hear themselves praised on record that they give the singer a Toyota jeep or a Nissan Patrol. Like having two women, these are status symbols for which, they imagine, everybody envies them.

There are two levels of mafiosi: the white elite who control the drugs trade and never appear downtown. Their money is safely stashed in Miami banks and they either live abroad or in the wealthy suburbs of the capital, Bogota, behind several rows of spiked railings and sentries armed with submachine guns. Then there is the black mafia, mostly of mixed blood (and known, therefore, as blacks or mestizos) who actually dirty their hands and take the risks. It was the black mafia who were the worst affected by the slump in the marijuana trade. During the drugs boom, they patrolled the area in shiny Nissans buying pretty girls

from their parents at 150 dollars a head. Often they enticed married women away from the boredom and squalor of their homes with promises of wealth and excitement. Hundreds of families were broken in this way. But when the drugs trade collapsed, the black mafia could no longer support these girls, and local bordellos – already a flourishing institution – expanded to absorb the new influx of unwanted women. A small town like Valledupar boasted some 20 or 30 such places which had become, ironically, the last retreat of the genuine street musician. There he could make a living, playing traditional vallenatos that had elsewhere been corrupted with mafia references or the promotional tactics of record companies that sponsored events like the Valledupar festival.

Astrid de Russo, an outspoken observer, described how vallenato music mirrored that society:

'It has become typically macho. They sing phrases about women like "I'm your owner". Machismo is characteristic of this whole region. Even worse, some musicians make their fortunes by mentioning the names of drug traders in their songs. Our black mafia delighted in their vallenato music. It was one of their trademarks. But now their lack of education and social standing has left them stranded with the decline of the marijuana trade. Now they are the victims of their own game.

'But the white mafia still control the cocaine. Those families that have been our ruling elite for generations still hold the power and the money. For them it is just a different sort of investment: it's cocaine instead of real estate. Most of them now live safely in Bogota.'

A few miles outside Bogota, beyond the sprawling suburbs, stands an incongruously modernistic concrete block with dappled cows

**The mountain villages have lost their men to the drugs trade: an elderly *conjunto de gaitas* is the sad musical legacy**

In an idyllic valley high in the Sierra Nevada de Santa Marta live the Ika tribe who belong to the Arhuaco Indians. Threatened by the drug mafia and by the Catholic missionaries, they struggle to keep their culture, music and language alive

grazing on the front lawn. It is a new recording studio, run and built by a rich young Colombian. His ambition had been to entice the Rolling Stones to record there with an offer of abundant technical facilities and drugs. Three years later, he was still waiting for a reply.

In the studio, a band from the llanos cattle lands was playing a beautiful and highly traditional form of local music known as llanero, on a large harp, quatro, capodirs and electric bass. The harp was introduced to Colombia by Catholic priests from Spain, the quatro is a small four-string guitar and capodirs are rattles. An

electric bass is added for recordings only and the results are both musically brilliant and beautiful.

The band had recently been playing at a new mock-Gothic building built by a cocaine dealer, Carlos Leheer, who was standing for election to the Colombian senate on the grounds that he had reinvested his money in Colombian real estate. This Teutonic edifice was to be a hotel with a disco dedicated to John Lennon and a wildlife park. Outside the front door and between the cages of wild animals specially imported from Africa stood a bronze effigy of

*Sometimes there were problems with the army*
*or police*
*But I promised my girl that I'd buy her a house*
*With the dollars I made from dealing in drugs.*

The heroes of these songs are, quite commonly, impoverished drug pedlars who escape capture from the police, cash in their one-way tickets to the ghetto and end up with a beautiful mulatto girl and a home.

Omayra Mendiola, a young sociologist, lives in the Valledupar backstreets where so many drugs find their way onto the market. She said:

'In some vallenato music they make heroes out of marijuana traders. They become our modern folk heroes and thus glorify the drugs trade in music. Now this is all part of our local legend. All this publicity had a huge effect on communities like mine in the Sierra Nevada. Men left their wives and children to rush to the marijuana fields. Some called it 'the Colombian gold rush'. After the drugs trade collapsed they could not settle down again – they had deserted their homes and towns for ever.'

On her advice, we drove to the mountain village of Atanques, which had furnished the drug industry with workers and mafiosi. It climbs almost vertically up a hillside of the Sierra Nevada, not far from Valledupar, in an idyllic setting with lush green fields filled with butterflies, lizards and magpies. It is halfway to the marijuana plantations. The men have gone, leaving women and little children staring out of the doorways of their painted huts, and adolescents who spend their days and nights in the village pool-hall. Here, amongst a few old men, we found a reminder of the region's former musical glory, a '*conjunto de gaitas*'. It comprised a singer (in this case an alcoholic who was unable to stand and sing at the same time) accompanied by a flautist, a drummer and maracas player. The flute was Indian, the drum had been introduced by the Spanish army and the maracas represented the black influence in the music. This tattered grouping reflected the 'tri-ethnic' roots of the music tradition.

All able-bodied men had left the village for

Lennon, naked and clutching a guitar.

Musicians in the other Bogota recording studios were the more typical vallenato bands singing about a very different aspect of the drugs industry. Their songs are about the victims, and the suffering:

*I went to the mountains full of hope,*
*I couldn't get money for food, I couldn't get a*
*  job,*
*The marijuana seed had just begun to grow,*
*I had no money for food or for a job.*
*Poverty tormented me and drove me to it,*

the marijuana fields and subsequently become armed drifters. They abused and shot local Indians and raped their wives. This meant that the Indians – the indigenous people of that area – either had to fight for their lives or move down to the city of Valledupar. Some are still fighting, while others gave in to the disease, boredom and disillusionment that goes with city life.

We wanted very much to visit the Arhuaco Indian community who now lived in the highest and most inaccessible ranges of the Sierra Nevada de Santa Marta. For two days we waited in the rain until we found a jeep that was willing to do the ten-hour drive across the river beds and deep ravines that led past the marijuana plantations and up to the Ika tribe of the Arhuaco Indians. High in the plantations there is a sort of halfway house where the jeeps and

**The Arhuaco Indians give special meaning to music, which is central to their own cosmic philosophy**

**The Ika chief plays accordion and sings songs that he learnt while visiting the town of Valledupar**

donkeys stop and their riders exchange news. The village is called Pueblo Viejo, and here we breakfasted on meat, soup and maize balls beneath a corrugated iron roof which covered bunk rooms filled with Indian bags, domestic animals, children and wooden crates. On the road outside a dead cow was being savaged by black vultures; rabbits and lizards scuttled intermittently across the road. Luck was on our side as our driver, Lydio Osorio, flagged down a passing jeep which happened to contain the governor and aides of the Ika community. We introduced ourselves and explained our mission. Gradually their suspicion subsided and we decided to go on up the ravines and along the precipices until we reached their 'hidden valley'.

Eventually, in the midst of a terrifying rainstorm, we found it. The jeep floundered in the mud and we waded across a river into a tiny hut and dined on tinned sardines and beer before falling asleep. The morning brought with it a miraculous transformation. The sun shone on a serene and beautiful valley surrounded by mountains. Wild animals roamed in the long grass and trees, and about a half mile from our hut stood an ancient stone-built Indian settlement.

The Ika people are justifiably suspicious of outsiders. Local traders cheated them, drug dealers abused and murdered them and Catholic missionaries attempted to convert them. Recently, the Indians had driven out the missionaries, discovering, they claimed, sophisticated radio equipment and other links with the American CIA. They believed the missionary conversion scheme was a convenient means of infiltration by intelligence forces. It is probable that we would never have been accepted by these Indians had it not been for another torrential outburst. We all rushed for shelter into what turned out to be the village community centre, a low thatched stone building with one electric light bulb swaying from the roof and a long table at which the Indian chiefs gathered. In the near dark, with everyone packed tightly together, the tension broke and people began to laugh. The chief picked up an accordion and played some local melodies he had learned in the city of Valledupar during one of his visits. We had been accepted as guests.

The next day, Luis N. Torres (the Indian governor) and his advisers explained to us the importance of their Indian music:

'It is an example of how western culture has penetrated our minds that instruments like the accordion have displaced our traditional flute. Recovery is going to be slow and hard. We have been so brainwashed and downtrodden for so many years.

'Our music plays a central part in our cosmology. Music was born in the struggle of darkness against the light and it reflects the tension between those two powers. Music was used to distract the opponent and win the battle. Just as fireflies and glow worms pretended they were light, so music was used to confuse the senses and deceive.'

They played their ceremonial and religious music in long slow meditative phrases on flutes and drums. The onlookers chewed the coca leaves they had ground inside the small earthen pots they carried with them. In Ika society, cocaine has always played a traditional role; when Indians meet, they do not shake hands or kiss, they exchange dried coca leaves and stuff them away inside their brightly embroidered bags. When the mafia attempted to steal the coca fields cultivated by the Ikas, the Indians appealed to the Colombian army for help. The soldiers came and burned the fields and thus also destroyed the Indian culture. Now the Indians no longer invite the army and live instead in constant fear of the horseback mafiosi with their rifles and six-shooters. Since the Ikas pushed out the missionaries, the (Catholic) government has withheld all support and finance. Their future is now very grim.

We took the same route back to Valledupar and then drove northwards around the Sierra Nevada and up towards the Caribbean coast. We passed through ghost towns like Santa Marta, the oldest colonial city in Colombia. A decade ago it was flourishing, but with the collapse of the drugs trade, the hotels were without guests. Musicians and croupiers, dressed in tuxedos, spun their roulette wheels in empty casinos – the violence, corruption and drug dealers had seen to that.

Around Santa Marta were picturesque fishing ports where cocaine was loaded for shipping to Miami. The smugglers were protected by the local militia and threatened us with submachine guns pointed through the windows of their Toyota jeeps. That evening nobody in Santa Marta would converse with us. We were warned that we were not safe to be seen with. So we left.

Not far west of Santa Marta, we came across the huge banana plantations that have been so important in Colombia's past. In *One Hundred Years of Solitude* García Márquez described the terrible massacre of the striking workers there, and people still talk of it. Around the plantations stand the remnants of the colonial plantation owners' houses. Behind them lies the vibrant black township of Cienaga. There we met an old plantation worker called Humberto Daza who nostalgically described the old days and the changes he had seen:

'Once the whole area depended on bananas for its wealth. Their decline affected everyone. It opened the way for a new economy of drugs. But now history is repeating itself. The same thing has happened to the marijuana trade that happened to bananas. The trade collapses and the people suffer. The old plantation days are just a dream now, when we picked bananas and played the old cumbias.'

The original cumbia music of the black plantation workers is almost impossible to find today. Humberto gathered around him a few of the old timers and played his caña de millo (a small cane flute), supported by pounding Afro-Colombian drummers who danced some of the cumbias that were once part of the everyday street life of Cienaga. Victor Lazala is a young and forceful musician who believes that action can right the wrongs his township has suffered:

'About ten years ago the mafiosi started coming in from other towns when the marijuana bonanza started. They took over our stores and our streets. It became dangerous even to walk in Cienaga. Mafia were everywhere, living off the proceeds of Colombian gold. Local kids left

**Banana plantations were crucial to the economy before drugs: cumbia music was a part of that life**

school to sell it. In place of school books the mafia offered them a Colt 45, a sawn-off shotgun, money, jewelry, a car. They went crazy. The women went crazy too. They left their families for rich gangsters only to end up homeless or on the streets. There were days when maybe 15 people would die in the night, and come morning the elders would ask how many dead bodies would be buried in the graveyard that day? It became an important topic in the social life of our town.

'Something very strange then happened in Cienaga. People built fences around themselves out of fear. The police became the pawns of the mafia. Instead of finding happiness in songs and dances, people found it in cars, revolvers and money. They lost their cultural roots. The cumbia, for example, was once heard everywhere. But when the mafia arrived, they brought their brash corrupted vallenato music to replace it. Today that's all you hear on the street.'

The final journey in our battered bus took us along the coast and inland to the tiny village of San Pelayo, near Monteria. This was cattle country; flat lands inhabited by a racial mix of black, Indian and Spanish people. We arrived at night. In the central square, a huge circle of flickering candles moved around a brass band who were blowing their lungs out in a sort of musical violence. The dancers were glassy-eyed with sweat pouring down their bodies and clutching in each hand half a dozen candles whose burning wax dripped over their faces and arms. The dancers and musicians went on, hour after hour, round and round as though hypnotized.

The next day, people rose from where they had slept on the ground and joined in a procession that wound its way to the local graveyard. Inside the walls, 24 brass bands had congregated, for San Pelayo is the village where, each year, a festival of bands is held. First the musicians wished to pay homage to their predecessors who lay beneath the ornate tombstones carved with cherubim and seraphim. They wanted to let their ancestors know that the competition was alive and well,

In the village of San Pelayo, brass bands are the voice of the people: an all-night dance to candlelight, a procession to the graveyard where they play for their dead ancestors and shout their continuing presence in life

and they planned to rattle their sleeping bones with a vast cacophony of sound.

First the local priest, swinging incense, intoned prayers. Then all 24 bands started blowing simultaneously. Some bands played fast, others slow, still others played whatever came into their heads. The village elders in their Sunday best squatted on top of the gravestones to get a better view. Finally, the bands trooped ceremonially out, preceded by a canopied Madonna. They left behind a thin and angry revolutionary who had apparently been shouting the whole time through a homemade

**The brass bands who compete in the San Pelayo annual contest aim to make their presence firmly heard**

loudspeaker system, though no-one had been able to hear him. Now the crowds filed out behind the bands for the start of the competition and he was left alone, berating the gravestones about the hardships and iniquities of the San Pelayo life.

The festival itself was a statement of defiance. The rhythm of the music, called the porro, was unique to that area. The whole festival had an obsessive intensity: the bands practised fanatically throughout the year, focusing on that one moment to gain public recognition and be heard. Until their turn came, they flopped nervously in hammocks, fidgeting with their instruments, polishing them with spittle and rags. Each band took its turn to play before the judges, and to a western ear the sound they made was crude, almost offensive. But the

purpose here was not to play with perfect harmony or balance or rhythm. In the words of its young organizer, William Fortich:

'The main purpose of this festival is to make enough noise to let people know we exist. That we're not "nobodies" in this region of the country. The porro rhythms that the bands play here are our very own. Rhythms that were born in the fusion of black Africa and Indian America.

'The trombones, the clarinets, the tubas and the trumpets may be European instruments but the statement that they make is ours. We are all fanatics.

'The main purpose of this competition is not to win, but to be heard. It is the only way we have to proclaim our identity in a society that otherwise ignores us. Here, for a moment, we are no longer victims. Music offers what the rest of life denies us.'

# 8 There'll Always Be Stars In The Sky
## *The Indian Film Music Phenomenon*

As dusk fell, a bus forced its way through a thousand sleeping camels, its horn blaring. Beneath their painted carts, parked in the desert sands of Rajasthan, the market people stirred, and chattered with excitement. They trampled sand over their fires and hurried over to where the bus had stopped.

It was November 1983, the moon was new and – after much argument and last-minute changes of mind – the astrologers and soothsayers had decreed that this night should be the start of Pushkar Fair.

Pushkar stands on the shores of a holy lake. It is a peaceful desert town with its ghatts, its river steps, filled each day with Hindus praying, bathing and purifying themselves. But, for a few days every year, the sleepy city is transformed into a camel and cattle market, invaded by thousands of buyers and sellers who camp with

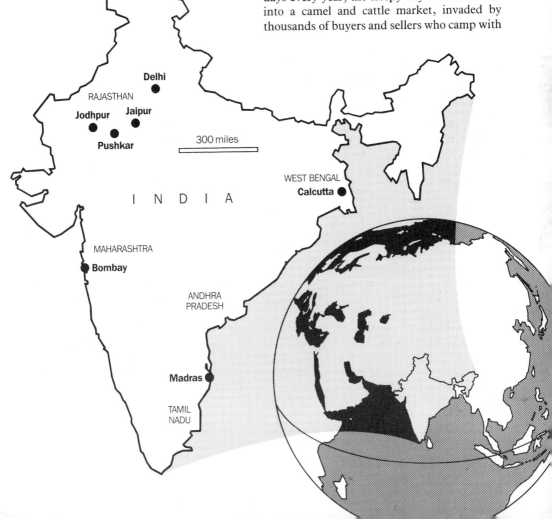

**Camel and cattle traders gather with their families for Pushkar Fair in the deserts of Rajasthan**

their families in the hot sands. This year had been a busy one: drought and poverty had driven many farmers to come and sell their remaining livestock.

Now they gathered round the hooting bus on which a makeshift screen was lowered from the roof and pinned across the windows. A hundred feet away, an antique projector flickered as the audience, swelling in size with every moment of suspense, waited for a black and white version of an Indian music film to start. Soon, their faces were lit up by the images on the cloth screen and stunned by the sounds of 100 violins. This was a typical travelling cinema showing an illegal print of an Indian film extravaganza to an audience some of whom had never seen a film before. The film was called *Upkar*; its music had been written 1,000 miles away in a Bombay film studio by a team of two music directors, brothers who are known as Kalyanji Anandji.

These travelling cinemas have been an aggravation to the authorities for decades. With pirated prints, they tour the least accessible areas of India, dodging police and tax collectors to say nothing of irate film accountants who chase them through the desert in old black Morris cars.

What they are bringing to these country people, just like the cinemas that fill every city and village across India, is a music fantasy. Visited by 100 million people every week, the Indian film musical is unique in the world. It brings together the scale of a Busby Berkeley musical, the action of a James Bond spectacle and the epic proportions of a spaghetti western. In every region of India the whole family goes to the cinema to share the emotion, the adventure and, most important, the music.

Indian film music is a synthesis: Indian classical and folk music blended with western pop and disco, with a generous reference to the western classical repertoire. Hundred-piece orchestras are mixed with traditional instruments – often reproduced on synthesizers. In Bombay we sought out Kalyanji Anandji who were unusually hospitable and helpful. Kalyanji had recently been travelling in Rajasthan (home of his Hindu saint who occupied a shrine in his music room) and had 'borrowed' a few themes from local musicians:

'We get ideas not just from the tunes of the folksongs but also from their lyrics. Then we adapt them. In India life begins and ends with music. For instance, a new-born baby is greeted into the world by songs. When you put your

baby to sleep, you sing him a lullaby. He is brought up in school with nursery rhymes. In his teens he sings romantic songs. There is song and dance when he weds and dies. Just as food is a must for the body, I feel that music is a must for the mind. We often get ideas for our music from folk songs from Rajasthan, like "Jodhpur kee jugnee" ("Jodhpur's sexpot").'

The two music directors were rehearsing that song, in Kalyanji's home, with a young girl protegée. They were taking her into a recording studio the next day, for the very first time: 'I am Jodhpur's sexpot,' she intoned sweetly and shyly, 'I'll arouse you and tease you until I make you cry.'

Kalyanji played harmonium, Anandji added percussion with hand claps. As they perfected the number, Kalyanji exchanged his Indian instrument for a Casio portable synthesizer and Anandji stopped clapping. They rehearsed with extreme precision through the early hours of the morning, repeating phrases over and over until the singer perfected them. Then Kalyanji continued:

'I feel that we are definitely ahead of other countries in music. In our classics, musicians have worked out the effects that various notes can have if they are played for certain periods of time. It has been proved, for example, that rain can start to fall or an oil lamp can ignite – of its

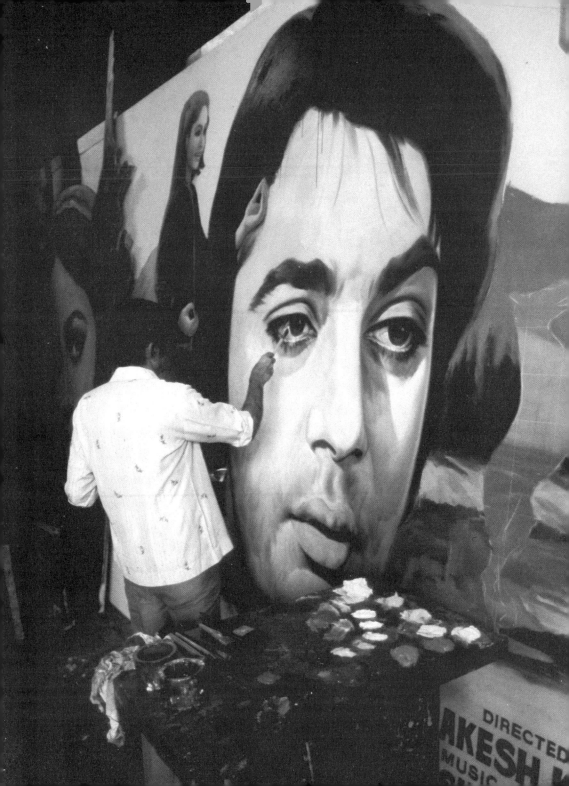

DIRECTED
AKESH
MUSIC

own accord – if certain notes are played for particular lengths of time.'

In terms of Indian record sales, the classics, surprisingly, account for only 2 per cent of the total. About 15 per cent is ghazals (light classics) and most of the rest – about 80 per cent – film music. This also dominates Indian radio despite past government attempts to ban movie music totally (as they did in the 1950s) as culturally demeaning and subversive. It fills the most popular programmes on television and spreads across the Far East and even into South America.

In India television is still available to only a privileged few, so cinema and its music are the principal entertainment. Some 750 feature films are produced each year and it is reckoned that 600 are in some stage of production in the Bombay studios alone. The success of these films depends on two factors: their stars and their music. Often the only names mentioned on the hoardings, dominating the roads of every major Indian city, are of the male star and the music director of the newest film. In the backstreets of Bombay, there is a thriving cottage industry of poster painting, since every film poster is painted by hand with as much loving attention to detail as in the music scores themselves. Often up to 20 feet in height, they are wheeled on barrows across the city in the early hours and then winched up the fronts of office blocks and cinemas, ready for the morning rush hour. With their brilliant, gaudy depictions of mythology, affluence and melodrama, they make an uneasy contrast with the street squatters below in their tents patched with plastic bags.

The music names most often appearing on these hoardings are Laxmikant and Pyarelal, Bombay's most successful music directors. As a film's market value depends largely on its music

**For the dozen or so new films appearing each week in India, giant, gaudy posters are painted by hand**

and lyrics, there is a great demand for their involvement. Laxmikant and Pyarelal are said to work on up to 30 films simultaneously. Rich and extremely powerful, they can financially make or break a film. I tried to meet with them on several occasions, but was confronted by a battery of aides and much arrogance and condescension by the great men. Laxmikant and Pyarelal constitute a small industry in themselves; they farm many arrangements out to a bevy of ill-paid apprentices because of the volume of work they have to complete. Like other music directors, they plagiarize all sorts of music from classics to pop, favouring western harmonies and a western-style orchestra. These are then matched with elaborate scorings for traditional Indian instruments, and what emerges is the hotchpotch that is Indian film music.

The sheer volume of scores required by the Bombay industry has resulted in formula music: directors often write for perhaps 100 films per year, each with six songs. In the 1940s and 1950s there was some genuinely original work by composers like S.D. Burman, but the Laxmikant and Pyarelal factory has become a musical conveyor belt.

The next morning, we joined the music directors Kalyanji Anandji at a sound studio where they were to record with their protegée. First they were rescoring someone else's film music which a producer had found unsatisfactory. So, after tidying up the music for a suggestive love scene (that dissolved from knickers dropping down a woman's legs to erotic statues at the temples of Khajuraho), they composed a new number to accompany Shashi Kapoor riding a motor bike into the sunset while his neck was nibbled by his pillion rider. Kalyanji explained:

'Music directors may be a most important element of a film, but we can seldom do what we want. When composing a song, we have to keep in mind not only the storyline that our producer gives us, but also the image of the leading stars. It is details like these that shape the songs that millions will later take to their hearts. Music

**Each poster is carefully wheeled across Bombay in the morning rush hour traffic**

directors must be like department stores, ready to supply anything and everything. We try to write songs so simple that they can be hummed by everybody. Every song should be as simple as a nursery rhyme. This is where our art as music directors lies.'

The 'catchiness' of a song must first hook the financiers. The way a film is born is unique. First the producer finds a star (someone as big as Amitabh Bachchan may be shooting as many as 30 films simultaneously) with the help of some substantial tax-free gifts. Then the producer gives a top music director a theme – usually extremely simple – on which to base a song. If the backer likes it, the music is choreographed and filmed as a dance sequence. It is then appraised, and if considered potentially commercial, other numbers are composed and shot while the rest of the script is written and acted out.

The prestige of the music director also depends on the size of the orchestra. For Kalyanji Anandji, nothing less than 100 musicians at any one session will do, even though the music could often be played on a synthesizer with two fingers (as Anandji demonstrated). Mostly the studios are old-fashioned; their 1950s ferrograph recorders jam and spill tape all round the mixing desk while the orchestra continues to scrape out lush melodies – a mixture of available manpower and antiquated technology. Like America in the 1930s, the industry still depends on Hollywood production values, with vast numbers of musicians, big stars, lavish sets, lots of extras, and, at the end, plenty of cut-and-thrust hype and promotion. There are no less than 600 movie fan magazines eager for gossip, scandal

**From far away
Bombay comes the
magic of the cinema
with its music, dance
and superstars**

and cheap publicity.

We left the brothers in a midtown studio. They were still having problems getting copies of the scores out to 100 orchestra members. All these scores were handwritten but there was only one copy of the violin part, so 34 violinists had to follow the lead player: six other sections had been hastily written the previous evening, but the brass were without scores at all and having to improvise, while the images were going through on the screen to meticulous timing, as precise, for example, as 3.7 seconds. The musicians had to get the emphasis correct, exactly on each cut. There was considerable confusion: sometimes three or even four conductors were beating different times simultaneously; the music director was shouting through a loudspeaker from the control room and the senior musicians were trying to look cool – difficult in a 100 degree temperature with no air conditioning. It was, of course, an extremely expensive procedure, given the cost of a 100-piece orchestra, soloists, engineers and studio time, In addition, every ten minutes, the power kept fading, as happens all over India. So the tapes ran slow and there was another spontaneous unplanned effect. Very few studios had their own generators. On top of that, the music directors probably had recording schedules in four other studios the same day. No wonder the producers seldom look happy. Only about 20 per cent of Bombay movies are ever completed.

An essential ingredient of a successful Indian movie is a top 'playback' artist who sings but never appears on the screen. The songs are all written and recorded prior to filming – which is done to 'playback' through a cheap set of

**Each film needs a top playback singer: still reigning supreme with 25,000 recordings behind her is the great Lata Mangeshkar**

loudspeakers attached to a tape recorder in the film studio.

We visited India's number-two box-office draw, Dharmendra, while he attempted a dance sequence with two starlets about whom there had been much recent hot gossip. The camera had been blessed that day and flowers placed upon its ancient lens to bring good fortune to all. They needed it. After spending time at the mirror with his makeup men, Dharmendra's ample figure tried valiantly to keep time to the taped song and the little starlets.

The voice on that tape belonged to a legend: her name is Lata Mangeshkar and her voice is one of the controlling forces within the Bombay industry. It is an accepted convention that (with the occasional exception of Amitabh Bachchan) the film stars never sing. Though they mouth the words expressively in the film and are featured on the record covers that accompany it, the voices belong to others – with a star system of their own. The greatest of all time is Lata Mangeshkar, known outside India for her entry in the *Guinness Book of Records*

which notes that she has made 25,000 recordings. Her power is second to none and she was described, by an intimate, as 'harder than steel'. In her heyday those who crossed her were finished and she can still make or break anyone in film music. When we were there, she favoured Laxmikant and Pyarelal, so they were riding high.

For all her power and wealth, Lata lives unostentatiously and with gentle dignity. She invited us to visit her on Divali – the Indian New Year – and was generous in her time and hospitality. She gave thanks to Laxmi, the goddess of wealth, at the private shrine in her apartment, explaining:

'I believe that music and God are one. My father always maintained that music has a power that leads to a short cut to God. Yes, I am religious and yes, I do pray, but not four hours a day like some people say I do. I pray according to the free time I have, when I'm not recording film music. After my father's death I had to work in films as a child in order to support my family, as I was the eldest. When I started work as a playback singer I had to rush around from place to place. I travelled alone on local trains and sometimes did not get home until two or three in the morning. Usually I had to miss meals too. I still work hard. I still practise every morning. Each artist develops his or her own individual style of singing. Whenever an artist sings someone else's song, his or her individual style always filters through. No-one can behave just like a tape recorder, at least not so far as I'm concerned.

'I've often made suggestions to music directors about either changing the rhythm or the melody of a song, and I've been lucky in having a lot of freedom to sing the way I think

**One of India's top stars, Dharmendra, tries out a dance sequence, miming to the taped voice of a playback singer**

right. Not only have they accepted my suggestions, but they've liked them; and it seems the public also likes them.'

Lata is in her sixties now; her voice is not quite what it was, and she is handing over the mantle of top female playback singer to Asha Bhosle, her sister and previously her rival.

Lata's voice has crossed regional boundaries and dialects, bypassing caste barriers and enchanting the subcontinent with sweet melodies. From cinemas, food stalls, pirated cassettes and radios throughout India come her pure, ingenuous tones. They are inescapable. It is said she will be deified at her death.

In order to assess the impact of film music on local ways of life, I chose Rajasthan, in the north, because of its rich assortment of tribal, folk, religious and ceremonial music. These have often been incorporated by music directors, like Kalyanji Anandji, into Bombay movie music. Ironically, now, the movies are feeding back and affecting local entertainment.

**The long tradition of puppet shows, a feature of Rajasthan culture, has changed with the pressure of the cinema**

Snake charmers have for centuries been playing traditional tunes on their flutes. But in the past decade, these have changed. They are now playing film music: Bombay movies updated the snake charmers' tunes and the next generation unwittingly adopted them. The snakes do not seem to notice the changes.

So too, in the puppet theatres, local Rajasthani myths have given way to film stories which themselves were originally based on the puppet mens' stories – a musical circle that delighted the audience we filmed in a slum settlement at Jaipur. It was a community of dropouts, low castes and a few petty crooks, whom we were discouraged from visiting by the local government officials. The puppeteers had been forced to adapt to the new age of the movies. Costumes and characters mirrored the Bombay stars and the music they played on an antique harmonium cleverly included the latest film hits. The myths and history which were so much a part of local life had given way to the fantasies, glamour and glitter of the movie world. Local heroes had lost their powers, local myths their relevance. What one Rajasthani described as the 'historical consciousness of our people' was being irrevocably altered in the space of a few years.

The Bhopas have one of the earliest forms of 'travelling cinema'. We saw a husband and wife arriving with a bag of instruments and a rolled-up screen, which was a painted parchment. They attached it to the branches of a tree, at dusk. The man took out a rebab (an upright, two-stringed fiddle) and ankle rattles, while the woman, her face covered with a veil, lit a candle attached to the end of a wooden pole. When it was dark, the performance began: with great intensity he sang, played and stamped his feet while his wife used the candle to illuminate the portion of the scroll he was describing. But their audience found them boring. They booed and catcalled and hurled insults. Halfway through the show, the restless audience left, joining their friends who were watching a real movie, a little way up the hill.

The Kalbelia gypsies have adapted better. Preserving all the grace of their nomadic forefathers, they have smartened up their clothes and now perform for tourists and visiting TV film crews, from whom they make a good living. While staying in their tents we were suddenly and unexpectedly invited to film with them the next night – at the wedding of two six-year-old children. Child marriages are now outlawed in India and this posed problems for us. Every film crew working in India has to sign a paper before entering giving the representatives of the Indian government power to determine what may or may not be filmed, and power over the editing too. We had no choice but to comply. Our government 'guides'

**The Kalbelia gypsies have learned to make a living from their own dances and music, performing for film crews and tourists**

had been helpful and we had found ways round most problems. But what would they say to our filming an illegal wedding? We had the good fortune to be working with Gattu Kaul (whose brother is the avant-garde film maker, Mani Kaul). She was determined that we should attend the wedding and not only managed to persuade the authorities, but also hired a generator from a local tradesman, mended it, hitched it to the back of a truck which she drove into the field where the gypsies lived, bought

vast lengths of cable from an electrical store, fixed the lights on poles and then went to buy food and gifts for the wedding. Gattu also served as a useful distraction; she dressed like a man, in jacket and trousers, with a short haircut. This was so unusual for an Indian woman that, when she was around, all eyes were on her rather than the camera or the recording equipment.

From the families' point of view, the wedding was a necessity. They had maybe a dozen children and needed to stagger their marriages so they could fulfil the dowry requirements. And they wanted to know that their children were going to be married and secure. Therefore, this family had found a six-year-old from another gypsy tribe, arranged dowry payments and this wedding. Not only that, they each had a twelve-year-old, and so turned the ceremony into a double child wedding.

After the blessings, the young couples circled the symbolic fire seven times. Then came chanting, followed by a dance to a massive, two-sided bass drum. The Kalbelia danced as though possessed, quite differently from the polished shows they gave for tourists and folklorists. This wedding was the only example we found of a musical tradition that had not been affected by the commercial cinema. These gypsies were outsiders, unacceptable to society and therefore unaffected by film music or social trends. Others, like the Kavad singers (with holy stories told in a fold-up wooden box, almost like a medieval comic book), were outlawed as beggars and had stopped their trade altogether.

Migrants from these rural places move in increasing numbers to the major cities. They go in search of work, often enticed by the glamour and excitement of the big cities as depicted in the Bombay films. They become manual workers in the construction industry, building roads and multistorey office blocks. Their leisure hours are spent in cinemas which they can enter for a couple of rupees. Other avid cinema goers are the minor civil servants, caught in the impenetrable web of the bureaucracy machine, where one piece of paper can pass for weeks around a single desk for scrutiny and signatures. Others are the young teenagers for whom dull reality cannot compare with the glamour and action of their movie heroes. For all these people, the cinema is bright, beautiful and escapist. This audience does not want social realism; they seek from the screen a way out into a larger, more vivid life than their own. A local laundry worker expressed this yearning:

'Watching films is a lovely way to pass the time. They make me forget all my troubles. I love to sit in the dark and dream about what I can never possibly have. I can listen to the music, learn all the songs and that way I can forget about my troubles.'

In India, popular films and their soundtracks supply a fantasy which stops people thinking too much about their real world and how it might be changed. This gulf between screen fantasy and experience is often carefully nurtured by successive governments, so politics and the film industry are closely intertwined. In Bombay, top officials, including the Mayor, are ex-movie stars. But the most obvious example of 'movie politics' is in the Tamil cinema of Madras, which specializes in huge mythological epics. A political party was built up around these whose leader was MGR (Marudur Gopalan Ramachandran), a hugely successful screen actor cast often in the role of god or king. In the course of his 45 years and 280 films, he acquired a mystical status as the ideal, benevolent father figure. MGR then broke away from the original party and branched out to form his own, finally becoming Governor of the whole Tamil Nadu province. He posed a real threat to Mrs Gandhi who had him replaced. When this happened there were riots in the streets and burnings and killings. For local people had included MGR – in the guise of a god – within their household shrines, and identified him completely with that role. When electioneering, he made capital out of this identification and dressed up as a deity with mythological powers to do good. He was swept into power.

Again, in the regional cinema of Andhra Pradesh, N.T. Rama Rao, often in films a mythological figure or god, has become a deified politician for his audience and voters – on and off screen.

In the Bombay cinema, politics has flirted with the film industry. Mrs Gandhi cultivated superstars like Amitabh Bachchan to gain, by association, glamour and popularity. Conversely, the movie stars were given political prestige and financial advantages. Now Rajiv Ghandhi, after his mother's death, has persuaded Amitabh Bachchan to stand for parliament and support him. The minority art-film makers, on the other hand, have an urban

**Two six year olds of the Kalbelia tribe are married: illegal but a necessity for the gypsies' survival**

intellectual audience of only a few thousand.
The impact of their films on the broad populace
is slight; even names like Satyajit Ray – which
for many people outside India means cinema –
can only raise an audience of a few hundred in a
Bombay art house.

One of the few producers of commercial
films who seemed aware of his political role is
Raj Kapoor. He is something of an elder
statesman of the Bombay industry, and very
hard to reach. Eventually we found him,
reclining on a couch in his ranch-style home.
Driving out to his suburb, our car radio played a
song from one of his earliest hits, his film *Shri
420*:

> *In this city people live . . .*
> *In the shadow of suffering.*
> *Living people and their hearts*
> *Are sold for money.*

Raj Kapoor's first films, heavily influenced
by Chaplin, did tackle real social problems,
featuring an Indian 'little tramp'. They were
immensely successful at home and abroad,
making him amongst other things 'A Hero of the
Soviet Union'. But his later films became
increasingly expensive and trapped within the
Bombay system; dependent on stars, music
directors and general razzamatazz. When he
tried to add a sense of social realism to these, he
failed. His 1970 production, *The Joker*, about a
city man trapped in a web of deception and
corruption, with himself in the principal role,
contained the final ironic lines:

> *Tomorrow we may or may not be*
> *But there'll always be stars in the sky*

As Raj Kapoor explained:
'The most entertaining film is one that does
not raise any controversy in this democracy of
ours. There are a lot of diverse factors in our
country, such as all the different languages and
people and castes. All of these can create friction
so one has to be very careful as to what kind of
fare is presented and how much truth you can

present along with it. By and large, we are
making escapist fare. Of late, I have realized
that the common man says: "Look, I go through
a lot of problems in life. I know that poverty is
there, all sorts of things that hassle my life are
there. Now, if you give me a film again depicting
me, for me to identify with, I don't want it. I
want a dream. I want to dream what I am not."
Hence the escapist fare. And it feels lovely, it
feels fine for that little moment, to dream. And it
is a dream that I sell.'

The Bombay dream machine really grew in
the years after World War I when the new rich
built cinemas and studios. That was a time of
strict political censorship by the British, a
censorship that has persisted in different guises
until now. But earlier this century, before the

**Ugam Raj is the last great travelling showman: dressed as a woman he dances and mimes the dramas of Rajasthan**

first cinema tents had been pegged into the ground, Parsi theatre offered much the same mix as its successor: a narrative melodrama with folk songs, dances and bit of gaudy mythology. A top actor of the Parsi theatre was Prithviraj Kapoor (later called the Errol Flynn of India), Raj Kapoor's father.

The forerunners of Parsi theatre were the travelling stage shows. We were fortunate to trace perhaps the last of the great showmen in

Rajasthan to the annual Pushkar Fair. His name is Ugam Raj, and it took a dozen messengers, some pigeons and two soothsayers to locate him. His show was a highlight of the fair, held on a proscenium stage in a tented enclosure at the edge of the desert. Accompanied by a band of musicians, dressed in glittering costumes and jewelry, he acted out ancient Rajasthani dramas of kings, queens, legends and morality tales – still a part of his audience's world. These he interspersed with 'praises' bought by members of the audience for friends or relatives.

His troupe are, in the literal sense, transvestites: playing and dressing as women. He explained:

'It is our tradition that men not only play the male roles, but also play the female roles.

There is no need for actresses. Anyway, in the past women were not allowed to act. It was not considered proper.

'In the *cinema* they play immoral scenes and they sing indecent songs. Nothing like that exists here. We only sing nice, old-fashioned folk songs and inspire people in the old values, like being a good neighbour. Because we preach through our plays, I suppose you would call us a kind of mobile social service.'

Between acts, we sat in his makeup tent, eating freshly cooked chapati from a fire. He was a proud, intelligent man in his sixties who had worked hard to give his children a formal education, for he considered himself to be the last of a line of great travelling performers. Ugam Raj explained how he had to think himself into a role: it was not just a question of dressing up, each time he carefully went into a meditative state to prepare, to think, breathe, walk and be motivated as a woman. On stage, he danced, his ample girth decked out in flowing skirts and bodice layered with coloured scarves and adorned with bangles, earrings and the brilliant costume jewellery he kept in little pearl-studded boxes. He had hoped to pass the skills that he had learnt in his epic career onto the younger boys in his troupe, but there was no longer the same discipline nor motivation for tradition. Local people respected him; he was the one traditional entertainer who could compete with the travelling cinema – at Pushkar Fair he drew a crowd of thousands every night, whole families who loved and appreciated him.

'The coming of cinema has finished us,' said Ugam Raj. 'Film makers have so many facilities at their disposal, like scenery, costumes and rows of chairs to sit on. The cinema has so much to offer that audiences would rather go there. We just have a very simple set with no special place for people to sit and no fancy lighting effects.

'But when I play one of our ancient dramas of Rajasthan, I am continuing a valuable tradition. It is not like escapist dreams of the cinema. For these people it is something real. A link between their past and their present.'

**With meticulous care and detail, Ugam Raj prepares for his role: he has no one to follow him, the cinema has taken over**

# 9 Roots Rock Reggae
## *Jamaican Music*

1977 was an exciting and creative time for reggae music in Jamaica. It had just begun to make its presence felt internationally and was spawning a great variety of talent on the island and overseas.

Since the making of this film, much has been written about reggae. It has been analysed and reanalysed, filmed and refilmed. But back in 1977, apart from Perry Henzell's *The Harder They Come*, few films had been shot about reggae music, and so it felt like a pioneering effort to organize the first documentary on the island that related the music to its society.

A year before, I had the good fortune to film some of reggae's best British musicians in a film ironically titled *British Reggae*. This had included the first generation of Jamaicans who came to Britain in the late 1940s to find work, as well as their children, for example, Aswad. But I wanted to get to the heart of the matter. I had become increasingly tired of the way music was presented on television, particularly BBC Television. It was either high art, consumer pop or, if a 'foreign' music form, it was given a demeaning, semi-colonial, folkloric presentation. It seemed that film makers were bent on going to the Third World and selecting to film the most comfortable and unrepresentative music they could find, usually artificially costumed dance troupes organized by the wives of lawyers and politicians. Everything was 'set up'. Nothing was natural. Crews seemed to spend their time avoiding reality rather than trying to record it. I had travelled enough to know how false a picture was being shown. This was also a time when reggae music itself was relatively unknown, both in the pop charts and among young record buyers generally in the UK and USA. I remember trying to find (without success) some Wailers records in New York. I did meet and talk to Jimmy Cliff, however, and determined to try to get to Jamaica and make a film about the wealth of music being born and recorded there, as well as the close relationship of that music to the history and social realities of the island. In the end, since none of the television companies

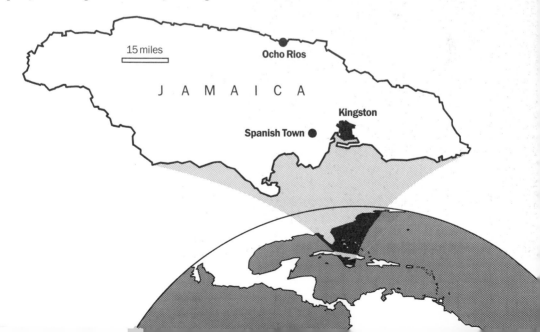

was in the least bit interested, we borrowed heavily from the bank.

Getting into Jamaica, at that time, was not easy. Political gang wars, street violence and the continuing conflicts between the socialist Prime Minister, Michael Manley, and the right-wing opposition leader (now Prime Minister) Edward Seaga, had thrown the island into greater ferment than ever. Any film that was likely to portray the realities of Jamaican life was not looked upon kindly by its bureaucracy. Particularly in the Third World, the government departments which issue the visas and permits that allow you to film only want the high art or the folklore portrayed as their culture, the very aspects I wanted to escape from. They are not unreasonably obsessed with film as propaganda and would like to manipulate it. What Jimmy Cliff was later to call 'the cry of the people' was a truth that few of the countries I dealt with ever wanted recorded and shown abroad.

The result, in Jamaica, was that we were forced to offer a film script based largely on calypso and jazz, virtually avoiding reggae and the realities it described. I had an uncomfortable week or so hanging about, waiting for the

**Jacob Miller formed Inner Circle with Ian and Roger Lewis in 1968, combining rock and reggae**

complicated, arbitrary decision-making to be finalized and the official paperwork to be completed. I spent days on the stoop of Tommy Cowan's 'music ranch' in Kingston (which was shortly afterwards burned to the ground by frustrated musicians or police). There I met the legendary Jacob Miller of Inner Circle, the Abyssinians, Gregory Isaacs and Ras Michael with his Sons of Negus. It was a time of little work or recognition for most reggae musicians, so there was a lot of lounging about, rolling giant spliffs and waiting for something to happen. Among the most unpleasant was Gregory Isaacs who chose to threaten almost every visitor with offensive language and a rusty knife. That reputation persists today. By contrast, Jacob Miller and the two Lewis brothers – three highly extrovert musicians who had taken Jamaica by storm – piled me into their battered silver-grey Mercedes Benz and took me up to stay with them in Kingston's 'Beverly Hills'. It was said at

**Michael Manley, the leader of the People's National Party used a populist approach: he looked to reggae musicians and the Rastafarians to increase his image and credibility**

the time that Jacob Miller had a 'direct line', not to God but to Michael Manley – the next best thing. Manley himself was making full use of the reggae stars: he had already conscripted Bob Marley and Jacob Miller to perform on his political bandwagon – though in later years, they were all to become distanced from the bloody infighting of Jamaican politics. Manley had plastered the ghetto walls of Trenchtown and Jonestown with clenched fist images of himself above the title 'Forward Together'. Other slogans like 'Heavy Wonderful' and 'Heavy Manners' were painted across record shops, bus stops and even the surrounds of the red prison. There, gun or drug offenders were sent to suffer in a sort of red agony – every prison cell, every table and chair, every cup and saucer was painted bright red, the theory being that the colour would deter offenders from further crimes by the discomfort afforded the eyes.

Michael Manley, like many other politicians in developing countries, used the popular street music to spread his message. One reggae number was played incessantly, enveloping him and his supporters in a wall of rhythmic sound:

> *Heavy Wonderful,*
> *Dupe them with the microdot.*
> *Socialism no fool*
> *No, socialism no fool*
> *We have them under manners,*
> *Heavy, heavy manners*
> *Michael Manley no fool*
> *Socialism no fool.*

As a reward for the top artists' commitment to his politics, Manley made vague promises about legalizing ganja and offering a square deal to the musicians who had suffered at the hands of the unscrupulous record dealers and

**Reggae brought the sect of Rastafarians to popularity, with its belief in Haile Selassie as deliverer**

recording companies. But if Miller and the Lewis brothers, by moving up into high-class Kingston, had isolated themselves from those areas that gave birth to the music they played, they still believed in the power of their music to do good, to voice problems and frustrations and to unify the people through a common language

and rhythm. It was a sad day for Jamaican music when in 1978 that silver-grey Benz, which the whole city of Kingston loved to recognize and wave to, finally drove 'at knots' off the road and smashed down a mountainside. Jacob's funeral was a national event. A day of mourning was held for the good-natured singer who had tried to unify his land by combining Manley and Seaga on his own reggae platform.

In those heady days of 1977, with visiting American record producers from CBS and Warners coming to discover what reggae music was and how best to exploit it, Jacob Miller and the Lewis brothers had sat on the porch of their new home and knocked out the latest of their numbers. Miller, a bigger name on the island than Bob Marley, who had by then left, swung heavily in a rope hammock, lighting and relighting spliffs as he worked his way through the lyrics. His 'manager', Tommy Cowan, would hastily scribble down the words while the Lewis brothers helped him out with a thudding bass line:

*Me say sing them songs of culture*
*Me say sing them songs of love.*
'Blow hole'
*Forwards ever and backwards never.*
'Now we need the next verse.'
*Songs for the people to unite*
*Teaching them not to fight.*
'Serious thing, this!'
*Come manners must turn to discipline.*
'Order in the court!'
*That's what justice should bring.*
'Man like it!'

A couple of days later we persuaded them to hold a free show at 'Tastees' – a Jamaican pasty maker – on a busy main street of Kingston.

The show was preceded by old enemies meeting, fists flying and a few stabbings. Jacob Miller rushed on stage appealing for calm and peace. 'Rastafari,' he shouted, 'Selassie rule the business.' The reference was, of course, to Haile Selassie who Rastafarians regard as Jah or God. At the time, many singers and musicians made their hair into locks and espoused the faith of Rastafari. Meanwhile, in a local church of the 'Ethiopian Federation', reggae hymns were being sung. One of the songs was 'Satta Massa Gana', a beautiful sad melody about the lost homeland, which the legendary Abyssinians had written. We were lucky enough to record them performing that number within the corrugated iron walls of an Ethiopian church. While children rattled dustbin lids and screamed outside, the Abyssinians contrived the most perfect vocal harmonies, accompanying themselves on rough, borrowed guitars. Their songs were imitated and recorded by many, but never with such intensity and simplicity.

The next day, we were given protection for our trip to Trenchtown. His name was Bunny, a thickset gangster with a six-gun, heavy scars on both sides of his face, dreadlocks and, of course,

**The Abyssinians were founded in 1968: their first song 'Satta Massa Gana' made history**

mirror shades. He was dressed in black leather and, while riding his Honda motorbike, smoked joints wrapped in old brown newspaper. Bunny was in with one of the political gangs fighting in Trenchtown. We filmed amid the burning houses, the screaming fire engines, the pistol shots and the ever-present thudding bass line of reggae that boomed from the houses. Suddenly, we were confronted by an advancing band of heavies who pointed guns at us. We turned confidently to Bunny, only to discover he had vanished. At the time there was – perhaps justifiably – an obsession about the power and

**Joe Higgs has been an important figure in reggae for many years: guitarist and singer, he influenced Marley and other musicians**

**Bob Marley formed the Wailers in 1963: after two albums for Lee Perry, they signed to Island Records**

presence of the CIA, who were seen by many Jamaicans as responsible for many of the ills that had befallen their island. The gunmen insisted we were American agents. We denied it. They threatened to shoot us unless we proved otherwise. I said I was from Camden Town. They did not believe me. Chris, the cameraman, explained he was from Yorkshire, where Freddy Truman came from. The gunmen hesitated, lowering their weapons: 'Freddy Truman – him a wicked fast bowler, man!' From being the enemy, we had become heroes, and were given a new escort to see us out of the Trenchtown ghetto.

Trenchtown has an almost mythical role in reggae music: it is commonly said that Bob Marley and the Wailers grew up there. At that particular time, Marley's name was not one to conjure with in Jamaica. Many felt he had deserted the island for the glories of superstardom, and certainly his image was heavily nurtured and promoted by Chris Blackwell and Island Records who had dominated so much of Jamaican music for the past decade. Bob Marley's 'teacher' was, by common consent, Joe Higgs who had coached many young hopefuls – including Peter Tosh and Bunny Wailer – in phrasing, control and intonation. He was unwilling to talk of this relationship with Marley when we met him.

'Music is a matter of struggle. It's not good that it's known you're from Trenchtown because it's quite evident that the less fortunate people are distributed in that area. Music originated from confrontation, so the roots really is from struggle. Reggae is a confrontation of sound. Reggae has to have that basic vibrant sound that is to be heard in the ghetto. It's like playing the drum and bass very loud. Those are the basic sounds. A classical reggae should be accepted in any part of the world. Freedom, that's what it's asking for; acceptance, that's what it needs, and understanding, that's what reggae's saying.

'There was a time when music was emphasizing more on the rhythm – in ska, rocksteady – but to break it down, to bring it down to a proportionate pace is to put the attraction not on the music but on the message. It's the message that really matters.'

That was Joe's concise analysis of the changes reggae had gone through since the days of bluebeat and ska up to 1977.

In the evening, Joe sat outside his house beneath an almost full moon: 'You have a certain love come from hard struggle, long suffering. Through pain you guard yourself with that hope of freedom, not to give up . . .' He sang the most beautiful of his compositions called 'There's a reward for me'.

> *Every day my heart is sore*
> *Seeing that I'm so poor.*
> *I shall not give up so easy.*
> *There's a reward for me.*

Around Joe's house were burned-out shacks and rubbish dumps piled high with the skeletons of cars and trucks. Beyond them stretched the waters of the Caribbean glittering in the moonlight, and beyond them the domes of giant petrol tanks in which the multinationals stored their oil. In the dawn light, men, women and children scrabbled amongst the rubble and dug amongst piles of offal and litter in search of anything eatable or of value. Posters proclaimed 'Socialism no fool' and 'Rob the rich, not the poor'.

Several Jamaican officials later criticized us

**Jack Ruby was one of Jamaica's toughest producers, in the '70s, always with a queue of young hopefuls**

for the bleak imagery shown in the film. But shooting quickly under pressure, the images seemed almost to select themselves. They were what the lyrics spoke of, they were what the musicians talked of. They were the realities of daily life.

In the next days, we drove up through the lush green mountains to Ocho Rios, at the time a resort of empty hotels, workless waiters and musicians. The bossman of the backlands of Ocho Rios was Jack Ruby, a tough, bearded, straight-talking record producer who was famed throughout Jamaica as a talent spotter. A weekly procession of young hopefuls came down through the hills to Jack Ruby's house, where they queued outside the gates for a hearing. On the day we visited, there were solos, duos, trios, with and without guitars, some accompanying themselves on matchboxes or newspapers or just tapping their feet: an incredible variety of real talent able to conjure up lyrics of meaning and harmonies of sweet subtlety out of their lives in the hills. If Jack Ruby liked what he heard, he would take the aspiring young reggae stars down to Kingston for a session in a recording studio.

The studios were cheap and had a fast turnover. Many people in Jamaica were illiterate or semi-literate; others simply did not believe what they read in the newspapers run by the government or other interested parties. So music, especially recorded music, played a vital role in spreading street news. Anyone, any toaster, could go into a studio and rap out a record about some particular grievance, violence or feud. The record would be out on the streets the next day and then carried by one of the travelling 'sound systems' all around Jamaica. At dances and parties in every corner of the island, toasters like U-Brown and U-Roy

not only played these records but dubbed their own lyrics over them as a sort of comment on the news. This was recorded music playing a traditional role: of the troubadour, of the African 'griot', updated to the sound systems and toasters of Jamaica in the late 1970s.

In stores like Randy's, reggae musicians and the buying public came to check out the records. In fact it was the only way they could assess how many were being sold – royalties were a thing unknown in Jamaica. Randy's was

a water hole for musicians. It was here I met Big Youth, another famous toaster of the late 1970s, whom I was later to encounter in a hotel room in Nigeria when he was hiding out from the authorities.

Because of the political violence, the lack of money and the dangers of going out at night, there was little live music at that time. People stayed home, shuttered their windows and locked their doors. Nor was dealing with musicians exactly easy in the atmosphere of

paranoia. Jimmy Cliff finally consented to be filmed only if we bought him either a refrigerator or half a carpet. We chose half a carpet. His musicians then decided that because we came from England, we must somehow be connected with the actor Clint Eastwood whose spaghetti westerns they adored and whose cool style of killing was much admired. They had read in *Playboy* magazine that Clint was earning a million dollars a movie. So at the last moment, with tape recorders and cameras in place, we had to postpone filming for another day, while

we painfully bargained the musicians down from a million dollars each. They were Jamaica's best: Sly Dunbar was on bass guitar and Robbie Shakespeare on drums. Jimmy Cliff had become obsessed with his own image in the film *The Harder They Come*, and seemed still to be playing that role. He told us about his hard life: how he used to dive for tourists at the Montego Bay resorts when he was 14 and how he was paid just 12 cents for his first record, 'Daisy Got Me Crazy'. He finally got himself signed up by Island Records and made 'House of Exile'

**Jimmy Cliff was one of the early ska singers. His lead role in the film *The Harder they Come* gave him international fame**

and 'Struggling Man', both vividly portraying racial and social problems by this intense and gifted singer.

But Jimmy had now moved on through Christianity and Rastafari to Islam, and was trying to fit his music into a broader perspective of life – the spiritual as well as the physical:

'People say justice is a notion, but it's something real for me. There's so much injustice going on in this business: I don't intend that I alone can fight the battle. But I would like to see some justice done. Get paid for what you're due. People don't feel no form of guilt if they use you and you're ignorant of that fact. So part of my job is to say what I know. To put people on their guard. I don't want to be the pawn on the chessboard – to be pushed around by whoever's playing. I want to be the pusher. To control myself and give opportunity to less fortunate people who are now in the position that I was once in.

'I went to England because I believed I had a mission to complete there. But I had to move around a lot of barriers I wasn't used to. The racial thing really got me down. It was the first time I had come upon that. And working with white musicians – there was a big mental conflict for me getting on with them. We have a spiritual side to us which is the highest part of us and that must be developed: my work is now along those lines. That's how I feel about this music. It's really to do with the people, not politically but spiritually. That's how I see reggae. It's the cry of the people.'

We left Jimmy and his musicians jamming in his garage beneath the palm trees on his front lawn, and made our way to the greatest of all record producers in Jamaica: the inimitable Lee Perry, nicknamed Scratch. The studio adjoining his house was called the Black Arc and had images of Haile Selassie and the Lion of Judah painted around it in Rastafarian colours. Inside, Scratch, together with Junior Murvin, The Upsetters and The Heptones were waiting for us. 'Drum and bass, drum and bass,' cried Scratch dressed in red boxer shorts, rasta hat and yellow T-shirt. 'That's the rhythm of the ghetto, drum and bass, with the lyrics of the street.' He and his musicians, with much good humour, had written a number specially for our filming:

*The chalice is burning*
*The cameras are rolling*
*Getting ready for the show*
*Play on Mr Music.*

Scratch's equipment filled his tiny control room: the walls decorated with the photographs of artists he had recorded, like the early Wailers, whose records displayed the rhythms and harmonies of a genuine creativeness and musical innocence that was soon lost in the superstardom imposed on 'brother Bob'. Marley had recently revisited Scratch to record two versions of a single called 'Smile Jamaica', another musical attempt to improve the image the island presented to the world outside. In fact, Bob had recently been machine-gunned at his home, but his life was saved by his agent Don Taylor who hurled himself in front of Bob and caught some bullets in his spine.

Before the end of our trip, we filmed The Mighty Diamonds in concert and the talented Third World, with whom we were invited to eat cucumber sandwiches on the lawn of the Foreign Minister's colonial dwelling. For me it had been a frenetic few weeks, working by day, negotiating and organizing by night, aided by an incredibly supportive team of Chris Morphet on camera and Bob Bentley on sound. When the film was edited, it was met by a barrage of indifference. I still remember the purchased programmes officer at the BBC looking at the enormous variety of artists and rhythms and remarking: 'The problem is, it all sounds the same. It'll never catch on.' Crisis followed crisis, until finally the film was bought for a pittance and shown by the BBC. Then it won some prizes and was picked up by television stations across the world, eventually covering its cost. This success encouraged us to make a series based on the role of music as a mirror of society – the mouthpiece of the frustrations, changes and aspirations of communities around the world for whom music provides life's rhythm, and lyrics a means of self-expression otherwise denied them.

**The Mighty Diamonds, three vocalists who formed in the late sixties, have had many changes of style**

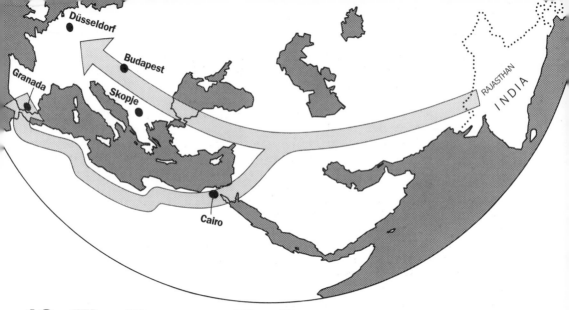

# 10 **The Romany Trail** *Gypsy Music*
*Part One: Into Africa*

For weeks we had been walking the hot, noisy streets of Cairo in search of a clue that would lead us to the fabled lost tribes of gypsies who were believed to have settled in Egypt several centuries ago. We were tracing the Romany trail which took the gypsy people out of their Indian homelands from the tenth century onwards, and up through the Middle East into Africa and Europe.

It was crucial to find the gypsies of Egypt, since they have a special place in all gypsy mythology and music. When their ancestors entered Europe in the twelfth and thirteenth centuries, they chose to call themselves the 'Dukes and Lords of Little Egypt', claiming to be from a lost biblical tribe of Egyptians. The name 'gypsy' (abbreviated form of 'Egyptian') stuck – a curious misnomer that has gradually become a word of abuse throughout the world. Many historians have asserted that on their great migrations out of India the gypsies did not in fact cross into northern Africa and then onto southern Spain. Yet the gypsies themselves claim that this was one of the main routes that took them into Europe. Egypt, as a gateway into

North Africa, was therefore central to the puzzle.

Before leaving England I had talked to many gypsies and specialists in gypsy affairs including Grattan Puxon (a part-Irish, part-English Romany), who was head of the 1981 World Romany Congress to be held that year in Göttingen, Germany. This would attract gypsies from every country in the world – delegates of some 10 million 'outsiders' would be united in a new awareness of their common customs, birthright and language.

But first, how were we to find these gypsies of Egypt? Everyone in Cairo claimed ignorance, especially the cultural institutes, through which we, as foreigners, were forced to go. In every country, gypsies are treated as third-class citizens, not to be visited, let alone filmed. Nor should they talk of their problems to outsiders. In Egypt we met a blank wall of silence. To be honest, it was partly ignorance: people either did not know or did not want to know. Gypsies were regarded as infidels or criminals. The Arabic word for gypsy is 'Nawar' and throughout the Arab world they are

The search for the fabled gypsy tribe led to the city of Luxor: Joseph Maazen is the head of the Nawar tribe; his daughter Soard is outcast as a ghawazi

despised as non-believers since they are rarely Moslems.

Having no success with other sources, we tried the Egyptian TV offices where we asked their music department if they had ever come across gypsy performers or dancers. Again there was a solemn shaking of heads. Suddenly the door opened and a bespectacled man in a knee-length trenchcoat entered, slowly and deliberately. He searched out a chair and sat down in a rather odd, stiff manner, half looking in our direction. He was introduced by the Managing Director as Mr Chowky Goma, the head of the arts and music department of Egyptian TV. Later, alone with us, Mr Chowky Goma explained that he was almost blind, a fact he tried to disguise.

Chowky Goma took us out to a noisy local restaurant. He leaned secretively across the table and whispered that some 20 years earlier he had known a beautiful young girl who lived in the ancient city of Luxor, several hundred miles down the Nile. She had in her turn whispered certain secrets to him: that she came from a special tribe called Nawar, so discriminated against by local people that she was unable to be

anything but a prostitute and that in the evenings she and her younger sisters danced to a special kind of music their forefathers had brought into Egypt. Moreover, they had a special language of their own which no-one else could understand. This sounded an interesting anecdote but was far from conclusive proof that the lost tribe of gypsies was living somewhere down the Nile. 'Wait,' said Chowky Goma. 'That's not the end. One day, Soard Maazen, for that was her name, was working on a pleasure boat on the Nile – her job was to dance for the tourists. She did one of her tribal dances, using the castanets with which her people accompany themselves. Afterwards, a passenger from Spain started talking to her. Then something strange happened, something I have never forgotten; that Spaniard spoke to her in her own tribal language. She could not believe her ears because no-one outside her family, let alone a foreigner, had ever spoken her secret language. The Spaniard explained that he was a gypsy and the language she was speaking was Romany, both words she herself had never come across. You should go, my friend,' said Chowky Goma,

**The three Maazen
daughters dress in their
finery and perform their
own private dances**

'and tell her that I still remember her. But I
cannot accompany you. I would not wish her to
see me as I am now.'

So we went to Luxor – in a horrendous
duststorm that had grounded all the planes and
stopped the trains. We hired a truck and drove
several hundred miles south along the Nile,
never stopping except to fill up with petrol and
sleep in the precincts of a police station as

protection against the bands of robbers that
frequented the road. But in Luxor, again,
everyone claimed ignorance: no gypsies, no
Maazen family, no secret languages and no
dancing girls. The local tourist officer assured
us that even were we to find such people, it
would not be possible for us to film them; it
would be bad for Luxor's tourist image. But
leaving his office, we noticed a dark and rather
dapper taxi driver polishing his pale-blue
Peugeot on which were stuck little paper
symbols of hands with magic numerals
patterned across them. I took a chance and
asked him if he knew the Maazen family. He

Its name was Nurel Hamamsha. It was called Nawar because of its founder's name; then Nawar became the name of all our people here. From Kurdistan we descended into Egypt many generations ago, having been cast out of our homelands because of our evil deeds and bad reputation; for in truth we would steal and plunder and some of us were even highway robbers. Everywhere we went, we lived outside society, but we kept alive our own traditions and our own language. Yet we were punished and driven out of Kurdistan and from Iran whence our forefathers had come. In the beginning we took after our ancestors, but we suffered, for the Egyptian people were against us. So that we could settle in Luxor, we encouraged our sons to become musicians and our daughters to dance. In that way, we might become accepted by the local people. So we invaded their hearts and their minds with our arts.'

Through Joseph Maazen, we had discovered not only the 'lost tribe' of Egyptian gypsies but also the means by which gypsies, throughout the world, had become entertainers, musicians and dancers. Their entire history seemed concentrated in this one proud old man resting beneath the Temple of the Pharoahs.

Over the next few days, we were introduced to his three daughters: we met Radia who was crossing the Nile on a ferry boat to do the family shopping, just beside the tombs of Tutankhamen. Respectable Egyptians did not want to be seen walking near her, and certainly not talking to her. Kharia was the middle daughter who had recently become a professional dancer and sometimes worked on the Nile pleasure boats. The eldest of the three was Soard Maazen, who had been forced, through hostility, to become the local prostitute. (It was she who had met Chowky Goma 20 years earlier.) She had just been widowed by the death of her latest and wealthiest benefactor. Soard too was a professional dancer, but because of her other activities was not accepted at her father's house.

stared back in astonishment. 'Yes, of course. I am of that family. My father is Joseph and my sister is Soard. But how could you, foreigner, know us by the name we never use in public?'

He took us down a hundred dusty little side roads, until we were almost at the walls of the great temple of Konarak, which the Pharoahs had built for the sun god, Amon Ra. There, in a tiny, pink house, in a room piled high from floor to ceiling with coloured carpets, sat Joseph Maazen, head of the family and of the gypsy tribe of Nawar, the keeper of his people's history.

'Our tribe originally came from Kurdistan.

Indeed, the very fact of our visiting her had led to an interfamily feud. Joseph Maazen refused to have anything more to do with us or to permit us to enter his house. However, over the following days, tempers subsided and the long-standing family feud was patched up to the extent that Joseph was happy to appear in the same film as his daughter, though not actually in her company.

Soard told us, in no uncertain terms, of the prejudice against her and her tribe and how she had been forced into prostitution. Young men who had fallen in love with her – she had been very beautiful – were chastised by their families for consorting with a *ghawazi*, which means literally, an invader of the heart. Colloquially, it means a whore, or in general terms, a gypsy. Soard remembered:

'I always wished I wasn't a "dancer" when a

man of another tribe fell in love with me or with one of my sisters. Their families would fight a war to stop them marrying a *ghawazi* – a girl of bad reputation. They would say: "How could you do such a thing to us? A Maazen, a dancer, a girl who 'performs' for others and from the tribe of Nawar." Marriage became impossible and it hurt terribly'.

Soard now lived comfortably in the house she had bought with her deceased benefactor's legacy, but her bitterness at her continuing ostracism had not diminished. She and her sisters and a band of local musicians gathered together and invited us into the intimacy of her home to film an evening of dance. The sisters were dressed in gypsy finery: long, shiny, gauze dresses hung with sequins, scarves knotted round their heads; gold earrings and, between their fingers, castanets of copper and brass. The dance music was played on typical Egyptian instruments, like the rebab (a two-stringed fiddle), drums and a tambourine. Curious passers-by stopped in the street below, staring up in the darkness, shaking their heads disapprovingly. They pulled their children into the safety of the street shadows, away from the light and music, away from those irrepressible 'invaders of the heart'.

Over the following days, we traced members of the family back to their small villages outside Karnak, in the dusty landscapes filled with camel trains, steam locomotives, flute-playing shepherds and poor farmers humping corn on their backs along the banks of the Nile. In the desolate little town of Kus, in a one-room house, sat Said Dowi. He is one of the last great gypsy epic-singers in Egypt – or anywhere else in the world. Amid small-town prejudice and indifference, he tried to teach his sons and other village children those epics, each of which could last a day in the telling. The story

**Mitkail of Kena
is a Nawar who, to
become an
international star,
has denied his origins**

we heard was of Abu Said, a dark gypsy hero who still has a special place in Arab culture. Later, over innumerable cups of tea and packets of cigarettes, Said Dowi told us where in Cairo we could find whole communities of gypsy entertainers, the very people we had been so hopelessly unable to locate.

Mitkail of Kena is the one member of that gypsy family to have succeeded as a commercial entertainer. He is also the only one to deny his origins. We met him in a flashy nightclub, half a mile from the pyramids, filled with French tourists. Mitkail was not permitted to sit at the same table with us, even though he was the star performer. When we asked why, the manager insisted it was because of the family he came from. Mitkail firmly denied this. 'I, a Nawar? A gypsy? Impossible!' he remonstrated, turning to us, 'Said Dowi is a liar.' But in the privacy of his own home, Mitkail admitted to his family

**The Nawar gypsies in Egypt include epic-story teller, Said Dowi, who tries to pass on the tradition**

origins: 'It is true that I was born near the temple of Karnak and that my family were very poor. One day I was told an important group of guests had come to hear me play – all the way from Cairo, no less, just to hear me. Well, they heard me play and brought me to Cairo and promoted me. From that day, I have never looked back.'

He became a singer and rebab player of great brilliance and charm who regularly plays abroad.

After achieving stardom in Egypt, Mitkail went to Paris where he was signed up to feature in French porno films. Now he is proud to boast

that in Egypt alone he has nine wives and 14 children. His music and his band are far more flamboyant and have far less depth than that of his poorer relatives living near Luxor. In nightclubs and expensive tourist restaurants, he calls on young girls in the audience to come up on stage and dance with him while he plays the rebab above his head in extrovert fashion, and spins in circles, his long robes swirling.

At our request, Mitkail led us into the poorer quarters of Cairo where gypsy street musicians and conjurers were still a daily sight. In fine costumes of red and gold, they balanced – on their foreheads or noses – long poles at the top of which were ornate fezzes, mirrors or even bicycles. They danced and pirouetted along the streets surrounded by the clashing of brass cymbals and the beating of drums and tambourines. These people were called Nakrazan, a term used to describe street entertainers of tribal origin. Most of them lived in a ghetto area called El Hashish which we were warned was far too dangerous for us to enter because of physical violence, squalor and rampant diseases like cholera, typhoid and smallpox.

El Hashish stretched across suburban railway lines on the outskirts of Cairo: the

**Hidden away in the poorer parts of Cairo are the gypsy street musicians and the entertainers, from acrobats to conjurors**

**Gypsy dancing girls who perform for the tourists and who call themselves ghawazis**

wooden shacks actually leaned within inches of the old diesels that thundered through the community. On Sunday morning, many of the citizens made their way to the markets of camels and oxen in their elaborately decorated wooden carts. There they performed as acrobats, dancers and entertainers. This is a role which no Islamic person could play, for such public displays of frivolity are not permitted to Moslems. A tattooist was surrounded by framed pictures from which a design could be selected for any part of the body – dancing girls, fat women on deckchairs, figures from tarot cards, symbolic fishes, lithe nudes. The tattooist turned out to be a relative of Said Dowi and, as he talked to us about his Nawar family, he tattooed the image of his customer's new wife on

top of that of the old. This he did with a blunt and rusty needle tied with bandages onto a battered green drill. In the centre of the market, three dancing girls, with earrings and castanets, swayed and tripped to the rhythms of giant two-sided drums pounded by gypsies. These dancers also called themselves ghawazis (invaders of the heart), but insisted that they were different from the Nawar. It was their ancestors who had gone through Turkey into Europe, becoming the belly dancers of Istanbul and the restaurant entertainers of Budapest. (Much later in the year, I met in Hungary an old dark-skinned violinist who had been back to Cairo and had played with members of his family.) The Romany trail was unfolding before us.

At the same market there were fire eaters, acrobats who jumped through burning rings, almost invariably setting fire to their shoes or trousers, magicians who pulled live chicks from inside their mouths and puppeteers doing an Egyptian version of Punch and Judy. Many times on our travels we were told that the Punch and Judy story, and much of the art of puppetry, had come with the Indian gypsies into the Middle East and up through Europe into England where it became a regular seaside event by the turn of this century. And everywhere, of course, were the gypsy fortune-tellers with gold earrings, nose rings and tattooed hands and faces, telling customers what they most wanted to hear – after cleverly eliciting from them what their hopes or fears might be.

It was one of these fortune-tellers who took us to an exorcism in the back streets of old Cairo. It had to be performed by gypsies, as they were the only non-Islamic people who could flirt with the Devil and the powers of darkness. Also, many of the local people were still superstitious about the gypsies' powers and were willing to pay for their 'magic'. Down a winding sidestreet danced a group of gypsy exorcists, spinning in cloaks of gold and turquoise to the hypnotic rhythms of flutes, drums and tambourines. In their midst they dragged a girl, her face covered by a hood. A young teenager, she was suffering

In the markets, the gypsy entertainers carry on age-old traditions brought with them on their migrations: fire-eaters, puppeteers, fortune tellers

from an illness that no doctor could diagnose or cure, and this was her family's last attempt to exorcize the ailment, along with the devils that were causing it. At the entrance to her wealthy house, a cockerel was sacrificed; its head was sliced off into the street and the warm blood that spurted from its neck was dipped onto the forehead of the sick girl.

Led inside the house in a slow procession, she was pulled first physically, and then psychologically or spiritually, into a ritual exorcism. Rows of enormous women, draped in black, swayed and chanted while playing tambourines and drums. Slim gypsy men with shoulder-length hair and scarlet waistcoats danced, clicking castanets, like puppets jerking on a string. And the gypsy congregation whirled in a self-induced trance around a white-decked shrine. Soon the girl's hood had fallen back and her ashen face became frozen. Into her hands were pushed live chickens – one black, one white – to symbolize the cosmic forces. The music increased in volume and speed until the participants were throwing themselves around the shrine in a frenzy.

The problem for the gypsies was to discover which devil possessed the girl's spirit. Until they could identify it, they would be

**Superstition about Romany power means gypsies are asked to conduct exorcisms: in Cairo, they visit a wealthy house to identify and drive out the particular devil possessing the young daughter**

unable to find the right words to exorcize it. First they dressed her in Arabian clothes, in a cloak with white headdress and a curved sword in a scabbard. But she did not react. So they changed her into Moroccan clothes with a white smock and a fez but still, amid the frenzy, she stayed calm. They then placed her in a Tunisian cape and immediately she became caught up in the same wild dance rhythms as the others. They had caught the devil – trapped him in the rhythms of their music in this symbolic journey through the lands of their gypsy migrations. Finally the girl fell unconscious to the ground and the music stopped. There was a deathly silence as she was carried away into the inner part of her parents' house and that was the last we ever saw of her.

The next day we left Cairo through the oasis of Fayum where nomadic gypsies, tent dwellers, rested with their donkeys and camels – the poorest of the poor, their only wealth the gold-plated ornaments attached to their ears and noses. Some were blind, others crippled, all were outcasts. Even as we passed through, we saw ignorant Egyptian children stoning them and their animals, for they believed that as infidels, they deserved their fate. These nomads were setting out westwards across Egypt to

**Gypsies from Egypt came into Spain with the invading armies as entertainers: those living in the Sacro Monte caves in Granada have been there for 400 years**

Tunisia and Morocco. What we had found in Egypt was evidence – if not conclusive – that the Nawar had migrated westwards across North Africa and might, as so many gypsies claim, have entered southern Spain with the invading Moroccan armies as their musicians and entertainers. We followed this evidence.

The gypsies of Guadix in southern Spain live in caves or beneath the ground in a desolate, burning landscape. One local gypsy, Pepe Albecin, put on his cleanest shirt, buttoned to

the neck, and a black-striped suit and stood beside the entrance to one of the caves to sing an unaccompanied song. This intense, emotional deep-throated singing is called cante jondo, or deepsong, and is strongly reminiscent of the Arab prayer chant. For the gypsies it symbolizes the continuing fervour of their people, unshaken despite centuries of hardship. Pepe's song ran:

> *The Lord brought me here out of Hungary and*
> *out of Egypt.*
> *Now I am a basket-seller so I can give my*
> *gypsy woman some food.*

By contrast the Sacro Monte caves that lie beneath the Alhambra Castle in the city of Granada, are filled with fiery, extrovert gypsies who have lived there since the fifteenth century when they claim to have accompanied invading

armies from North Africa. Now they are an important part of the tourist trade, visited by coachloads of north Europeans anxious to taste the flavour of the exotic gypsy life.

The Cortez family, who were related to Pepe Albecin, invited us to film a private fiesta in their cave. La Maraquilla, one of the finest and most flamboyant gypsy dancers, was among the guests. Against the chalky white walls, next to the refrigerator and the TV, the whole family participated in a 'zambra'. They regard this as the flamenco dance rhythm that owes most to the gypsies. Flamenco is a mixture of Andalusian, Moorish and gitano (the Spanish word for gypsy) music and dance.

If this flamenco is, in essence, little different from that which the nightclubs offer up for after-dinner entertainment, another,

**The Cortez family hold a fiesta in their cave; they dance one by one while the family claps its accompaniment**

deeper sort of gypsy music does exist. We found this in Jerez (the sherry town) at the home of a 70-year-old gypsy singer, La Perata. Her family was quoted by Garcia Lorca as 'one of the true repositories of the flamenco spirit'. Accompanied by her son on guitar, she sang with deep inner sorrow, yet made no movement other than waving one finger and stamping one foot. We had found her through Pepe Heredia Maya, a member of the famous Maya gypsy family. Pepe was unique: a Professor of Flamenco at Granada University, where he lectured to non-gypsies about the traditions of his people's music.

While attending a local wedding, Pepe also introduced me to a tall handsome gypsy, half Irish, half Spanish, with a white powdered face and slicked-back hair, who was committed to improving the awareness of local gitanos. Miguel Haggerty did this by teaching in Callo – the Spanish gypsy language that is based on Romany. I was carrying with me a book published in the Punjab called the *Romany-Punjabi-English Conversation Book*. It had been written by a Mr Rishi who had devoted his life to compiling a dictionary which aimed to prove the Indian origins of the Romany (and Callo) language.

Haggerty was teaching the gypsies about their rights. 'This is a very poor neighbourhood. It's a wretched part of Granada. We are teaching these people to count, to multiply, add,

**Much of the public gypsy music in Spain is popular night club flamenco: La Perata expresses a deeper, older tradition**

subtract, read and write. Things that are necessary. We do not want to integrate ourselves completely into the *gauja* (non-gypsy) way of life. But we want to handle ourselves with more ease in the non-gypsy society around us. Gypsies have always been accepted as folkloric and this has been taken advantage of in Andalusia. Yet here they have real day-to-day problems: not all gypsies can sing, dance and play guitar. Their families are very large – this is a big problem because it leads to unemployment and rejection. Certain prejudices show. Whenever you have an economic crisis you look for a scapegoat, and gypsies have always been that scapegoat, in almost every society.

'As in all gypsy communities, music is the most important element. It is the binding factor

**Teenage gypsy boys make up their own flamenco songs — relevant for them**

of all our cultures. In Spain the music is flamenco. This is the way nomadic peoples have preserved their oral traditions. Music has preserved our Romany language, which has never been written. Dictionaries are now being compiled, but music has qualities which do not need to be written down. It expresses in its rhythms and words all our frustrations.'

Miguel Haggerty's words were reiterated

**An Egyptian madonna in a French church has an Indian name**

by the boss of the ghetto suburb of Virgencica, where many gypsies had been rehoused by the authorities when forcibly removed from their caves. Now teenage boys, who survived by petty crime and drug dealing, sat around all day making up their own flamenco songs about being criminals and living in a ghetto. 'Our music is the very basis of our lives', said the gypsy boss, 'because it allows us to survive. It helps us feel and forget our sorrows.' Others, who had been rehoused in multistorey blocks, were ill-adapted after centuries of nomadic life. Many took their sheep and donkeys with them, leading them up and down the stairs or into the lifts. The authorities had worsened, rather than eased, their 'gypsy problem'.

Despite the laws that now prevent gypsies from travelling freely within Spain, there is one annual pilgrimage which none of them would wish to miss. The journey takes them up through Spain to the southwest coast of France to the Camargue and to the tiny town of Les Saintes Maries de la Mer. Although this is now a commercialized and popular celebration, the service in the Catholic church of Les Saintes Maries does symbolize the gypsies' power to adapt to other peoples' way of life at the same time as preserving the heart of their own culture.

As a dozen nationalities from all over Europe accompanied the service with music and song, an ornately painted box was lowered from the church roof, containing the remnants of Saint Sarah, gypsy patron saint of travel. To gypsies, she is known as Sarah the Egyptian, because they believe she travelled here from Egypt. A huge queue formed to touch the feet and kiss the face of the black Madonna. As the box was slowly lowered by ropes into the congregation, their hands reached up above the flickering candles to touch and be blessed by her presence. In Romany, her name is not, in fact, Sarah the Egyptian but Sarah the Black One or Kali. Kali is the name of the Indian goddess of time.

## Part Two: Into Europe

Ironically, in India the word 'gypsy' has been introduced through the western media. The gypsy has now become a stereotype in popular Hindi films like *Sapno Ka Sadugar* in which a gypsy girl is seen as the alter ego of a respectable Hindi bride-to-be: a non-conformist, uninhibited and unconventional. In major cities like Bombay there are many real gypsy street performers who have migrated from the countryside in search of a way out of abject poverty and discrimination. They end up as acrobats, snake charmers or wandering musicians who walk the Bombay streets and beaches with monkeys, hoops and high-wire acts.

To find the original gypsy tribes from which migrants travelled into Egypt and Europe, we went to the north Indian state of Rajasthan. The Persian poet Fidursi described how, nearly 1,000 years ago, a prince of the Sassind dynasty took gypsy musicians out of India to entertain him in the Persian courts. After that, there were many migrations in search of work or to escape famine and wars. But many still remain in India. The Luri and Banjaras of Rajasthan are musicians and puppeteers who once dwelt in tents around the palaces of the maharajas, for whom they were court entertainers or tinkers. The Gaduliya Lohars are cartwrights, their whole families living

under elaborately carved carts, the wheels of which are draped with coloured blankets. We found acrobats and bear trainers whose relatives we were to meet later in Greece and Yugoslavia. The Lovari tribe even today travel Europe in covered trucks with their bears. And the tribe of Dom (from which the word 'Rom' may be derived) make their living from basket weaving and entertaining. Here were the original customs, language and music – with its distinctive passion and ornamentation – that the gypsies have preserved for centuries across Europe.

After leaving India for Persia, the Romany migrations followed two main routes. One went through the Arab countries into Egypt; the other continued up through the Turkish empire till it entered Europe, probably early in the fifteenth century when the gypsies frightened people with their wild, dark appearance and alien customs. Today, the largest Romany population in Europe – nearly 1,000,000 – lives in Yugoslavia. We visited one of their communities in the gypsy suburb of Shuto Orizare near Skopje in Macedonia.

Life is not easy for gypsies in Yugoslavia: they are still discriminated against and watched for 'dissident tendencies'. The Yugoslav

**Many of the original gypsy tribes from India have migrated: the Gaduliya Lohars have stayed on**

authorities' attitude to these people was made clear to us by the way we were treated when trying to film and record their music. On the first three occasions that we took out our equipment, we were immediately arrested. Police cars appeared over the horizon and screeched to a halt beside us, our equipment was searched, threats made and it was even suggested that we had hidden a camera inside our camera so we could film secretly what we were already filming! All this, despite having received official permission to film from the central government in Belgrade.

**Bear training has been the speciality of the Lovari tribe who have travelled to Europe from India**

In a church in the
south of Yugoslavia,
Moslem gypsies
come to worship, to
the accompaniment
of swirling zurla
pipe music and
resounding beats of
the drums

Some 40,000 gypsies live in Shuto Orizare. We arrived there on 6 May, which is the date of one of their major festivals. At a Greek Orthodox church in Skopje, hundreds of Moslem gypsies gathered to light candles and touch the silver icons inside the darkened building at dawn. The women wore Moslem headscarves, a legacy of their predecessors' faith absorbed on their historic migration through the Arab countries. At a Christian church, in a Communist country, Moslem gypsies were recalling their Hindu past from India – it was the Festival of Indra. Two-sided drums and long zurla pipes accompanied their acts of worship. The purifying rituals of water which we had so often seen amongst the gypsy tribes of Rajasthan were replaced here by milk bottles wrapped in brown paper. We saw tinkers of the Kaldaresh tribe and bear trainers of the Lovaris.

On 7 May, the corpses of over 1,000 sheep hung from every tree in town, sacrificed to bring good luck and serenaded by the playing of Indian film music records. Amin Ramadan, one of their spokesmen, described how they were fighting to establish a national minority of Indian origin which would give them the same rights and privileges as other Yugoslav citizens. They described to us the police harassment,

false arrests and even blackmail. For these reasons, they have rejected the name 'gypsy' in favour of 'Rom' or 'Roma'.

On my first trip to Shuto Orizare, I had stayed with Professor Saip Jusuf, a vice-president of the World Romany Congress. He is a gypsy who taught himself the Romany language and even introduced it into the official school curriculum. He had done this cleverly, writing the first-ever book in the Romany language in praise of President Tito. This gained him official approval and recognition. Saip lived in a wood-frame, two-room house decorated with a massive alpine landscape and the same Arabian wall hangings that appeared in almost every gypsy house I visited. When Saip was not teaching, he was writing books; when he was not writing books, he was travelling; and when he was not travelling, he was farming his small plot of land. He seemed to work 24 hours a day with an energy and enthusiasm that never ceased, until he met with a tragic accident. In the army hospital at Skopje they cut off his leg – some say unnecessarily. It effectively put an end to Saip Jusuf's life, a man who, just a year or two previously, had been personally invited by Mrs Gandhi to visit Delhi as a spokesman of 'our Indian cousins in Yugoslavia'.

The Festival of Indra celebrated in Skopje: with Romany language, Indian music and dancing, and pelivani wrestling in oil

In the Budapest clubs and restaurants it is gypsy musicians who entertain with cleverly adapted tunes of Hungarian origin

Indian consciousness was extremely strong in Skopje: queues of youth encircled the local cinema which showed Hindi movies. At the May festival, women danced in the streets wearing saris, headscarves and jewelry. They spoke and sang in the Romany language. There was pelivani wrestling in oil and amplified musicians played their popular music of Indian films or Macedonian gypsy songs on accordions, guitars and drums. Juro Jasarevski and the Romany Drama Troupe managed to evade official censorship at the festival by telling a story of gypsy history without words – just with actions and grunts. It was a symbolic play about how one oppressive dictator (Hitler) had been replaced by another, dressed in red. But still the gypsies suffered. As Juro Jasarevski explained:

'This theatre is still something very real to our people, retelling their past with their music, their happiness, their hopes and tragedies. They cannot remain indifferent and the only means they have of learning or remembering the past is to watch our drama. For them it is the only way of knowing their own history.'

When we visited a number of state-run schools, the teachers gave a very rose-tinted version of post-war gypsy history. In fact, most gypsies grew up without education and with enormous popular prejudice against them wherever they tried to settle. As non-conformist travellers, they were seen as a threat to Communism and were compelled to settle into fixed housing in selected areas. We followed the route some of them had taken out of Yugoslavia, through Romania (we were warned that if we were even to unpack our cameras in that country, we would be immediately imprisoned), and into Hungary where still some half million Romanies live.

The capital, Budapest, with its 65,000 Romanies, has an acknowledged 'gypsy problem'. Many of them live in bleak, forbidding workers' hostels where they sleep in dormitories. But these are not the gypsies any visitor to Hungary would come across. They live separately from their cousins who play in the Budapest night spots and restaurants. Some 10,000 gypsy musicians and over 90 Romany orchestras play in the restaurants and hotels of Budapest alone. But what they play, as they serenade the clients with sweet violin melodies and sentimental tunes, is not 'gypsy music' at

**Young violinists
from gypsy families
are taught the tricks
of the trade at the
Ryko music school**

all. It is Hungarian folk tunes, music the gypsies
know their clients want to hear, played with a
little extra sentiment and ornamentation.

The most successful of these, like Sandor
Lakatos, whose comfortable home we visited,
send their children to the state-controlled Ryko
school of music where they are trained to
become restaurant performers. They are taught
all the tricks of the trade: a little more rubato,
slipping into the minor key, sudden speeding up
and slowing down, gestures and theatrics. But
this is far from the indigenous gypsy music
which we found with the help of some
Hungarian gypsy friends. We drove out to
Transylvania with them and filmed in the damp,

thatched huts where gypsy families,
accompanied by a violin, spoons (used like
castanets) and mouth music, sang ancient songs
and danced to the vital rhythms that their
ancestors had brought from India. For these
people, music is not a public performance, it is a
private act of celebration.

On Sunday, we went with the Rostas family
to a Catholic mass in their village church. The
entire service was held in the Romany language
for these gypsies. It is the only such church in
the world. A thin Hungarian priest gave the
sacrament to dark-skinned gypsies, their heads
covered in brilliantly coloured headscarves, all
accompanied by music from electric
instruments played by gypsies behind the crypt.

This Hungarian priest was acting as
a missionary in his own country. What was
happening in this church, like the one in Shuto
Orizare, was a process of syncretism. The
gypsies were using the images and symbols

**Away from the clubs and the cities the gypsy music is very different, retaining the Indian tradition**

of Christianity to recall, privately, a faith, a history and a myth far removed from these Catholic rites. It was also an example of how far the Hungarian authorities had moved to assist these Romany communities. In general, we found this government's attitude to gypsies the most enlightened in Eastern Europe, though still highly patronizing and often discriminatory.

Before leaving England I had been given some useful gypsy contacts by the late Bert Lloyd, a dedicated folk-music collector. One was Manyat Lakatos, the foremost Romany novelist of Hungary, whose books depict, with a poignant realism, the problems of the gypsy

people in Budapest. 'It's extremely important,' he pointed out, 'for minority groups to preserve their own culture. For the gypsies of Hungary, despite all the official attempts at integration, our own inner culture remains very strong. At first people tried to destroy our culture and they called us outsiders. But despite all popular prejudice, gypsies want to integrate since they belong to their country like all other Hungarian citizens.'

As a Romany spokesman, he has to tread carefully and toe the official line while maintaining the respect of his own people. One fiery young gypsy radical, whom we later met again at the World Romany Congress in Germany, was Agnes Daroczi. She said:

'Gypsies are probably the only people left in Europe with a folklore that is still living and growing. Our songs, dances and traditions are not just some sort of staged presentation, they are the very means of describing our everyday lives. Let me give you an example which I heard the other day: the husband of an old gypsy woman had been sent to prison but just before his release, the old lady suddenly bursts into rhyme:

*God give me that day*
*And liberate the poor prisoner*
*Liberate the prisoner from captivity*
*And myself from sadness.'*

That evening Agnes took us to a workers' hostel where the gypsies played spoons, and sang and danced against the backdrop of a Caribbean island sunset that hid the bleak exterior of their hostel. It reminded me of the migrants workers' hostel in South Africa. These gypsies were Eastern Europe's 'blacks'. The train that brings migrant workers from the Transylvanian countryside into Budapest is called the 'Black Train'. We were forbidden even to film it passing, though we did so. Gypsies are the only passengers other than the police.

**In their isolation or ghetto conditions in the Balkan countries, gypsies have preserved traditions such as stick fighting**

**In Hungary, gypsies seeking work have to live in bleak hostels in the cities, far from their families**

Conditions in the countryside are bleak: many gypsies suffer from tuberculosis and malnutrition. In the cities they can find work, though it means leaving the family and living in a hostel hundreds of miles away. Unlike the Yugoslav gypsies, Hungarians are not permitted to travel abroad as migrant workers. However, they are spared the indignities we were later to discover amongst the Yugoslav gypsies in Germany.

On my last day in Budapest, I attended a surreal event at the new Hilton Hotel. It was the annual Gypsy Ball. Romanies from all over Hungary congregated in dinner jackets and ballroom gowns and danced stiffly to a rotating selection of professional bands. Curiously, what they played was restaurant music – Hungarian folk tunes with a gypsy styling. I sat at a table covered with artificial flowers and bowls of plastic fruit, watching a dance floor filled with impeccably attired and formal dancers whom Agnes Daroczi cursed with open hostility as she wrote Romany graffiti across the starched white table cloths.

Given a chance, many of these Hungarian gypsies would migrate to western Europe the way the Yugoslavs have. I remembered the words of one of the Rostas family who was forced to take the Black Train to find work: 'We are often called "guest workers" here but we have to travel as there's no work to be found in the countryside. It's hard leaving your family behind. Workers who aren't educated – like gypsies – do manual labour earning only a few pounds a week if they're lucky. We really are the "guest workers" of Hungary.'

The gypsy 'guest workers' of Germany are better off financially but suffer worse insults and discrimination. Against the belching chimneys of a Düsseldorf steel works, in his claustrophobic one-room attic, we talked with Ismail, an activist for the Romany community in Germany.

'We came to Germany because there was no work for us at home and because we couldn't get enough education. Here we have a better chance of owning our own homes or giving our children a decent education, so gypsies come to German cities from Turkey, Greece and Yugoslavia, because the Germans don't care about your education. They just want people to do their dirty work. There are tens of thousands of gypsy workers in Germany doing semi- or unskilled work that the Germans don't want to do. You can't get a job at all if they know you're a gypsy. So gypsy workers pretend to be Turkish or Albanian or Serbian, anything that stops your boss finding out that you're a gypsy. We even pretend to speak other people's languages or make up languages that don't exist.'

Most of the gypsies we met pretended to be Turkish – part of the 'Turkish immigrant problem' the Germans are trying to solve by repatriation. They hide their culture and their language except when they come together in the evenings and mix with the local German gypsies known as Sintis (the name of the original Indo-Aryan tribe). The music played at these gatherings owes much to Django Reinhardt, the great gypsy jazz guitarist, but there are bursts of Macedonian and even Indian music. An ironic story was told by one of the members of a band called Swing Gypsy Rose. Its founder actually changed his Romany name, Kroner, to Rosenburg: with a gypsy name he had been out

of work for months, but with a new Jewish name he was highly employable. 'The German conscience is very selective,' he laughed. He told me a chilling story about how his father had suffered in the concentration camps where almost half a million gypsies perished during World War II. One evening, 20 years later, his father was driving to Düsseldorf and was stopped by the police. Not having the compulsory registration form that all gypsies are forced to carry in the Federal Republic, he was taken to the local police chief. His father would never, he said, forget the wave of panic and terror that ran through him as he found himself confronted by the same camp commandant who had previously ordered the torture of his family and who was now back as the local chief of police.

Until 1970, a special police bureau existed in Munich whose documentation about German gypsies was composed from files inherited from the Third Reich, including the fingerprints of all gypsy children. It is believed the police are continuing to use this bureau's records and local gypsies are still protesting.

Rosenburg, sitting beneath a striped awning outside his caravan, played a song he had learnt from some survivors from the gypsy holocaust – a song, he told me, that they sang in Auschwitz:

*Don't wake me from my dreams,*
*So I needn't understand this world.*
*Soon darkness will surround us*
*And daylight stay only in our dreams.*
*My love, don't look*
*So you don't have to see*
*How a gypsy is treated.*

Rosenburg, with his Polish gypsy friend, Rudko, has made a few records and plays in bars around the German cities. They had written a song whose lyrics accurately described what almost every German gypsy I met, whether a Sinti or an immigrant worker, felt about life in Germany today. They sang it together for us and a group of other gypsy friends.

**Rosenburg is a gypsy musician who writes and sings songs about his experience of living as a guest worker in Germany**

*Just because my eyes are dark*
*And my hair isn't like yours*
*You've been after me since I was born*
*But I've been here just as long as you.*

*At school it had begun already*
*As a gypsy you get the worst of everything.*
*There, right from the start they call you*
*A stupid, lazy pig.*
*That's what they think we gypsies are.*

*Tell me, where can we go?*
*Damn it, can nobody understand us?*
*Why are we scum?*
*Why are we always moved on?*

Rudko and Rosenburg joined delegates who came from all the countries of Europe to debate their problems at the World Romany Congress in Göttingen, West Germany. The only exceptions were those prevented from attending by the governments of Romania, Bulgaria and the USSR. This congress stood for the unity of language and culture of gypsies everywhere, and the delegates called for the name of 'gypsy' to be replaced once and for all by 'Roma', recalling the Indian birthright of all the Romany peoples and giving them the historic identity they have lacked for centuries. I recognized the delegates from Yugoslavia and Hungary, from France and Spain. Here again, I met Grattan Puxon who brought the whole question of the Romany identity up to date:

'Generally, you can say that there is still a steady migration of peoples out of north India, as there has been over the last ten centuries. For my part, even when I meet Punjabis who arrive in England today, I see them as part of the same movement, though this might be a strange thing to say. But for instance, at the First World Romany Congress, when East-European Roma came and saw for the first time a Pakistani family in London, they would automatically assume they were Roma. And in a sense they are.'

The World Romany Congress began with music. A simple zither tune was played on stage by an elderly Turk, for whom the congress fell silent. At the end, Punjabi drummers called all the delegates up on stage to dance with Romanies of every nationality. Meanwhile, an Indian woman, dressed in a crimson sari, shouted into a microphone: 'We are Roma, we are one. Let us unite. At last we have come together. Now we must link arms in the struggle to be free.'

# 11 Two Faces of Thailand
*A Musical Portrait*

On a cold December morning just before Christmas 1982, saffron-robed monks solemnly filed out of their Buddhist temple in a southern suburb of Bangkok and entered the home of the actor Khun Bunyang. His brother, one of the master musicians of Thailand, began to strike his xylophone, and call down the spirits of dead ancestors with secret melodies. He played a distinctive Thai version of that instrument, a ranatek, which has wooden keys and is shaped like a boat. His assembly of musicians followed him with the first notes of a 'wykru' spirit ceremony.

Praying and chanting, the monks purified the ground upon which the ceremony would happen. With long slim hands they unwound ribbons which were passed down the line towards an altarpiece where images of many different spirits, each identified by a dramatic coloured mask, were set around the central image of a golden Buddha. Incense was lit and a feast prepared for both the monks and spirits: expensive shellfish, animals' heads, even beer and brandy had been laid out for their nourishment. Dancers, exotically dressed in traditional Thai manner, moved around the room as the musicians played their secret tunes. A huge carp – an offering – suddenly leaped from the ornate plate on which it had lain and landed, twisting and jerking, among the worshippers.

The participants of this urban spirit ceremony were not quite what we had expected: mainly young, they were dressed in jeans and T-shirts, while a few elders were more formally dressed in western clothes. Children, too, waited in line to receive the spirits of the different gods from Bunyang. As he held each mask above a kneeling supplicant, he breathed its power into them. The younger people remained composed, the children wide-eyed, but towards the end of the ceremony, as the music and atmosphere became much more intense, several others started to writhe and cry and twitch as the Bunyang blew spirits into their faces. Helpers ran forward

100 miles

THAILAND

Nakhon Ratchasima (Korat)

River Kwai

Kanchanaburi

Bangkok

**Monks in a buddhist temple: they prepare for a wykru spirit ceremony in great detail**

COURTESY OF THE THAI INFORMATION SERVICE

to hold them steady and even deliver a karate chop to the backs of their necks to stop them falling into a state of possession.

This whole ceremony seemed to me essentially Thai, with its mixture of modern dress, ritual formality, youthful following and absolute acceptance of an ancient tradition. It merged Buddhism with an earlier pagan spirit ceremony in the urban atmosphere of contemporary Bangkok. Above all, the ceremony displayed the Thai obsession of keeping face, which means not showing real emotions and feelings. Even when they communicated with dead ancestors during the ceremony they had to avoid being visibly affected and falling into a trance – an appearance of normality and self-control was crucial.

Behind their courteous smiles Thais are shrewd, calculating, sometimes even ruthless. This quality has for centuries preserved the independence of Thailand against would-be colonizers and invaders, while other south east Asian countries have continuously fallen under foreign yoke. Similarly, Thai arts – including popular music – are not always what they seem to be on the surface: they reflect many of the inherent contradictions of Thai society.

In every house and on every slum, school and factory wall are portraits of the King of Thailand. Bhumibol Adulyadej has been on the throne since 1950, fronting a military rule under a succession of marshals, for whom the King is a constitutional show figure, genuinely adored and revered by the Thai people. A modest, kindly, devout Buddhist, he has done much to help the disadvantaged. Even so, his position seems to many Thais to be anything but secure.

Born in Massachusetts in 1927, he became King after the mysterious death of his predecessor. He is an avid jazz musician and together with Mr Manrat (an American-trained jazz pianist) started a palace band specializing in 1940s and 1950s American jazz. Once a week he would don shades and play clarinet with the palace band bopping away behind him. Every year he used to invite one of America's top jazzmen – like Dizzy Gillespie – to play and record in the palace with him. He built his own recording studio there, where his music could be mixed and then fed to local Thai radio stations. Each Friday evening, an hour of the King's music is still nationally broadcast. He has also written many of his own tunes: I was given a double cassette of His Majesty's compositions which show an influence of traditional black American jazz mixed with saccharine Thai pop music – an extremely strange combination for western ears.

Several years ago the King became desperately ill and had to stop playing the clarinet and saxophone, his two favourite instruments. It had been his therapy, his escape from the pressures of political intrigue which are never far from the throne. Every taxi driver in Bangkok would tell in whispered, secretive tones, a variation of the story of palace intrigue that put an end to his playing. The most popular version was that His Majesty had been poisoned or else deeply shocked by a conspiracy against him by the Queen and Crown Prince. The official version was that the King had suffered from a virus or heart attack.

Trying to find the real music of Thailand behind the polite public image is not easy. The official institutes are full of their traditional Thai ballet dances called khon and lakhon in which brilliantly costumed, beautiful young men and women with ten-inch fingernails parade in lacquered papier-mâché masks. In costumes sparkling with jewels, they dance in exquisite postures to religious stories from the Ramakian (a Thai version of the Indian Ramayana). But Thai music today is not about historical ballet. This is an official cultural relic put on for tourists and visiting dignitaries. Questions about the real popular music of Thailand, about likay or luk tung, were usually met with vacant stares or an apologetic evasion.

Kukrit Pramoj used to be Prime Minister of Thailand. A wily, elder statesman, he is now head of the opposition. I had met him once in Hong Kong and he had been frank about the way the Hong Kong authorities, like the Thais, use high culture to present a diplomatically civilized front. Kukrit himself runs a traditional khon dance troupe and travels widely with his beautiful dancing boys. When I contacted him in Thailand, he kindly gave me a few minutes of his time during a Shadow Cabinet meeting and ushered me into the back room of his ancient Thai home. To my astonishment, he then put a record on the turntable, turned the volume and the bass up high and the whole house, including the Shadow Cabinet, shook and rocked to a wild, contemporary Thai music called luk tung. It was partly western pop, partly a traditional big-band sound, with heavy brass featuring saxophones and lyrics in a shrill, high-pitched nasal tone. This, announced Kukrit a little smugly, was the music that the bureaucrats never mentioned – it was the real music of Thailand. He thereupon returned to his opposition Cabinet meeting to discuss the Kampuchean border crisis, the overflowing refugee camps and the Burmese heroin smugglers who were firing Russian rockets at the Thai army.

In the following days I found two advisors – from very different backgrounds – to work with me. The first was Bruce Gaston, an American who had dropped out of the Vietnam war. A

**A keen jazz fan, the King of Thailand, Bhumibol Adulyadej, gets out his sax for a night of cool jazz in the palace**

trained musician, he had once played the organ for Billy Graham during his long evangelical tours of the West Coast of America. After Vietnam, Bruce had stayed on in Thailand, deeply enthusiastic about Thai music, and now ran a school where he wrote TV jingles and modern orchestral music combining Thai and western instruments. My other advisor was a Thai, who was extremely well connected both with the police and the underworld. His car was fitted with a short-wave radio and half a dozen assorted handguns. One evening we visited a fairground on the outskirts of Bangkok. Amongst the trade stalls and balloons were the Disney cartoon characters and the other gaudy paraphernalia of what a neighbouring Thai described as 'American economic colonialism'. Our man was talking about his guns and his preference for six-shooter automatics – 'They don't jam'. When our cameramen asked him naively, 'Why do you need so many guns?' his answer was equally naive, 'To kill people with'.

Our advisor had friends in many areas of low life – in Thai boxing and in the big luk tung music circuits. Luk tung, to which Kukrit had introduced me, is the most distinctive, popular music of Thailand. At the same time as fusing eastern and western styles of dress and performance, major luk tung stars live luxurious and secluded lives in mock-Tudor English mansions protected by Dobermann Pinschers or Alsatians.

Surachai Sumbatcharon is one such star; he lived in his Tudor mansion with his mother, brothers and girlfriends. But unlike most western pop stars, Surachai approached life with an essential humility and calmness, with a belief in the dictates of fate that made him more the servant than the master of the people for whom he performed. After his father, the

**One of the stars of luk tung is Surachai Sumbatcharon; he has a life of wealth and danger on the road**

greatest of all luk tung singers, was murdered while singing in Thailand, Surachai had been sent for his own safety to Birmingham in England. Organized crime controls much of Thai society: the big money that is made on the luk tung circuit, and the glamour that goes with it, attracts violence and protection rackets.

In the shade of the willows by his garden lake, we picnicked with Surachai while he distinguished between his own luk tung and the syrupy international-style pop music called Thai sakon.

'Luk tung songs are usually made up from folk tunes or some old Thai melody,' he said. 'Whereas the Thai sakon singer might sing words like "If I loved you, would it be very wrong?" sweetly and in a quite bland way, the luk tung singer has to shout, "*Ai nong ai Noi, eeetoy, eeetoom*, come and get together." The voice must be loud and clear with a much firmer sound. Most of the lyrics of luk tung songs are about real life and real events that have happened, rather than about imaginary things or dreams. Luk tung is not a music for escapism. Most of the people who listen to luk tung live in the countryside; some of them have problems which correspond closely to the lyrics in the songs. For example, they leave their villages or their sweethearts and try to find work in the city because they are penniless. When they listen to luk tung they feel they are experiencing their own lives through our music. Sometimes a man is broken-hearted because his village sweetheart has gone off with a city guy or a gangster; the village boy is deeply hurt, but when he listens to a song about that he is very moved and touched. For example, a song called "Parting from you" which I often sing, has the lyrics: "Parting from you in the middle of the sixth month, the sky cried thunder, the rain fell, my heart wailed . . ." Mostly our songs are about love, melancholy and grief, but they are not sentimental. They are too realistic for that. When there is a flood and the crops are destroyed, there is nothing left. People starve and have to go to Bangkok to find work. Tens of thousands do this every year. So our luk tung

songs tell their story: about how people live and
work in the countryside.

'But it's troublesome being a luk tung
singer on the road. First of all I have to care for
the whole band, who treat me as their father.
That means not just the band, but also the 40 or
50 dancing girls, some of them very young,
whom we take with us. Then, almost
everywhere we go in the country, there are local
gangsters or protection racketeers who threaten
us. But we always try to remain cool, calm and
modest. Sometimes we are treated unfairly by
those bullies; sometimes we get threatening
phone calls. They murder some of us, just as
they murdered my father. At times there are
bombs and gunfire. Then, the only thing to do is
pray and ask God to look after us. Once,
travelling back with my driver and uncle after a
show, a car pulled alongside and started to shoot
at us. My driver was killed and my uncle was
badly injured. I escaped. The car nearly went off
the road but luckily I kept hold of the steering
wheel. And then, just a few months later, there
was another bomb attack while I was singing.
Many people were hurt, and over 100 died.
Once again they missed me. It was the same
people who had killed my father'.

Surachai spent 40 weeks of each year on the
road travelling from gig to gig. He had his own
chauffeur-driven limousine. The rest of the
band and the dancing girls travelled in two large
green coaches inside which costumes and props
were piled across the seats. The driver hummed
the lyrics of some new luk tung number they
were learning. As the Thai countryside flashed
by outside the windows and the coaches hurtled
to their next location at a death-defying speed,
the 70 dancing girls inside broke into a typical
luk tung song:

> *This year it's very cold and the rice has failed,*
> *The rice is dead and there is no rain.*
> *The sky is red like a fever,*
> *My love, you must be crying, and so am I.*
> *You starve for rice and the buffalo starves for*
>   *grass.*
> *There is no money to spend,*

*I have to leave you now.*
*It is as if the sky intends to make us sad.*

Occasionally the buses screeched to a halt,
the dancing girls went tumbling off into the rice
fields to relieve themselves, and then returned
to the bus which thundered on its way. When we
arrived with them at their new venue, the first
items erected were the enormous posters of their
sponsors – in this case, Honda motorbikes.
Ironically, the location was the Bridge on the
River Kwai at Kanchanaburi, which was built
during World War II. The Japanese army
worked 16,000 allied prisoners of war and
50,000 enslaved Thais to death during the

**A luk tung show is an extravaganza of song and dance, and outfits from coy Victorians to Superman attendants**

construction of that bridge which was finally bombed by the British during 1945 (many of the bombs actually fell on the prisoners of war who were building it). There, where a Japanese concentration camp had once stood, luk tung was to be played, and the commercial sponsors were Honda! Trains still crossed the bridge silhouetted in the evening light; the rails read 'Made in Japan'. When I walked to the local graveyard behind the newly erected stage and looked at the 7,000 white crosses on the neatly kept graves, I noticed that many of the prisoners had died on the day I was born.

The luk tung show itself was unlike anything else: a vibrant, brilliant, non-stop flow of sound and colour. The costumes of the dancing girls became increasingly bizarre. The first on stage were dressed as fairies, then came western-style ballet dancers doing a badly choreographed version of what appeared to be 'The Sugar Plum Fairy' to a heavy rhythm and blues backing and sweet Thai vocals about a doomed love affair. Next came Surachai, garlanded in flowers, to the screams and adulation of the crowd. Between verses, they pushed forward to lay more and more garlands on his body until the flowers swamped him, covering his waist, then his shoulders and finally his head. He could see nothing and staggered round the stage with the aid of several henchmen. On came more dancing girls who had frantically changed in the ankle-deep mud behind the stage, for it had rained all day at the River Kwai. One group of girls was in their late teens – another barely in their teens at all. They were smeared in makeup, still tearing at the costumes as they raced on and off stage in a desperate attempt not to be left behind by the next number. Often they charged back on from the wrong entrance, at the wrong time, colliding and stumbling across the stage and desperately trying to pick up the choreography pattern for that number. They reappeared on stage in English Victorian costumes: the men in leotards, the girls in corsets and high frilly neck ruffs. Finally came the highlight of the whole performance: a portrait of Surachai's father was displayed on stage by male dancers dressed as policemen. They marched and saluted while something like an early blues was played. Then the disembodied voice of the dead luk tung singer echoed out of the loudspeakers, across the thousands upon thousands of avid listeners crammed tight around the stage, many still clutching garlands and flowers for Surachai. When the voice stopped, the portrait disappeared in clouds of smoke that had the band choking and spluttering, and it was time for the whole ensemble to dress as Superman. Surachai, still weighed down with flowers, wound up the show with a satirical number about modern Thai girls:

*I was born a Superman with special powers.*
*But I'm afraid of those girls with sharp*
*    tongues and itchy fingers,*
*Those girls who cry: 'He's magical.'*

Seated on a deckchair in the mud backstage was Surachai's mother. She was never far from his side. She had survived the killing of her husband and had sent Surachai abroad, but she was determined that the rival luk tung shows and gangsters should not triumph. She brought Surachai back from England and secretly trained him, night after night, week after week, year after year, until he had perfected the manner and delivery of his father. Then she presented him in public. She was a proud and beautiful women to whom Surachai and the rest of his family paid constant respect. She, in turn, pointed out the importance of the luk tung performer's respect for his audience:

'I tell my children they shouldn't be too loud and they must smile when they come out on stage. They must also *wai* [pay respect to their audience]. When on stage they must stand up straight, they mustn't bend their backs. I don't really know a lot but I learnt from experience when their father was alive. I learned that for a luk tung song you must stand up and sing the words clearly. You don't slur and croon like a pop idol. My son tries to do what I say, but sometimes he forgets and gets carried away and I have to remind him. But he has his father's gift and if God wills it, he will be an even greater success'.

Within minutes after the show, the stage was dismantled and packed, the costumes were bundled into the buses and show girls were flirting with their audience. Surachai and his henchmen ran for the cover of their limousine in the darkness. The fairground behind the Honda posters was playing Surachai's latest hit and the lights of the big wheel and the candy-floss stalls were shining in the waters of the River Kwai. No-one was going home that night: they would drive on to their next location and sleep on a temple floor. The next day they would erect the stage and perform all night. In this way they would travel up to the north of Thailand, playing to audiences of tens of thousands, even millions in the course of a year. These would all be country people, not city folk, everyone identifying with the music, with the extravagance of the costumes and with the songs' sad stories. The luk tung show was a brash, extraordinary, show-biz circus complete

**Each young Thai girl's dream is to be picked by a talent scout as a luk tung showgirl — with all its show-biz finery and money**

with midgets, clowns, fat men, superstars and nymphet chorus girls. Its mixture of western rhythm and blues, Thai popular music and Thai classics was in deliberate bad taste, as the show's fat man explained:

'Luk tung is an expression of stress. It's the split between the country and the city, like my favourite song, "I knew a girl on a Honda". These country boys once in the city are frightened of losing their identity or their loved one at home. It is the city that is seen as jazzy, as tasteless. That split is what makes the whole show tasteless, deliberately so. It is a self-contradiction, a clash of opposites. It is hard for any foreigner to understand that luk tung is as traditionally Thai as any khon performance churned out for the tourists: more so. Ours comes from the heart. The other comes from the pocket.'

That is not to deny that money plays a large part in luk tung. In many ways it is about material success. The fairgrounds all around the country were filled with hopeful young luk tung singers, willing to do anything that might lead them to stardom and glamour. Young girls sat astride collapsible wooden bars, perched above huge buckets of ice-cold water. Customers bought wooden balls like those at coconut shies to throw at the wooden support. If they scored, the bar collapsed, dropping one into a gigantic cauldron of freezing water where she totally disappeared, then hauled herself up, dripping, to climb back onto the bar again. Between plunges, between those moments when her eyes closed with the realization that she was falling once again into that huge tin tub, she sang fragments of luk tung songs.

Another girl in a miniskirt was singing and leaping about on a stage on which a gleaming motorbike was parked. Behind her, customers filed into a shaky wooden tower. At the end of her song, and when sufficient customers had paid to enter, she leapt onto the bike and drove inside the tower. This was a wall of death and she roared around on her 500cc Japanese machine, pulling her T-shirt up over her breasts and across her face and placing her hands before her in a gesture of prayer, thundering round and round the wooden walls, supporting and controlling the bike only with her naked knees.

The customers chewed corn and gazed down at her. Afterwards she went back on stage to sing another luk tung song and wait for the next batch of customers. Somewhat tamely, we asked her if she had ever come off the bike. 'Of course,' she laughed. 'Do you want to see my scars?' And she explained the lyrics of her song, which were about losing her virginity.

> *Tomorrow I shall be a lady, not a child any*
> *more.*
> *I'm telling you, tomorrow I'm going on a bus,*
> *Tomorrow I may lose it, and you won't find it*
> *any more.*

All these girls were desperate to leave the countryside. They could see no future in the cornfields or the rice paddies and they wanted to get away from the poverty and inevitability of the peasant woman's role. They had seen the

Sport as a way out of the country slums: boys practise boxing and hope to get a place at a Bangkok training school

city lights on their TV sets and heard the city stories from those who had returned. They wanted to be part of 'life' in the 1980s. In every country town, girls grabbed the opportunity to sing luk tung at talent shows. They might be spotted, or might pick up a recording contract, or be picked up by a touring luk tung star who could take them onto stardom or a brief stay in a Tudor mansion. The talent show we visited in the township of Korat took place under a huge canopy whose ropes were being tugged at by the wind and eventually blew away down the dusty main street of the town. Girls as young as six or seven clutched the microphone and sang lyrics of lost loves to an amused and cynical audience:

> *The golden heads of rice in fields are waiting to*
> *be reaped*
> *And I am also waiting.*
> *The girl in the fields is still waiting for you.*
> *Come back from the city, my love,*
> *Or I shall come and join you there.*

**Music to box to: up in the north of Thailand, boys learn kick boxing to the rhythmic Molam music**

Young boys also tried their hand at singing – luk tung stardom after all is a male-orientated affair and is often handed down to the sons in the family. But for boys, there is another popular way out.

Just as music has been a means of escape from the ghetto for young people all over the developing world, so too has sport. Sport in Thailand is male-dominated and it is a route that many boys choose to follow. One that involves glamour, fast money and prestige is Thai kick boxing. In the countryside boys learn to box in muddy courtyards. With a punchbag and a pair of padded gloves, they practise the delicate but aggressive art of Thai boxing. If they are spotted in local bouts, they stand the same chance of making it as the luk tung singer spotted by an agent at a talent show. The young boxer is taken to Bangkok and interned at one of the many boxing schools. He lives, eats and sleeps there, subject to a heavy and unremitting discipline and a tough communal existence. The school becomes home, the trainer becomes a new father, and the school chief the focus of the boy's loyalty and faith. Boxing schools are also dominated by gangsterism and gambling: the head of the school we visited had recently been the victim of a hand grenade attack and was still recovering in hospital.

Music is also crucial in boxing, at all stages. Out in the countryside, by the wooden dwellings that stand on stilts above the marshy ground, boxing is accompanied by molam music. This is the traditional local music of the northeastern countryside. Molam is unique: it sounds astonishingly like American mountain music with its vibrant, syncopated rhythms played on a stringed instrument and accompanied by a khan – a large panpipe made of many reeds vertically fixed together. However western it may sound, the Thais insist that molam is a purely local music: it began as a verbal courting contest – a competitive play on words between a male and a female singer backed by the nasal, reedy sound of the khan. Troupes of molam singers still tour the northeast, playing in villages and temple fairs and as the entertainers in slum districts.

When it comes to a real Thai boxing contest in a major Bangkok stadium like Rajadamnern, which is decorated with giant illuminated effigies of Thai fighters, music plays an essential role. No boxing can take place without it. The music starts slowly with beating drums and the high-pitched wavering tones of Thai flutes; then gradually speeds up throughout the fight, stopping abruptly for a knockout or a win. Whether the music reflects the tempo of the fight, which inevitably increases during the three rounds, or whether it spurs on the fighters, we never quite discovered. But when, for filming purposes, we tried to stage some close-ups, the next day, when no audience was there, our fighters refused even to enter the ring, let alone pretend to box a sequence, unless the musicians played the ritual music that was such an indispensable part of the boxing experience.

Boxing in Thailand has deep religious and spiritual traditions. No female is allowed to enter the boxing ring because of the belief that her influence will destroy the boxer's knowledge of his art. Boxers often wear a sacred cord around their head with a small Buddha charm inside. All pay homage to the guardian spirit of the ring by kneeling outside it before the fight begins. On entering the ring the contestants crouch on the canvas facing the direction in which they were born. Sometimes they walk slowly round it with their hand on the top rope to discourage interference from spirits or unrequested advice from the seconds. Most off-putting of all for an opponent is when one boxer does a sombre grave-digging movement which ends in stomping down the earth that will cover the grave of his rival. Our fight programme described the boxer in the blue corner as 'the aggressive agent of kicking practice who seeking bang-and-break until the opponent's head-no-thinks on canvas'.

Thai boxing is much more than a musical spectacle; it is an integral part of the criminal and gambling empires that the Thai mafiosi have organized for themselves. So there is no room for failure. The triumphant boxers are paid a small percentage of the purse, offer a prayer, have their photographs taken and race off to find a girl – a rewarding break from the rigid discipline of the boxing school. For the losers there is nothing but abuse. We saw them roughly assaulted by their trainers, even by their mothers; slapped, kicked and sworn at. They were not physically hurt, just humiliated – they

**In the big stadium in Bangkok, the boxers will not begin a contest without the sound of the music of drums and flutes**

had lost face, not only for themselves but for their trainers and their school.

Failure for these young people can be costly. They may suffer the same fate as tens of thousands of girls and boys who find themselves on the Bangkok streets. Most come from desperately poor families in the countryside who make 'arrangements' for their children to find work in the city. It seemed impossible, to us, that their parents did not know what horrors awaited them. Many children below the age of 12 end up as slave labour in Thai garment factories; they work 15-hour days, sleeping on the factory floor where they work. They are thrown out after a few years when their fingers and brains are no longer as agile as they were and when their eyesight has faded. Other girls are conscripted into prostitution: an estimated half million Thais serve their own Thai customers as well as the many Europeans and Japanese who come as sex tourists. These girls are mostly found in enormous mob controlled massage parlours where up to 400 sit in a window with numbers round their necks. Customers select one by announcing a girl's number to a madam who then shrieks it through a loudspeaker system; the girl, smiling and demure, exits from the window, taker her customer's hand and disappears into a gloomy darkness to the piped musical accompaniment of 'Jingle Bells' or 'My Way'.

Stories about the underbelly of Thai society are often acted out in another local form of entertainment – a music-drama called likay. Bunyang, who exhaled ancestral spirits at the wykru ceremony, is one of Thailand's master likay performers. He has his own troupe and sometimes performs on TV. His performance is a whole day affair on Sunday, during which convoluted, part-traditional, part-modern plots unfold, interspersed with hair cream commercials and luk tung stars advertising the latest in motorbikes. Most likay can be seen on the streets during festivals, temple fairs and King Bhumibol's birthday. It is a pantomime with social satire, garish costumes and androgynous makeup; with slapstick humour

The King enjoys a genuine popularity in Thailand; on his birthday he reviews the troops from his fifties Cadillac

and bawdy lyrics. The exotic performers are accompanied by a small but heavily amplified band of traditional musicians.

I first found Bunyang through a typical Thai ruse. I was sent to Korat, a few hours drive from Bangkok, to meet him – but he did not show up. I was put in the worst hotel in town where no-one could speak English, where there was no food, and where black rats ran vertically up the walls at all hours of the night. In the morning there was still no Bunyang. He arrived casually at lunchtime with an entourage of 20 actors and

actresses who seated themselves around a table in the most expensive restaurant and ordered more food than they could conceivably eat. Bunyang kept watching me. We talked about likay and what I wanted to film. Somehow I managed to remain polite.

At the end of the meal Bunyang turned to me and asked provocatively: 'I hope you didn't mind spending so much money on my friends?' I managed, following local custom, not to show what I was feeling as I answered: 'No amount of money, Khun Bunyang, could ever compare with the honour of your presence at my table.' Bunyang stared at me and asked: 'Did anyone prompt him in that answer?' The others shook their heads and giggled. Bunyang turned back to me and said: 'Whatever you now wish me to do will be done. I will organize the best likay that I have ever done. What is more, I shall ensure that the cost in all respects is negligible.'

The likay performed by Bunyang and his troupe was a modern morality play about two boxers, one a thug and the other a fool. The fool won and got his girl. In these travelling theatre

**Likay drama blends
elements of music,
pantomime and
topical reference**

shows the dramatic lead is idolized by his
audience and his frequent liaisons with married
women, who come and watch the performances,
are legendary. Like luk tung, likay offers a
glamorous mix of old and new, funny and sad,
that translates directly into the experience of its
audience. Likay is a musical, with reed
instruments, drums, cymbals and flutes
supporting and punctuating the action.

The day of Bunyang's show was also that of
King Bhumibol's birthday – two men at
opposite ends of the social hierarchy. For the
King's birthday celebrations, on a parade
ground in the centre of Bangkok, the army was
assembled in its finest regalia of purple and
gold. Thunder pealed and scattered raindrops
fell. King Bhumibol arrived in a gleaming 1950s
Cadillac, and the army greeted him with one of

his own compositions – 'His Majesty's blues'. It
was previously known as 'Hungry man's blues'.
The King had written all the music that his
bands played at his birthday parade. In
Thailand the unlikely always seems to happen.
It was a huge pageant, a sort of military musical.
Painfully, His Majesty alighted from his
Cadillac and climbed the steps beside his Queen
to a golden throne. The royal salute was given.
The generals who control both King and
country chanted: 'We are like the dust under
your Majesty's feet on the occasion of your
birthday. Long live the King.' Above them all
the thunder pealed and storm clouds gathered,
blowing their way from Kampuchea across
Thailand and to the west.

# 12 Spirit of Samba
## *The Black Music of Brazil*

In a corrugated tin shack – one of thousands sprawled across the steep mountainsides above Rio de Janeiro – Leci Brandao tapped out a samba rhythm on a matchbox. Her *favela* (the local name for a shanty town) rose above the haze of belching chimneys and the soft white sands of Copacabana bay, within sight of *Christus Redemptor*, the gigantic statue of a compassionate Christ. Some miles below his outstretched arms, Leci – a slim black girl in her twenties – described with anger the rejection of her latest samba. She had composed it specially for the carnival celebrations. But its outspoken lyrics about the place of blacks in Brazilian society had led to her expulsion from the samba competitions.

Rio Carnival is highly competitive. Each of the samba schools, which evolved in a different *favela* round Rio, selects a theme for its floats,

costumes and sambas. These are then paraded on the streets and one of them becomes the winner for that year – a decision that carries with it much prestige and money. The carnival parades originated from a mix of pre-Lent festivities (called the *enturdo*) which the Portuguese colonizers brought with them from their motherland, and the black percussive rhythms of the African slaves who were imported to work the plantations.

Initially carnival music came from woodwind orchestras playing polkas and waltzes and Portuguese folk songs. But soon these yielded to African percussion and a hip-swivelling dance called Semba – an Angolan belly dance. This then became the samba. A Brazilian tourist magazine, however, offered a different official version of the story:

'Our samba was born of the people in the

picturesque houses of the Praca Onze, long torn down to make for Rio's 100-metre-wide Avenida Vargas, in the hills where the lyric view is itself a source of poetic inspiration; in the shanty towns where life and love were as simple as the stars up above and in the distant suburbs lit by flickering oil lamps. Every Brazilian has an innate sense of rhythm'.

These are cosy and self-perpetuating fictions put out by the state propaganda machine. Brazil, in fact, was the last western country to abolish slavery, less than 100 years ago. Today, after much 'mixing of blood', there are more than 20 expressions to distinguish the variations in colour of Brazilian citizens. A person's place on the social scale more or less corresponds to the darkness of his or her complexion.

Leci explained the place of her music:

'All my songs reflect my daily life; my loves, my emotions, my problems. I try to picture everything I feel in my lyrics. I try to point out to people the difference and inequality between the social classes. Too many people are interested in taking culture only to a certain privileged class. In Rio, all the theatres are located in the south, the rich area. But I think culture should go everywhere, to shanty towns and suburbs as well, because everyone can understand music.

'I've always tried to be myself and act naturally. When I went to agents with my songs, I'd say: "Look, if you like my work, that's OK. If you don't like it, I don't care. I don't need you." That's how I've been all my life. Except, that is, with my samba school, where there was prejudice against me for being a woman. So much so that I always lost the samba competitions. So I just got up and left.'

Song writing for the samba schools is male-dominated: it has been since the very first carnival hit song – 'Pelo telefone' ('On the telephone') – was recorded in 1917. It was and is a reflection of the machismo of Brazilian society. The songs are composed and performed in a cut-throat atmosphere since each of the schools will select just one on which to base the entire theme of its carnival presentation. The fantasy parade of exotic costumes, gigantic floats and deafening samba bands all depends on this one song. For the author of the successful carnival samba comes fame, wealth and musical immortality.

In the New Year of 1980, carnival preparations had been under way for nine months and were building to a climax as

**From her favela shanty town high above Rio, Leci Brandao travels down into a club to sing the sambas she composes herself**

February approached. The finishing touches were put to elaborately sequinned silver costumes, and huge papier-mâché masks were being painted and fixed to the floats which would decorate the parades in four days and nights of musical oblivion. We chose to film the oldest samba school in Rio, the Manguiera, situated near the Manguiera favela – a shanty town where thousands lived.

The Manguiera School hit the headlines for the first time in the 1926 carnival with a smash-hit samba, 'Morro de Manguiera', written by the immortal Manoel Dias:

*I went to a samba*
*On Manguiera hill*
*And there a high yellow girl*
*She gave me a thrill.*

Leci's songs, which are rooted in her tough living conditions, stand no chance against these bland lyrics. Carnival is not about real life: it is about forgetting who and what you are behind a frilly costume and a painted face, in an orgy of music and dance. Subsidized and politically manipulated, it is a safety valve for a society that edges towards explosion. It is a politically harmless means of diverting the energies of the most underprivileged. Carnival means, literally, to give up meat (*carnem levare*). It became Carnevale, meaning 'meat farewell': the last explosion of pleasure before Lent in the Catholic calendar. In Rio, it is a socially stratified event: the upper classes, mostly white, attend indoor balls and private parties, while the lower classes, mostly black, parade outside in the streets.

With Leci Brandao, at the Manguiera School, was a young black activist (who preferred to remain anonymous). He described the place of the samba schools and their music within favela life:

'Once the samba school belonged only to black people. It was a black cultural place. But the dominating white class took it over. Today we make a distinction between the black samba people who have sold out, and those like Leci who still write and sing committed sambas.

'Favela society continues to be one of the most important areas in Brazilian black culture. It is the centre of black resistance to all the forms of oppression we face elsewhere in the city. In fact, these shanty towns are still called Quilombo, because back in 1697 there was an African state here called Quilombo which was a nucleus of resistance by black African slaves to their white oppressors. History books today claim that it was only peopled by black layabouts, so now our educated dominant middle class, supported by the government, believes that the favela is where all the black layabouts are centred. We cannot participate in decisions made by the middle classes and we are marginalized.

'But the favela is an important centre of cultural resistance in terms of music and religion as well: the two most important things we have as weapons of resistance. And basic to the samba rhythms are the Macumba and Candomblé spirit ceremonies with their Yoruba drumming rhythms which were brought here from Nigeria by our forefathers.'

As we left the samba school rehearsals, literally thousands of dancers were gyrating, semi-nude, swivelling their hips to the thundering beat of the huge bass drum (the surdo), accompanied by rico-ricos scrapers, friction drums and tambourines. The leader of the samba band, which was perched on a balcony above the milling dancers, controlled the rhythms with a choice of whistles, all of which were made in Britain. A peal from the Acme Thunderer, for example, got the band going and the beat was then accelerated or slowed by blasts from the Rocket International 51.

We descended through the favela and

**Spirit ceremonies like Umbanda involve rituals with the gods brought by the slaves from West Africa**

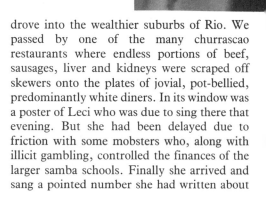

drove into the wealthier suburbs of Rio. We passed by one of the many churrascao restaurants where endless portions of beef, sausages, liver and kidneys were scraped off skewers onto the plates of jovial, pot-bellied, predominantly white diners. In its window was a poster of Leci who was due to sing there that evening. But she had been delayed due to friction with some mobsters who, along with illicit gambling, controlled the finances of the larger samba schools. Finally she arrived and sang a pointed number she had written about

the poor black servants who remain in the kitchens of the rich, while the ladies of the house go out to gorge themselves in restaurants. The song was politely and mindlessly applauded. Having eaten, our advisor on this film joined us – a tiny, rotund, beaming Brazilian called Djalma Correa, who is one of Brazil's virtuoso percussionists. He was taking us to a spirit ceremony held by the local favela people.

Umbanda is Rio's largest spirit cult, which began as late as the 1930s. It is an urbanized version of the more primitive and secret

Candomblé cult, which we were to encounter later. In the early hours of that morning, we stopped our car outside a yellow shack, hurried up a steep flight of steps and into a stiflingly hot Umbanda spirit house. There, a dozen or so old ladies swathed in white and puffing on giant cigars were spinning in circles beneath a huge green fan. They were making contact with the spirit world and inviting the gods to possess them and then work for them. The ladies twitched and juddered in silk frocks and red-indian-style feathered headdresses. Thick cigar

smoke filled the room, enveloping religious effigies that ranged from St George and the Dragon to the Exus devils of Umbanda. Jesus Christ was there, as was Mary, but both of them represented spirits of the Yoruba pantheon. Olurun is the chief god who plays the role of Christ, and Yemanjá who is the mother of the secondary gods called Orixás, wore the face of the Virgin Mary. Each god had its own drum beat and song at which it would awaken and emerge to occupy the bodies of the dancers and 'ride the horse'. The old ladies staggered, rolled on the floor and choked on their cigar butts. Then the medium, who puffed on the largest cigar in the room, took on the voice and gestures of the spirit, moaning or howling. To the pounding of Yoruba drums, hymns called *canticos de Umbanda* were incanted. On record these are sometimes accompanied by machine-gun and artillery fire.

Umbanda originated in the northwestern district of Brazil called Bahia. It was there that we next travelled to find the earliest roots and expressions of black Brazilian culture.

**Gilberto Gil is from Bahia, an area rich in music traditions. His own music, now known internationally, has its roots in Bahia**

Bahia's capital city, Salvador, was founded in 1500. In the following centuries over 1,000,000 slaves from the west coast of Africa were landed there. Salvador is a city totally unlike Rio. It is an enduring remnant of colonialism with elegant but crumbling churches and colonnades set in picture-postcard streets. On the hour, every hour, 100 church bells sound across the city, for despite the abundance of spirit cults in Brazil, 90 per cent of its citizens still profess to be Catholics. In a society with little time for social welfare, faith and its accompanying spiritual and emotional counselling fill a void.

Music was everywhere in Salvador. At the harbour there were drummers and singers of praise songs; the shoe-shines serenaded their customers, and in the central square of the old town, among the travelling salesmen, street vendors and barbers, itinerant musicians came to sing local tales or news. A blind accordionist accompanied his wife's songs about the village she had left, with the aid of a cheap microphone and amplifier swinging from the branches of a tree. Our adviser, Djalma Correa, himself from Salvador, was proud of his city and its black culture which had spawned so many fine musicians like himself and the man with whom he had recently toured Europe – Gilberto Gil. On the porch of the wealthy pop star's house in a smart suburb of Salvador, Gilberto Gil and Djalma played a number about local girls who all too quickly lose their traditional values and virtues. 'The first sound impression,' explained Gil, 'is of a very traditional Bahian folk song. One that blends the old with the new, the supermarket with a Candomblé spirit hall, side by side. All my music reflects the black roots from which it comes. However successful I am, I cannot escape that.'

Despite his pop star status, Gil has on several occasions run foul of the authorities. The military dictatorship which took over in the late 1960s found his lyrics and life style too threatening and imprisoned him.

'That was in 1967 and 1968, when we had the beginning of military rule in Brazil. It was disturbing and a little dangerous for me from the cultural point of view, so I got into some trouble and had to leave and live in London. But in 1972 things had cooled down again and I came back. Now I am relatively free to do what I want.'

Although the political situation was now less extreme, Gil's relative freedom depended largely on his affluence. For other black Brazilians without his money or status, freedom of expression was harder to achieve.

In a dilapidated house in the backstreets of Salvador lived Batatinha, one of the oldest and

proudest of Bahia's current entertainers.
Printed curtains shut out the sunlight from a
room lined with trophies and yellowing
photographs in elaborate frames. Batatinha,
with white hair and a sad, drawn face, was seated
on a three-legged settee. Compared to the favela
dwellers, he enjoyed a modicum of comfort and,
as the walls informed us, had made several
records for a local company. Joined by a few
musician friends, he sang one of his favourite
compositions, a soft Brazilian blues:

> *Nobody sees my sorrows,*
> *All they see is false happiness and smiles.*
> *Someone must be responsible.*

Like many of Brazil's black citizens,
Batatinha was not happy with the society in
which he lived. He did not like being a third-
class citizen because of the colour of his skin and
laughed at the official propaganda: 'They say
there is no racism – only discrimination!'
Outside his home, however, Batatinha became
the professional entertainer, giving the public
what it wanted. When he played in the local bars
and restaurants, the contrast between his
private and public lyrics was ironic:

> *Smiling at the world,*
> *I'm a very happy man,*
> *With no problems at all.*

In the bar, Batatinha's turn was followed
by his friend Riachão, dressed in a loud blue-
check jacket, jockey cap, shades and red-striped
shirt. Riachão sang about his success with girls
and money. The crowd loved it.

Next day, we drove through the flat Bahian
countryside, lush green in the February rains, to
the village of Sobara. Pigs and mules splashed in
the river among a dozen little children whose
mothers beat their washing on the stones along
the banks. Sobara is a typical Bahian country
village. Its narrow streets climb a small but
precipitous hill lined with pink and green
houses where old-timers rock back and forth on
creaky wicker chairs in the heavy shade. Sobara
is unique because it has preserved the *samba da
roda*. This is perhaps the original samba form
that was brought from Africa and which gives
the lie to the absurd tourist brochures which talk
of the samba's invention in a shady avenue of
Rio.

At sunset the villagers formed a circle and
the musicians brought out their percussion: a
snakeskin stretched on a wooden frame, kitchen
plates and knives, spoons and rattles and two old

banjos. The villagers clapped and chanted as each one improvised a dance, shaking their bellies and undulating their hips in the manner of the original samba. The celebration continued for hours while night fell. Round and round each villager spun, young and old, dancing his or her own version, to the clattering percussion of kitchen utensils, in a sensual, extrovert display of physical prowess.

By the time we returned to Salvador a different sort of celebration was under way. That night was the festival of Yemanjá, goddess of the sea, in whose presence we had filmed the Umbanda ceremony in Rio. Now in Salvador, she drew crowds of worshippers down onto the beaches and rocks, lit by candles flickering in the dawn light. They came loaded with flowers in bunches and baskets to be cast into the sea, as offerings to her. They believe Yemanjá has the power to determine human fate. If the flowers were swept out to sea, they were accepted; if swept back, they were rejected and ill fortune would come to those who had offered them. The worshippers were falling into a trance and dropping to their knees – even throwing themselves from rocks into the sea with their offerings of champagne, brandy, plastic-wrapped dolls and perfumes which they emptied into the cold, grey water and the sweeping spray. One mother with a family of six or seven children raised her skirt and leapt into the waves, shrieking in a piercing, squeaky voice and laughing coquettishly, taking on the manner of the goddess Yemanjá, whom she felt possessed her.

By the time the sun had risen, many participants were weeping, others were walking in a trance barefoot through the water and still others had fallen asleep on the sand or wooden benches. Out at sea, boats bobbed up and down, their lights still glowing and samba bands playing on their decks. Those who hired the boats were carrying their offerings of flowers far out before throwing them in the water to guarantee they would not be washed back on shore too soon.

The black music and religions of Brazil are based on the religious cult of Candomblé which brought the goddess Yemanjá from Africa. Candomblé is very secretive and regards the act of filming or recording as akin to stealing spirits. I had spent much time with a priest of the Candomblé cult, whose hall was based a few miles outside Salvador. I persuaded him to let us film the initiation of a young girl to her god. This was one of the few genuine Candomblé ceremonies ever to be filmed. When he finally agreed, it was on condition that we used no artificial lights. Ingeniously, Chris Morphet, the cameraman, located a dozen paraffin lamps which he hung from the ceiling of the hall and which supplemented the existing source of light.

First the priest told us how he came to be there.

'We are of African descent, but my father denied any belief in the god Oxalá . . . Terrible things happened to him. Two nuts appeared in his throat and he died. Then my sister Rosa began to feel ill, and she died: she joined Yemanjá. Then I too fell ill. I took part in fights. I was arrested and imprisoned. People around me died and I became terrified. One night I had a dream: a handsome black man told me to leave my home and go to the house of "hypnotism". When I awoke, I ran to that place. It was a house of Candomblé. A lady said something and I fell into a trance. After 12 days, my head was shaved and I was initiated into the priesthood of Candomblé.'

Later that night, after grabbing a few hours sleep in the car, we entered the hall, which had been decorated in white. Over many, many hours, the ceremony unfolded to hypnotic drum rhythms that never ceased during the whole initiation. The priest himself chanted in the Yoruba language of his Nigerian forefathers. After the participants had prostrated themselves flat upon the mud floor at his feet, the ceremony began. A novice, dressed in layers of white with silver decorations on her head, wrists and waist, was led out to dance. She circled the hall in a trance, carrying silver offerings and flowers for her god. When finally

**Musicians in the
village of Sobara
assemble to play the
samba da roda: all
the villagers dance
one by one**

exhausted and in the possession of Oxalofu (the husband of sea goddess Yemanjá) she collapsed among her elders, and the priest led in another girl with shaved head and axe in hand who danced ecstatically round the hall, hour after hour, to placate the god that possessed the novice and ensure her safe journey through the spirit world. The drumming had become so hypnotically intense that one of my British companions fell unconscious and had to be carried out.

In a country which has lost many of its traditions and where families have been torn apart by migrations to the cities to find work, the paternal role of the priest holds rural communities together. So the secret sect of Candomblé is a social as well as a spiritual focal point. Over centuries, the Yoruba gods have been preserved through syncretism: many black Brazilian slaves were forcibly baptized and were subjected to religious education by their owners. They simply absorbed the outward forms of Christianity, but behind the effigies of saints, they kept alive the Yoruba gods and spirits. So Candomblé has survived as the strongest religious and cultural link with their past and as the basis for the drumming rhythms of the ceremonial and popular music of black Brazil.

The black activist who had talked with us in Rio came from Bahia, and he described these local traditions for us:

'The black person's culture here is an improvised culture – passed down from father to son. And in just that way Candomblé teachings are passed down through words and rhythms. Nothing is written. In Candomblé we use the term "made in the mind". It's a verbal tradition. Ours is a society governed by folklore. So in reality, there are two sorts of Brazil: one that belongs to Europe and the USA which we call "blue-eyed Brazil', and another which still belongs to the greatest African population outside the African continent.'

Not far from the Candomblé hall, in the salt marshes where horsemen rode among the washerwomen, we were fortunate to find capoeira dancers. Their leader was a friend of the priest and had helped preserve an ancient form of martial art, supposed to be of Angolan origin. The dance and song were accompanied by string instruments called berimbau and the vocal repetition of short phrases which, increasing in speed, inspired the fighters into faster and more violent action. Capoeira is a sort of African 'aikido', incorporating acrobatics, kicking, dancing, handstands and somersaults but also the offensive use of elbows, feet and hands. Angolan slaves were apparently forced to fight in the front line by their colonizers. So, armed with this aggressive art, they claimed to be invincible and terrorized their foe. Just as Candomblé used a religious syncretism to survive, so capoeira used the guise of dance to preserve a unique form of resistance amongst slaves. During the nineteenth century, it was adopted by black youths to counter police harassment, and it was used in sprawling cities like Rio that sprang up almost overnight.

One young migrant from the north, who had recently settled in the Rio favelas and joined the gangs of black youths on the city streets, was Melodia. He had just become an overnight recording sensation and we met him in a Rio studio where his record company executives painstakingly printed his lyrics on cue cards, in letters two inches high, so he would get them right while singing. Later we accompanied Melodia into a vast stadium where, that night, he gave a heavily promoted show with the black starlet, Zeze Morta. His hit number was 'El Gatto Negro'. It purported to tell the story of a local revolutionary leader called the Black Cat whose base was a Rio favela from where he fought for his people's freedom. In fact it turned into a drug-induced hymn to all that is worst in western pop music, as Melodia and Zeze Morta writhed around the stage to a crude rock-'n'-roll backing with a touch of bossa nova.

The bossa nova probably did originate in Rio. Stemming from the samba, it added a few jazz breaks and some white sophistication while extracting the passion and subtle cross-rhythms

**Candomblé is an important religious cult in Brazil: the ceremonies are held secretly and are rarely filmed**

to create a sort of smooth, urbanized version of the samba.

Everywhere in Rio, that February of 1980, sambas were playing. On the city beaches groups of bathers gathered with drums and whistles. In the streets, bands marched with trumpets and trombones while girls and their carioca boyfriends (a term for local sun worshippers) danced through the dense traffic and pollution. Sambas played from every radio, every car, every restaurant, every café.

Since my arrival in Rio two months earlier,

**An old form of fighting – Capoeira, involving acrobatics and dancing, is now a means of defence in the guise of dance**

I had been anxious to interview and film the two most important names in popular Brazilian music: Chico Buarque and Milton Nascimento. Although not black, Chico has done more than any other musician to raise people's political

**Milton Nascimento, who grew up in the northern outback of Brazil, has become a top singing star who is also politically committed**

consciousness through his art. His work is startlingly imaginative, incorporating Brazilian and European traditions in a unique and aggressive style of music which all the while keeps close to the lives of poor blacks. Milton Nascimento, on the other hand, is a brilliantly accomplished black musician and poet, whose music reflects the pulse and hardships of the black Brazilian people.

Ironically, both superstars had just been signed by a Germany company, Arista Records, who were breaking into the South-American market and had paid 1,000,000 dollars each to acquire the prestige that was attached to these names. In a week when Frank Sinatra jetted into Rio to perform in an exclusive restaurant at 500 dollars a ticket, Milton and Chico had tried to set up a free show in the main football stadium. The embarrassed authorities just managed to prevent it. But it meant that they were both in town, and eventually they agreed to play together for us. We met at dusk in the garden behind Arista Records' suburban mansion. Chico was nervous and highly strung, and had endless trouble tuning his borrowed guitar. Finally they sang a duet together – one of Milton's most beautiful melodies called 'O cio da terra'. It was about the fertile land of Brazil and its natural cycle, about its frailty and its imminent destruction.

Afterwards, Milton invited Chico to speak for them both:

'My music is aimed at all sections of society. I would like it to reach and be meaningful to many more people, especially those who suffer discrimination. But here in Brazil those people are deprived even of our music. It is almost impossible for them to have access to it. But the popular artist in Brazil has a most important role to play – sometimes I feel it is too important – because he is forced to substitute for the many voices that have been silenced in Brazil. And that happened very often until recently.

'It is true that the censorship which is so damaging to music and to all other areas of culture has lessened now, but with the law as it stands, it can return at any moment. The laws and the people who strangled our music over the last ten years are still around and waiting to come back.'

As we left Rio, the carnival celebrations were under way. The parades and their floats were on the streets, decked out in a kaleidoscope of colours, accompanied by the deafening rhythms of competing samba school bands. This was the black music of Brazil that their government and media continued to promote, drowning warning voices with a cacophony that deafened the ears, dazzled the eyes and numbed the mind.

# 13 Sukiyaki and Chips
*The Japanese Sounds of Music*

Contemporary Japanese music is popularly thought of as being hi-tech and based on the electronics revolution that symbolizes modern Japan to outsiders. But Japan is a highly traditional country and even in the extremes of its popular culture there is much that is authentic.

First impressions of the new obsession with youth (which in a country that has for centuries venerated old age is a break with tradition) come from television. Pop shows jam the airways with teeny-bopper bands, like The Goodbyes, who are popularly known as Lollipops.

After the Goodbyes had mimed ineptly to their latest record in a TV studio, we watched them being groomed for a press conference at teatime on a Sunday afternoon. They were led into a tented enclosure on the roof of one of Tokyo's most fashionable department stores from where a stream of screaming girls stretched down five flights of stairs, several times around the block and up the road as far as the eye could see. All the fans had cameras and cassette recorders with which to record their fleeting moment with a Lollipop. The rituals were distinctive: the girls presented their idols with combs which were run through the stars' locks and then returned to be treasured; gifts were

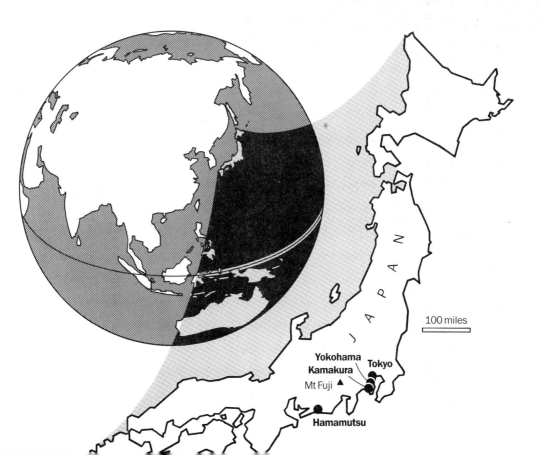

proffered, mostly Disneyland toys and muppets. Others gave silk handkerchiefs or paper tissues which were used for wiping away a bead of sweat from the brow of a Lollipop, who acknowledged the gift with the hint of a ritual bow.

Most of the girls were also clutching a comic book. A thousand million such comics are sold each year in Japan. They are filled with strip cartoons of idealized teenage youth without the neat Japanese features and dress of most of their readers: many of the heroes are westernized, blonde and tall, presenting an unattainable ideal to their impressionable consumers. These comics are not, however, only read by teenagers. In most subway trains, middle-aged businessmen, elderly executives and young housewives scan them. Scan is the right word since they only spend a few seconds on each page. Like everything else in Japan, the subject of comic books has been meticulously analysed, with the conclusion that the average

**Teeny pop groups are in great evidence in Japan with enormous record sales and a nice clean image for the girl groups on TV shows**

Japanese spends an average three seconds on the average page of the average comic. Yet, in that time, he or she succeeds in absorbing character, plot and dialogue. Some educationalists see this as the reason why the younger Japanese are more visually literate and have a higher IQ (especially in spatial logic tests) than the equivalent age group in other countries. After being read by its purchaser, each comic is distributed though the family and then on to friends at school or work, so the thousand million bought annually represents a readership of possibly ten times that number.

One of the dominant images of the cartoon strips, alongside some grotesque violence, is the glamorous pop singer: the Lollipop. These Lollipops play in standard four-piece rock-'n'-roll bands. They look back to the 1960s for style, and sound like the Monkees.

An equally powerful commercial force is the so-called New Music, aimed at the 16- to 22-year-olds. Between them, Lollipops and New Music account for 85 per cent of record sales, since most Japanese tend to stop buying records

IAN OWLES

**The Goodbyes are a typical Lollipop group: teenage fare with rituals for the girl fans — part of Japan's youth culture**

**Leading the world in
the electronics market,
the Japanese Yamaha
factory is a model
of organization**

soon after they start working. New Music is
based on the technology of electronic sounds
where computers recreate a range of music from
synthesized brass band to a classical Japanese
koto instrument.

We visited the factories of Roland and
Yamaha, two of Japan's leading synthesizer
manufacturers. Yamaha still build grand pianos
in a cavernous warehouse beside their electronic
components factory, but even these are tested
less by ear than by sophisticated electronic
tuning devices. Amid an intense cacophony of
scales as every keyboard was tested stringently
for its full range of sounds and rhythms, a tea-
break siren howled. The machines were
silenced. From behind the conveyor belts and
robot testing machines, emerged human
beings, spectacled and white-coated, some even

with masks and gloves. They converged into
disciplined lines as from loudspeakers across the
factory came the synthesized sound of Duke
Ellington's 'Caravan'. All the workers then
began a carefully choreographed callisthenics
routine until the music stopped five minutes
later and they returned to their tasks.

Each manufacturer guards its latest
electronic inventions from numerous spies sent
out by rivals in the cut-throat struggle to stay
one step ahead of their opponents.
Technological espionage has become an
everyday affair in Japan.

The aims of the rapidly expanding Yamaha
company were described to us by their executive
director, Mr Hayoshi:

'This is a new technology and it is always
growing. In the past, synthesizers were
designed for specialist musicians, but now they
will become available for the masses. By using
the memory facilities of this electronic
technology, people who could not play an
instrument can now make their own music. So
while advancing the technical side with digital

computers, we are taking our new electronic technology to the people and affecting their hearts and souls with it. This is what we are researching into.'

The biggest New Music group of all time in Japan is Yellow Magic Orchestra (YMO). Their music is entirely computerized and synthesized. We were fortunate to meet them before the original group finally split – the effect of which was as devastating as the break-up of the Beatles. The three YMO stars were fashionable and deliberately flip in their answers. Takahashi: 'We're doing what we want to do, the way we want to do it. The Japanese public is so terribly limited in its taste that if we started considering our listeners' interests we would have to make all sorts of compromises, so I'd rather not think about that.'

Ryuuchi Sakamoto, now a leading film actor and personality, continued:

'Because we have to record our music to a deadline, we try to concentrate on making it commercial. I want my records to be hits. There's no point in making them otherwise. I'm not "selling out" and I don't think it matters whether you're black, white or yellow. How your music sounds is more influenced by your environment, by the social background and education you've had than any racial differences. At the beginning, about five years ago, the motive for our band was to sound like Kraftwerk [the German synthesizer band], but now our music is based more on our individual styles and on the backgrounds we come from.'

The third member, Hosono, explained as he fed information into his drum machine: 'This is computer-based data. First I drum a short phrase and then repeat it, then play it back and then insert a ring drum sound. Then I mix it all down and make a guide track. On top of that basic rhythm I add other percussion ideas and I build on it.'

Despite the commercial dominance of New

**Vast numbers of comics in Japan mix aggression and an idealized image of youth**

**Ryuuchi Sakamoto, one of the founders of the synthesizer group Yellow Magic Orchestra is now an international star: a popular alternative to convention is still to dress up and dance to rock'n' roll in Harajuku Park**

IAN OWLES

Music and Lollipops, Japan has an extraordinary diversity of live music. There are clubs, bars and pubs in every city offering jazz, both modern and traditional, reggae, country and western, ballads, avant-garde music and of course, a flourishing of the classics, both western and Japanese. There are also smatterings of musical dissidents who, to the discomfort of many within their society, make themselves available to foreign media and suggest that the stringent conformity of Japanese society is not total. This conformity applies as much to appearance as to taste and behaviour. One of our Japanese production team told me how her naturally wavy hair had meant that during her school days in the 1950s, she always had to carry a doctor's certificate verifying that her waves were not artificial. Otherwise, they would have been instantly removed as 'non-conformist' – Japanese just don't have wavy hair.

On weekends at Harajuku Park, in central Tokyo, the musical dissidents dress as punks or 1950s rockers. The girls are in white ankle socks, full skirts and denim jackets; the boys appear tough and dangerous in classic Brando, biker style. Their leather gear and chains gleam defiantly in the watery sun that peeks out between the rain clouds as the rockers hop and jive from puddle to puddle. Massive ghetto blasters fight each other for decibel dominance, with American hits from the 1950s and 1960s. These rockers scorn their schoolfriends who queue for hours outside department stores to worship Lollipops. With their rock-'n'-roll music, their leathers and shades, they feel they belong somewhere, even if it is another time and place. They look down on Lollipop bands with the same contempt that they have for other consumer goods with an inbuilt obsolescence: 'They're groomed and trained like monkeys,' sneered one rocker, 'to sell several millions of records and the kids are conditioned to buy them.'

I spoke to a couple of Harajuku Hells Angels who enjoyed their rebel image: 'This is the best place for me in Japan,' claimed one girl, 'I can forget about what I'm supposed to be or do and lose myself in rock-'n'-roll.' Another added: 'Our parents don't approve of this, but

since we'll have to conform sooner or later, we're doing what we want to while we can.' Another explained how she had renounced the Hells Angels to become a rock-'n'-roller: 'If I had my way, I'd build myself an office block right here and dance in it all day long. It may be wrong to take drugs and drink, but dancing here can't harm anyone, can it? My day-to-day life is terribly boring. But here I can really live!'

For these teenagers' parents, and more particularly their grandparents, there is something very special and precious about the Japanese way of life and its accompanying aesthetic. They are afraid of losing it, just as they almost lost the music hall tradition that flourished in the pre- and postwar years.

As in most countries, music hall has in Japan been superseded by television. We managed to find the last one still operating in Tokyo: the Shochiku Engei-jo. This was in the

**Japanese music hall is not yet nostalgia: one of the last in Tokyo still operates with its fifteen minute acts including conjurors, musicians and a comic trombonist**

**Despite the new technology in Japan, old traditions are still valued, as in the shamisen player in a Tokyo music hall**

disreputable Asakusa district, in a street filled with strip shows, porno shops and a market selling wartime paraphernalia and stuffed African lions. With its ceaseless flow of 15-minute acts, it was a faithful mirror of the old Japanese music halls: an aged conjuror in pinstripes performed his act with bamboo stick and a plate decorated with peonies; a Shamisen player, with a leather-covered three-string instrument resembling a banjo sang nostalgic folk tunes and a magician produced white rabbits from a hat. Mrs Shasiko Kuroda and her family (an ensemble with shamisen, accordion and wooden sticks) sang strange vocal harmonies against a backdrop of painted bonsai trees, and Mr Bon Sight, a trombone player with

a resplendent moustache, made impressionistic sounds of steam trains. Then, as if by magic, he hoisted a miniature Japanese flag up the side of his trombone while playing the William Tell overture.

In the theatre's shabby back rooms, the artists made up and rehearsed their gestures. We paid our respects on entering and removed our shoes. Mrs Shasiko's younger sister tied back her hair and painted her face with loving care, patiently, slowly, as if in a place other than this knockabout backstreet music hall. What they had to say about their role in Japanese society was even more poignant than their performances:

'Of course it's a very hard life. None of us would do it out of first choice. The pay is poor and the work repetitive. The days are good or bad, depending on the audience's whims. If we don't look as though we're enjoying ourselves, and doing it all for the first time, then that's the beginning of the end. It's not just music, it's a show. We have to be entertainers. For this reason, we've incorporated western instruments like the accordion to make it seem more gay, to make the show happier and louder.'

Mr Bon Sight continued:

'I had been a jazz player for 26 years and had even been to England's Covent Garden. But I wanted to get into mass entertainment. I was not really interested in high art. I wanted to make people laugh. I got many ideas from American movies. Japanese people hear the sounds and music in a special way. If you listen to the speech of children, a child says, "*Kiyoshi-kun wa konai no?*" ("Won't Kiyoshi come?") or when a green pea drops from a mountain of fried rice, she says, "*Omame ga okkotta*" ("The pea fell"). These phrases are spoken in certain scales, in a certain tune – it's the way we speak. That is also the scale of the Japanese folk songs we've been playing. It is the same with nursery rhymes, the cries of street vendors or goldfish sellers or the "*Sao-ya, Aodake*" of the bamboo man. It even appears in pop songs for children. So we think that if we train Japanese children in European music like we do today, we may be forcing something unnatural on their sense of hearing. We may be producing musical cripples.'

This strong sense of national identity was shown very clearly in the work of Dr Tadanobu Tsunoda, whose laboratory resembled that of Frankenstein's rebirth. He had pioneered a new theory of the brain: that the Japanese use different hemispheres for hearing sounds from westerners. Dr Tsunoda:

'Language and music are closely related, so if our language interpretation in the brain is different from others', then our interpretation of music will also be different. As Japanese is quite distinct from any other language, it seems interesting to research into ancient Japanese instruments and see how these act within a person's brain. We discovered that whereas western people, listening to Japanese music, will take it in on the right side of the brain, a Japanese takes his music in on the left side. On the other hand, both westerners and Japanese people take western music in on the right side of the brain. From this I discovered also that human voices and animal and even insect sounds are all taken in on a different side of the brain by Japanese people – different from everybody else in the world.'

He demonstrated this in his experimental chamber packed with wires and dials by providing a 'human guinea pig' who was also a trained musician (which somewhat negated the experiment). By a complex system of feeding different sounds through different ears and then asking the subject to tap out cross-rhythms, Dr Tsunoda proved to his satisfaction that if a Japanese shakuhachi (a five-holed bamboo flute) plays Beethoven's Ninth Symphony, a westerner and a Japanese will hear it on the same side of the brain. But if that same Shakuhachi plays *Japanese* music then the Japanese person reacts with a different brain hemisphere. This, Dr Tsunoda pointed out, is not a genetic difference but rather an environmental one based on the 'unique quality of the Japanese language'. Most Japanese attribute a very special aesthetic to natural sounds like temple bells or the wind in the leaves of a bamboo tree, which the shakuhachi instrument is supposed to resemble.

One of the great living masters of the shakuhachi is Watazumido. He has the habit of changing his name quite frequently and was therefore extremely difficult to trace. It took us a couple of days to find him in a Tokyo backstreet, living in a minute, traditionally styled Japanese house. He was disappointed that it had only taken us two days: 'My intention,' he explained, 'is that it should take no-one less than three years to find me and in that way I can be sure that they really want to speak to me.'

Watazumido is regarded by some, even in Japan, as a little eccentric, but he is both a master shakuhachi player who has influenced a whole generation after him, and a uniquely inspired Master of Zen. He deliberately appeared humorously simple-minded, but behind that – in the Zen tradition – resided a sharp intellect. When a colleague asked the meaning of 'one-hand clapping', Watazumido leaned over the table of a fashionable Japanese coffee house and slapped him across the face. 'That is the answer to a foolish question,' he said, laughing. Watazumido had many extraordinary stories. To prove his 'oneness' with the sound of the natural world, while in New York, he chose to sleep beside a bulldozer

The shakuhachi flute has a special place in Japanese music culture. One of its greatest masters is Watazumido, a Master of Zen, who with his clarity of vision has floored western visitors who seek musical truth

that was excavating on a night shift at a Fifth Avenue building site. He slept like a baby. Later, however, he was arrested by some astonished New York policemen as he ran naked back to his hotel clutching his jo stick. This is the long, hard wooden pole with which he stretches, exercises, massages, pounds and invigorates his body every morning at 3.30, preferably without clothes.

That was the hour that we agreed to start filming with him, having arranged to do so in the peaceful gardens behind our Tokyo guest house. The management had given us cautious permission on condition that Mr Watazumido was silent while doing his exercises beneath the guests' windows. Unfortunately, he stripped off his clothes and proceeded to scream and howl. Unknown to us, this was his habitual behaviour before exercising – so as to clear the grounds of evil spirits. On this occasion, it also cleared the hotel of guests.

Watazumido had his own philosophy of music which was closely linked with the long-standing Japanese aesthetic towards sound and its role in everyday life. The shakuhachi flute he played was originally about the only instrumental music used in Buddhist worship. It is therefore highly spiritual and improvisational – perhaps more so than any other Japanese traditional instrument. Watazumido explained:

'During the war, I became an instructor of the National Guard but afterwards the absurdity of this discipline affected me. I would run up to the wall and smash my head against it until I knocked myself out. I had to get away from it. I then became a Zen priest. I studied Rinzai Zen, attaining the title of Roshi or Master, but finally I gave up organized Zen because the silence which stems from discipline is not silence at all. I left Zen to start mobilizing my body – to breathe more deeply, because breathing is the basis of all life and music. At the

centre of music is the pulse.

'When you play music, you probably read the notes on the page, but that is no good. You should not feel you are dependent on written music to play. You must look deeper at your own power and strength. One time I was at a conference with John Cage when I described even the sound of boiling water as a form of music. He asked me what I was talking about. I explained that to me music is not composed of a scale of seven notes. You must listen to all the sounds around you – to the falling leaves, to the sounds of the birds singing and crying, of the mouse scuttling behind the walls. This is also music. Music is not a formality predetermined by people, it is much wider and freer. For example, if I pick up my shakuhachi and play next to something which is boiling or cooking, then there will be the sound of my instrument and that of sukiyaki cooking – that blend is music too.

'John Cage and the others could not understand what I was talking about, especially when I mentioned the "one sound" which is the basis of my philosophy. Everyone wanted to know what the "one sound" was. "Please, Watazumido," they begged, "tell me what it is." I said: "It is everywhere around you – listen for yourselves." They were still confused, so I said that, if they insisted, I would show them the "one sound". I clapped my hands. Everyone looked worried. I said to them, "Now do you understand?" I pointed to each one in turn but none of them had understood. I said: "You fools, have you not even understood your own question?" Well, apparently not. So instead of trying to explain what the "one sound" was, I picked up my shakuhachi and played.'

When Watazumido played for us, it was a

**The Japanese response to sound is very acute: Watazumido describes his playing as a fight between himself and nature**

startling experience. His shakuhachi flute was made of untreated bamboo and required extraordinary control, yet he pulled from it, in what he described as a battle between himself and nature, the most beautiful sounds; some fierce, even frightening, others so soft that we could hardly hear them over the singing of the birds outside. It was all done with an intensity and concentration that this 70-year-old master musician maintained through the discipline of his physical and mental daily exercises. After playing, he concluded:

'The "one sound"? It is nothing special. It is the wind blowing or the waves breaking. It is sounds in the home like the chopping of vegetables or the dripping of a tap. All these are part of the "one sound". Man is very clever. He has made instruments which can imitate natural sounds – like the big drum that recreates the breaking waves. So for me, music is but a tiny part of the oneness of sound.'

Percussion plays a role in Buddhist and

**Sumire Yoshihara is a percussionist of great musical standing in Japan — unusual for a woman**

Shinto religious rituals. Often, during Shinto festivals, huge floats of pounding drummers pass in the streets or play at tented shrines erected by the roadside. 'In Buddhist temples,' it was said to me, 'there is no music save the moment of reverberation after the striking of a gong.'

A modern percussionist who has incorporated both traditional and modern ideas into her music is Sumire Yoshihara. We drove to the smoggy, rainy city of Yokohama where we found her house in a quiet suburban road. Her instruments were set up around a back room which was soundproofed from the rest of the world; it needed to be, for the volume and intensity of her percussion was almost more

**Enka music is one of
the great popular
forms in Japan:
the queen of enka is
Miyako Harumi**

than our equipment could cope with. Sumire is a modern musician in the Japanese style who has incorporated a special sensitivity to sound into her music. 'Being Japanese,' she explained, 'means being sensitive to the noises of our traditional activities, social as well as religious. So it is not possible for my music to exist without taking all those sounds into consideration. Therefore, indirectly, my music is influenced by my environment.'

Her instruments ranged from cow bells to kettle drums, from buzzing children's toys to kane metal gongs and cymbals, from the tsuzumi hand drums to wooden clackers and castanets. Her music was especially written by her country's leading composers. But being a women is not easy in the competitive world of Japanese professional music. There are, of course, Lollipop stars in the same fashion as western girl idols, but on the concert platform, there is no place for a woman. Yoshihara added: 'Generally speaking, it is a man's world here; even in a big corporation, it is a fact of life that women are discriminated against.' The crying

of her small baby interrupted us: 'The system is not made so that women can have a family and still go to work. That is what I mean when I say it is very hard for me.'

One almost exclusively male preserve in popular Japanese music is enka. In popular music surveys, enka accounts for 15 per cent of the market. It is said to appeal almost exclusively to 'middle-aged' men, particularly executives. Enka has its roots in old Japanese folk songs called naniwabushi and is mixed with the 'sound' of western ballad crooners like Paul Anka, Neil Sedaka and even Elvis Presley.

We were lucky to be introduced to the 'king' of enka, Hideo Murata. (In Japanese the family name, Murata, would normally appear first). He is a tough, thoroughly traditional entertainer, who always performs in a kimono and who is supposed to have had close connections with the Japanese yakuza (a secret society of gangsters). Certainly he has some powerful, wealthy sponsors. He said:

'I have been singing enka for 48 years, but since the last war, it has changed its character, with the economic upsurge here and the new Japanese ideals. Basically enka is words with a melody. That is the essence of this music which is still extremely popular in Japan. It is all about our daily lives – a sort of kitchen sink music. Once it was fashionable to sing about the flowers or the sea or the meadows, but now it has to be about our day-to-day life. It is my job to present people with a musical mirror, a map of their everyday lives and problems.'

We filmed Murata as he was making a record at the EMI Toshiba studios. He laid his vocals over a prerecorded orchestral track of bittersweet violin melodies. He refused money, since he regarded it as his 'privilege' to perform for people in the west. After recording he explained how companies like Toshiba-EMI had combined the technology of video cassettes and laser discs with enka music to create a whole new entertainment form called karaoke. This, in recent years, had taken over Japan and was now becoming increasingly popular in the USA and Europe.

**Hideo Murata is the king of enka, singing what he describes as a sort of kitchen sink music**

Orchestrated versions of popular ballads, mostly enka, but with a smattering of international hits like 'The green, green grass of home' or 'My way', are put onto disc or cassette and installed, like jukeboxes, in bars and restaurants all over Japan. But there is no singing on the cassette, it is 'music minus one', ready for all the eager, amateur performers to fill the space in the lush arrangement. The bar customers step onto a compact stage and sing into the microphone. Now a new element has been introduced: a video or even a film screen on which images, more or less related to the song, are projected together with the lyrics. So the customer can become every bit as professional as the professionals. Murata added:

IAN OWLES

**Karaoke or 'music minus one' is the latest form of enka: everyone can sing to backing tracks**

'Once people only wanted to listen to professional singers. Then they would go home after clapping their hands in appreciation. It was almost impossible for amateurs to get up on stage and sing. But the Japanese record industry came up with the idea of karaoke backing tapes over which anyone could sing in public places. And now every evening throughout Japan everyone has a chance to be an instant star.'

With some karaoke machines, a blushing singer can even be graded on his or her performance by a black box computer which judges accuracy of pitch and marks the singer out of ten. Murata was realistic about the therapeutic effects of this essentially sentimental music:

'Karaoke can be a release from the stress and worries of a working day. If you have had a terrible time in the office, just singing a karaoke ballad is not going to help very much, but it does give you the strength to carry on.'

We visited a number of such bars throughout Japan. In the evening they were filled mostly with factory workers and businessmen gathered to drink and sing instead of going home. In one tiny bar in an alley beneath a railway bridge, a group of businessmen were watching images of kamikaze pilots smashing into American warships. At the same time, to a backing of violins, they were singing a maudlin, nostalgic song full of military heroics, evoking the suffering and sacrifice of the Japanese people during the Second World War:

> *We who are the flowers of youth,*
> *Must be prepared to die.*
> *Die honorably*
> *For our country.*
> *Both you and I were contemporaries*
> *Like flowers in the same garden*
> *We belonged to the same squadron.*
> *We may not be blood brothers*
> *But we are comrades in arms.*
> *Why did you have to die?*
> *Why did you have to fall?*

In other bars, couples stood in the limelight and crooned, arm in arm. A young girl broke down in tears, overcome by the sentimental lyrics she sang. A sympathetic audience applauded her emotion and then helped her back to her seat. But for the most part, karaoke is for tired businessmen who wash away their cares and the very real competitive pressures of their work with bottles of saké and a deeply felt performance on the microphone.

One of the more bizarre outposts of the karaoke industry is Mr Sorita's taxi. He picks up singers when they are too drunk to drive. But those passengers are able to prolong their karaoke night inside his taxi. A Tokyo salesman slumps in the back seat and sings into the microphone while the backing tapes play; as a bonus, Mr Sorita accompanies his fare while he drives and records the whole dawn performance. He then hands a completed tape to the exhausted and hungover salesman who exits either into his home or straight back into the office.

Despite the common stereotype of the Japanese as excessively hard-working and orderly, Tokyo is very much a 24-hour city. Many young Japanese people explained that they stayed out all night long because life was too short for sleeping: one or two nights a week were dedicated solely to entertainment. Many of the karaoke bars ran soft porn videos for the predominantly male customers. As one barman explained:

'It alleviates the necessity of employing girls here and I can keep my customers drinking longer with this sort of entertainment.'

The Nichigeki Music Hall in Tokyo offered the 'best in erotic entertainment for discerning customers'. It always seemed to be packed with Japanese and foreign visitors. It was an up-market version of the sleazier strip clubs in areas like Asakusa where we had found old-time music hall. But here, on a computer co-ordinated, cheaply glamorized stage, came erotic fantasies in the high Japanese tradition. *The Story of the Burning Lady* was one of several based on the famous Japanese medieval classic, *Yaoya Oshichi*. This was the equivalent of a

**The Nichigeki Music Hall in Tokyo mixes tales from classical drama with hi-tech erotic glamour**

Shakespeare tale adapted to an 'exotic music-hall style'. It concerned a lady who became demented when her lover was gruesomely beheaded. She stripped and danced her way from one phallic symbol to another. It ended with her execution, for which she climbed, in the nude, up a shaky ladder to the gallows against a blood-red sunset backdrop. This was accompanied by music which adroitly combined traditional Japanese melodies and western electronic instruments. The themes of some of the Nichigeki dramas were even taken from the old Noh theatre classics.

Noh epitomizes the serious classical Japanese music values, although it derives from something much less serious – originally sarugaku or 'monkey music'. This originated in shrine pantomime plays which later became comic theatre and, later still, combined with Chinese acrobatics. It all became ossified into the highly disciplined patterns of Noh theatre, where all music, sound effects and staging suggest psychological states.

After the show we talked to a star actor of the Kanze Noh troupe about the Japanese concept of rhythm.

'Rhythm is not the same all over the world. People have a different sense of rhythm. It is determined by the life style of the people. The Japanese are agricultural; when planting rice

**Noh theatre, in origin a popular form, has become a highly ritualized and very disciplined form of theatre**

and working in the fields, one stands with the surface of one's feet touching the ground and lowering the centre of gravity. They move backwards and forwards, quietly lifting one foot and then the other. That is the basic beat of Japanese music – it is quite different from the pounding, rhythmic music of hunters and stock-raising peoples in other cultures.'

This insistence on a distinctive sense of skill, rhythm and sensitivity to environmental sounds filters through on many levels of Japanese life, from the music industry to the cries of street vendors, and from the Shinto drums to the martial arts.

Several years previously I had met one of the great masters of Japanese archery, Professor Ogasawara, who comes from a family of thirteenth-century samurai warriors. Japanese archery, called kyudo, is much more than a sport or a means of aggression: it is a philosophy and a way to enlightenment, and it has been closely linked to the practice of Zen Buddhism since the middle ages. Ogasawara is a proud,

**An actress in the Nichigeki Music Hall entertains with dark tales of woe and blatant sexual images**

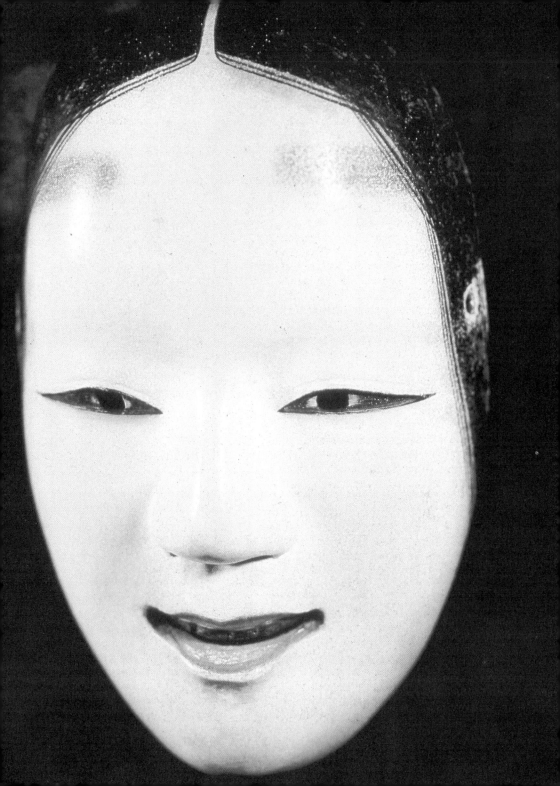

The great cry of the horse archers as they release their arrows has to come from deep within. 'The sound of the arrow has a physical and spiritual quality.' Professor Ogasawara is a master of kyudo, the ultimate in Japanese archery

formal disciplinarian of the 'old school' who was supervising the annual Yabusami horse archery festival in the coastal town of Kamakura. The riders, controlling their horses with their knees, gave ear-piercing yells as they released their arrows at targets while galloping down a narrow path lined with camera-clicking onlookers. Ogasawara explained:

'In horse archery, the quality of sound is important: there is yin and yang in all things, in the sun and moon, in light and dark, in male and female. This balance is the basis of the archer's shouts. Generally in life, those who shout the loudest are the weakest people. A man who shouts is like a dog who barks – a weak and cowardly thing. That is not the way. When you shout in archery you do so with an inner force. This is the meaning of the "yin yo", which the horsemen shout when they shoot their arrows.'

On this trip to Japan, I found Professor Ogasawara weaker and in pain; he had suffered a terrible heart attack. On a previous visit, he had, in full regalia, shot a ritual whistling arrow into the evening sky from his dojo (archery hall). Too weak to do so now, he explained the significance of that ritual:

'Both sound and silence are of greatest importance. For that reason, ours is different from archery elsewhere in the world. There is a great relevance in the sound made when you shoot an arrow – you can tell whether any archer is good or bad just by listening to that sound.

'However, the ceremonial shooting of the whistling arrow is to frighten the devil. The idea is to push back the enemy, not by killing him, but by the force of sound alone. This applies to the supernatural powers of evil that surround us. While the Zen priest carries the shakuhachi flute as an instrument of beauty and enlightenment, it is also a weapon by his side. So too – in the art of archery – the sound of the arrow has a spiritual and physical quality. As with music, all this is part of the spirit of Japan in sound.'

# Discography

Some of the music featured in *Beats of the Heart* is difficult to find outside its country of origin. For example, no Thai luk tung music is available except on cassette in Thailand. The following records offer a guide to the music in the films; where possible, they have been selected for their availability.

1. **No. 17 Cotton Mill Shanghai Blues**
'Ancient China: Exotic Music'
(Lyrichord, LLST 7122)
'L'Art du pi-pa chinois (Cheng Shui-Cheng)' (Arion, ARN 36.766)

2. **Rhythm of Resistance**
Ladysmith Black Mambazo, 'Induku Zethu' (Earthworks, ELP 2006)
Johnny and Sipho, 'Universal Men' (Not generally available)
Malombo, 'Pele Pele' (ATC, 8003)
'Rhythm of Resistance' (Virgin, V2 113)
Mohotella Queens, 'Thina Siyakhanyisa' (MGG, 618)
Abafana, 'The Cockerel Boys' (LR, 44 009)

3. **Chase the Devil**
'Children of the Heav'nly King – Religious Expression in the Central Blue Ridge' (Library of Congress Records, AFC L69 and L70)
Hazel Dickens, 'Hard-Hitting Songs for Hard-Hit People' (Rounder, 1026)
Virgil Andersen, 'On The Tennessee Line' (Country, 777)
Vernon Oxford, 'A Better Way of Life' (Rounder, 1038)
Joe Freeman, 'There'll Be No Black Lung Up In Heaven' (Jewel, 400)
Larry Richardson, 'Walking and Talking with My Lord' (MKB, cassette)

4. **Salsa!**
Celia Cruz, 'Homenaje a Los Santos' (SCLP, 9281)
Celia Cruz/Pacheco, 'Eternos' (Vaya Records)
'Salsa' – various artists (Island, HELP 20 and 21)
Tito Puente, 'Tambo' (Arcano, DKL 3174)
Willie Colon/Ruben Blades, 'Siembra' (Fania, JM00 537)
Ruben Blades, 'Buscando America' (Elektra for WEA, 960 352–1)
Charlie Palmieri, 'A Giant Step' (Tropical Buddha LP003)
Moliendo Vidrio, 'Maravilla Encarcelada' (Alhandra, ALS 156)

5. **Konkombé**
Sunny Ade, 'Ju Ju Music' (Island, ILPS 9712)
Fela Kuti, 'Suffering and Smiling' (Phonogram, PMCP 1005)
Sunny Okosun, 'Papa's Land' (EMI, NEMI 0232)
Lijadu Sisters, 'Horizon Unlimited' (Earthworks, DWAPS 2089)
Alhaj Mamam Shata Katsina, 'Mai Girma Sarkin Zazzan' (EMI, NEMI 0118)
Oriental Brothers, 'Oriental Brothers International' (DWAPS, 59)
I. K. Dairo, 'Iya O Yemi' (DWAPS, 2190)

6. **Tex-Mex**
Little Joe Hernandez, 'Live for Schlitz' (Freddie Records, FR001)
Flaco Jimenez, 'El Sonido de San Antonio' (Arhoolie, 3014)
Flaco Jimenez, 'Flaco Jimenez y su Cónjunto' (Arhoolie, 3007)
Santiago Jimenez Junior, 'El Mei'o Mei'o' (Arhoolie, 3016)
Placido Salazar, 'Placido Salazar' (Joey, 3009 LP)
'Texas Mexican Border Music Volume 1 – An Introduction, 1930–1960' (Folklyric, 9003)
'Texas Mexican Border Music Volume 4 – The String Bands' (Folklyric, 9007)

'Texas Mexican Border Music Volume 5 –
Norteño Accordion' (Folklyric, 9006)
Lydia Mendoza, 'Lydia Mendoza, Part 1'
(Folklyric, 9023)
Steve Jordan, 'Lo Mejor de Steve Jordan'
(Hacienda, 7940)

7.  **Shotguns and Accordions**
Fiesta Vallenata (CBS, 24 1638)
Diomedez Dias, 'Cantando' (CBS,
Colombia)

8.  **There'll Always Be Stars In The Sky**
Laxmikant and Pyarelal, 'Prem Rog'
(EMI, PEALP 2056)
Kalyanji Anandji, 'Upkar' (EMI, LKDA
190)
Lata Mangeshkar and Kishore Kumar,
'Satyam Shivam Sundaram' (Supreme,
PEALP 2011)
Lata Mangeshkar, 'Magic Moments'
(MFPE, 1044)
'Gouri Devi – songs from Rajasthan'
(EMI, ECSD 3008)
'Dhola Dhol Majira Baje – Hits from
Rajasthan' (EMI, EMGE 23005)
'All-Time Favourites of Music Director
S. D. Burman' (EMI, EALP 4074)

9.  **Roots Rock Reggae**
Joe Higgs, 'Life of Contradiction'
(Micron, deleted)
Mighty Diamonds, 'Right Time' (Virgin,
2052)
Jimmy Cliff, 'Struggling Man' (Island,
ILPS 9235)
Third World, '96° in the Shade' (Island,
ILPS 9443)
Gladiators, 'Trenchtown Mixup' (Virgin,
V2062)
Abyssinians, 'Satta Masa Gana' (US
import only)
Bob Marley and the Wailers, 'Burnin''
(Island, ILPS 9236)
Gregory Isaacs, 'Mr Isaacs'
Jacob Miller, 'Forward Ever' (Top
Ranking/ABC)

10.  **The Romany Trail**
Gypsy Songs from Hungary
(Hungaraton, SLPX 8028 29)
Sándor Lakatos, 'Sándor Déki Lakatos
and his Gypsy Band' (Hungaraton, SLPX
10153)
Juan Peña, 'Persecucion' (Philips, 91 13
004)
Zingaro, 'Voz de Luna' (CBS Spain, 40
835 61)
Duo Z, 'Ganz Anders', German Gypsy
songs by Tornado Rosenburg and Rudko
Kawczynski (Pläne, 88257)
'Egypte: Les Musiciens du Nil', Volumes
1 and 2 (Ocora, 558 514/558 52)

12.  **The Spirit of Samba**
Leci Brandao, 'Coisas do meu pessoal'
(Polydor Braz, 3175 102)
Batatinha/Riachão, 'Samba da Bahia'
(Fontana, 6470 506)
Chico Buarque, 'Chico Buarque'
(Phillips, 6349 398)
Candomblé, 'Candomblé' (Phonogram,
6470 598)
Milton Nascimento, 'Milton Nascimento'
(A & M, SP 4611)
'Les Grands Carnevals d'Amerique
Latine' (Arion France, 33 440)

13.  **Sukiyaki and Chips**
Watazumido, 'Watazumido' (Phillips
Japan, PH 8505)
Sumire Yoshihara, 'Sound Space of
Percussion, Volume 5' (Camerata, CMT
1086)
Yellow Magic Orchestra, 'BGM' (A & M,
SP 4853)

# Index